THE DEATH OF WEB 2.0

With all our contemporary connectivity, are we really connected? What does the nature of connectivity tell us about interpersonal and community relationships? What ethical concerns are raised through an always-on culture?

Communication in today's world is characterised by a condition of persistent, semi-permanent connectivity, which seems to bring us closer together, but which can also be profoundly alienating. *The Death of Web 2.0* takes a retrospective look at a moment in recent media history that has had, and will continue to have, a lasting impact upon the predominant attitude towards cultures of connectivity. Greg Singh draws from a range of approaches, intellectual traditions and scholarly disciplines to engage key questions underpinning the contemporary communications media ecosystem.

Bringing together influences from communitarian ethics, recognition theory and relational and depth psychology, Singh synthesises key approaches to produce a critical inquiry that projects the tensions at the heart of connectivity as a principle of Web 2.0. He argues that Web 2.0 is a cultural moment that is truly over, and that what is popularly described as 'Web 2.0' is an altogether different set of principles and practices. *The Death of Web 2.0* recognises the consequences of our 'always-on' culture, where judgments are made quickly and where impacts can be far-reaching, affecting our relationships, wellbeing, mental health and the health of our communities, and it concludes by asking what an ethics of connectivity would look like.

This unique interdisciplinary work will be essential reading for academics and students of Jungian and post-Jungian studies, media and cultural studies and psychosocial studies as well as anyone interested in the social implications of new media.

Greg Singh is Associate Professor in Media and Communications and Programme Director of Digital Media at the University of Stirling, UK. His previous books include *Film After Jung: Post-Jungian Approaches to Film Theory* and *Feeling Film: Affect and Authenticity in Popular Cinema* (both Routledge), and he has also published on topics including celebrity, YouTube and lifestyle television. Greg is Co-Director of the RSE Life in Data Research Network and is a Senior Fellow of the Higher Education Academy and a Fellow of the Royal Society of Arts.

THE DEATH OF WEB 2.0

Ethics, Connectivity and Recognition in the Twenty-First Century

Greg Singh

Routledge
Taylor & Francis Group

LONDON AND NEW YORK

First published 2019
by Routledge
2 Park Square, Milton Park, Abingdon, Oxon OX14 4RN

and by Routledge
52 Vanderbilt Avenue, New York, NY 10017

Routledge is an imprint of the Taylor & Francis Group, an informa business

British Library Cataloguing-in-Publication Data
A catalogue record for this book is available from the British Library

Library of Congress Cataloging-in-Publication Data
Names: Singh, Gregory Matthew, 1976- author.
Title: The death of Web 2.0 : ethics, connectivity and recognition in
     the twenty-first century / Greg Singh.
Description: Abingdon, Oxon ; New York, NY : Routledge, 2019. |
     Includes bibliographical references.
Identifiers: LCCN 2018039347 (print) | LCCN 2018051474
     (ebook) | ISBN 9780429020032 (Master Ebook) | ISBN
     9780415703796 (hardback) | ISBN 9780415703802 (pbk.) |
     ISBN 9780429020032 (ebk.)
Subjects: LCSH: Internet—Social aspects. | Internet users—
     Psychology. | Web 2.0. | Social media.
Classification: LCC HM851 (ebook) | LCC HM851 .S5584 2019
     (print) | DDC 302.23/1—dc23
LC record available at https://lccn.loc.gov/2018039347

ISBN: 978-0-415-70379-6 (hbk)
ISBN: 978-0-415-70380-2 (pbk)
ISBN: 978-0-429-02003-2 (ebk)

Typeset in Bembo
by Swales & Willis Ltd, Exeter, Devon, UK

For my girls.

CONTENTS

ACKNOWLEDGEMENTS

This thing you hold in your hands (whether on paper or screen) has had a long birth, and in the time it has taken to build from initial conception, through research and thinking, to writing these final words, five years have passed. Five years are to the Web what we might think of as several generations of family history, or perhaps equivalent to a period as tumultuous and eventful as the Cold War. Indeed, that is the only comparison I can think of in my living memory that might compare to some of the extraordinary cultural shifts I document here. I have a bunch of people to thank for being so patient with me when I mentioned 'I'm *this* close' all those times. I find it difficult to remember who helped with what, when and in what capacity. I have been lucky enough to work with some incredibly talented and resourceful people over the years, and each of them have taught me not only something about my subject matter, but also about myself.

First, Kate Hawes, Susannah Frearson and all of the production team at Routledge Mental Health. I owe, as always, a massive thanks for their support and belief in yet another of my strange project ideas. As always, my publisher has given me an immense amount of creative freedom and intellectual licence. I hope that this book lives up to the promises I have made these last years. Next, hello and thanks to my old colleagues at what was the School of Arts & New Media, University of Hull – Darrens, Mundy and Stephens; Toni Sant; Robert Consoli; and Chris Newell. In giving me a job, you provided me with the lifeline I needed to remain in academia (no really, thanks!) and keep the wolf from the door. A big hug to my wonderful colleagues in Communications, Media & Culture here at the University of Stirling. There were a handful of us just a short while ago, and now there are loads of us, so I shall not name you all individually, but the cake and fine wine, and the foods of the world make everything bearable. So thank you all for those things. A special mention should go to my predecessor (Doctor Who regeneration springs to mind here) Graham Meikle who so kindly provided me with a firm steer and sage advice in the early days of this project. Luke Hockley, whose guidance is always insightful and calming, and of course John Izod, whose wisdom and energy is a constant source of inspiration. In addition, my *compadre* Eddy Borges Rey for numerous symposia. Finally, a big thank you to Chiara Bernardi for the meticulous and much-needed feedback in the later days of the manuscript for this book – you have a real talent for cutting through deadwood, coupled with some amazing insights into what I had thought were throwaway ideas.

At various points in this book, I mention the Life in Data Research Network. This is a project I co-direct with Eddy Borges Rey, and is made possible through generous support from the Royal Society of Edinburgh Research Network grant. More information about this network can be found at http://www.lifeindata.org/.

INTRODUCTION

Whatever happened to Web 2.0?

Web 2.0 is dead and kicking

This book essentially tells the story of a cultural moment which defined a media decade. In such a fast-paced culture of change and obsolescence, I anticipate that a little future-proofing is in order – and so this book's themes and concerns will be examined through an intersection of multiple perspectives whilst at the same time acknowledging that none of these necessarily prevail and, certainly, that none are considerably more important than the others. This book concerns what we might describe as Web 2.0, and what happened to Web 2.0 as a cultural and historic moment. Above all, however, it concerns how Web 2.0 as a cultural expression articulates rather deep-seated and serious questions around connectivity, ethics and recognition, and how connected social technologies have contributed to a transformed understanding of these aspects of human interaction.

Web 2.0 is, perhaps, most popularly thought of as a read/write version of the Web whose user-friendly interfaces and opportunities for creativity and creative entrepreneurship echo earlier moments of DIY ethos in popular culture, but with the added protocols that enable the conditions of a semi-permanent state of connectivity. This semi-permanent state has been described by commentators as a state of 'always-on' (Turkle 2008, 2011; boyd 2012; Rheingold 2012; Jenkins, Ito and boyd 2015). Antecedents for the popular practices found in Web 2.0 arguably include punk subculture, with its fiercely independent and anti-establishment principles. But along with it, remnants of a late twentieth-century cyberpunk imaginary which yielded future visions (far from ideal) seem to form a background radiation to the popular discourses of Web 2.0 connectivity. One is reminded of the cyberspace of William Gibson's *Sprawl Trilogy* in the pre-Web era: disembodied assemblages of utopia disentangling the human race from the messy business of old flesh and removing us from the post-industrial deadness of a scorched sky. Yet these nightmarish visions of a techno apocalypse seemed to all but vanish from the popular imagination – endless cat videos, ubiquitous social media feeds and college-level courses in interaction and game design have pretty much erased the negativity from view. Web 2.0 is, essentially, made up of affirming stuff.

I started thinking about writing this book not so long after the initial promises of Web 2.0 had effectively passed on. But these are promises that we are now in a position to look back upon with the advantage of hindsight – with a fond, almost nostalgic, regard. There were promises to unshackle, finally, a democratised using public from the yoke of soulless consumer culture, dictated by faceless corporations and uncaring governments. There were promises to let the voiceless be heard, to allow creativity to flourish and to empower people with the status to realise Toffler's vision of a 'prosuming' society. These promises were simple and familiar enough: through the architecture of the Web, overlaid upon the communication infrastructures of the Internet, life online would be an enabling, freeing, enriching experience. Smarter processing, faster broadband connection, elegant experience design, and user-friendly applications would all but make the actual architecture vanish (that messy, mysterious, otherworld of code *The Matrix* films had made us all aware of). The Web had become a book without a face, a search without the engine. The Matrix had become in some ways a reality, except that in this reality it was we, the users, who were in control.

We can now see that very special promise of 'No Child Left Behind' for the spin that it was; by the very fact that every child would have access to a laptop in their schools, so it would follow that they would be able to put their spare-time tinkering with tech to good use within and outside of the classroom. Such familiarity with technology in everyday learning contexts assumes that children can write and publish through a few clicks of the mouse, customising the background of a blog post with a choice template available through a quick Google search. Even in considering the basic standards of hardware available to the domestic consumer, we find examples of accessible technology in the everyday that would have seemed impossible just a few short years ago. For example, music software such as Garageband, included with basic computer and tablet purchases as standard, is far more powerful than anything The Beatles ever had at their disposal. Therefore, it follows that budding musicians can finally realise that sound they hear in their heads. Historically speaking, new and successive distribution platforms such as MySpace (and more recently, Bandcamp, SoundCloud and BandLab) gave musicians the forum to realise their dreams of being heard all over the world and collaborate with like-minded talent without having to indenture themselves to the record companies. After all, if the Arctic Monkeys and Lily Allen could do it, then so can anyone. This logic translates as creativity direct from craftsman to consumer, and speaks to the indie-DIY ethos alluded to a moment ago.

By these tools and mechanisms the children at the dawn of the Third Millennium shine, and their creative enterprises can be broadcast for all to see; a permanent stamp of one's identity, forever *Out There* – fixed, immutable, certain, reassuring. We can 'plug-in-and-play' – that is to say, anyone can – with the popular promise that anyone can become designers, entrepreneurs and experts thanks to the munificent presence of connected technology.

I use the phrase 'plug-in-and-play' here to distinguish a consumer-friendly application from professional creative software packages. 'Plug-in-and-play' applications mean that the user need not have any skills in programming or knowledge of Web design or architecture to get quick results. More professional packages traditionally have often demanded more of their user: from a ground-up design process which engages code, design principles, security issues and copyright, to programming skills and knowledge of interfaces that only designers with expertise in the field can utilise effectively, and with a degree of flair. I have found in my experience of teaching creative design students, for example, a default attitude characterised with a view that they are not being taught enough about the software, and that making something using Illustrator or Final Cut Pro means that they can design something. This may well be the case sometimes – I have seen some formidable student work produced using programmes like these over the years. But the point here is that, just because you can use a piece of kit, some proprietary software or a widely available app, it doesn't make you a designer; nor does it mean that you understand creativity as a concept, a process or an act within the digital realm. For that to happen, an altogether higher level of engagement is required. All it means, in the end, is that you may have watched and followed a tutorial series on YouTube. Besides, anyone with a decent laptop, a fast broadband connection and a cracked copy of Adobe Creative Studio can accomplish a similar standard of aesthetic, given the time and a willingness to put in the graft.

This much I sometimes point out to student cohorts, and it may be an obvious point to some of them. But for others, it's a shock too, not to mention a betrayal of sorts. It is a betrayal by me as a tutor, for not lessening its impact (conventions in the higher education sector in the UK, as well as government policy, demand a consumer-driven attitude to satisfaction). And it is a betrayal by society, for not protecting these young people from the ravages of a free-market economy where one lives or dies by the strength of one's competitiveness. In essence, students on prohibitively expensive design courses, accruing massive graduate debts, compete with kids who have spare time, access to kit and a natural flair for design – and, crucially, no graduate debt – for jobs that may not actually exist.

I just indicated that one of the promises of Web 2.0 was that, by virtue of educational policy in the US, and in the UK, to place technology in the hands of schoolchildren as part of their learning experience, they are able to engage their own relationship to the technology itself. For those of us fortunate enough to be able to discuss ideas about technology for a living (whether at school level, in the university or in policy-formation) we are aware that this ideal engagement does not always materialise. A general example from anecdotal experience: when I ask students to critically engage with social technologies, they seem to have a habit of reverting to their identities as consumers. Whether this expresses as spontaneous log in to Facebook during lab sessions, or perhaps reverting to Wikipedia articles for information when asked to retrieve data on a topic (and not in the sense that they refer to article histories or talk pages underpinning the wiki). These kinds of actions are in substitution for research processes that are meant to develop critical thinking and theoretical engagement beyond factual sound bites.

One might suppose, though, that this default has something to do with the technology itself – that if you allow the tech into the classroom, the students inevitably play around. And in honesty, I would hardly blame them. Speaking from the perspective of many years teaching both film and media studies courses around the UK, I can assure you that it isn't *necessarily* so. Plenty of my students, past and current, have been excellent in terms of focus and attention, and I learn new things about my subject area from discussions with these students all the time. I learned of the comparative strengths and weaknesses of Snapchat use, for example, in an undergraduate class a few years ago. E-sports and other relatively marginal practices such as live streams of gaming walk-throughs, so students tell me, are key growth areas in mass media and communications services, as well as entrepreneurial career pathways, that are transforming our traditional understanding of television. And students have informed me of the alternative virtues of Vine and Reddit over and above Facebook and Twitter. But plenty of others have cultivated bemusement at the idea that anyone should treat film or media formats as anything other than entertainments, distractions and things to help one 'switch off' from the hassles of contemporary lifestyle. The disengagement then, it seems, is not the fault of the presence of technology in the room. Of course, its novelty might provide a distraction from the learning experience occasionally. What I refer to here, though, is the idea that disengagement itself is almost a default way of being – and that technology is, in some sense, an inhabitation (and a habitat) of distracted and omnipresent consumption which exists parallel to the tech itself.

In variants and using different languages, these arguments have been rolled out many times in media histories; in each instance identifying newer or newly named aspects of our relationships with technology. For example, Clay Shirky (2008) has spoken out about the effects of 'information overload' upon our ability to engage fully in the processes and procedures of knowledge acquisition. Sir Ken Robinson's well-known TED talk (2006) on education reform and the distractive effects of technology upon the attention spans of children is another salient example of these issues. The political implications for Robinson's stance is of particular interest to me; he doesn't condemn the technology itself, which is an important factor. However, he is quite critical of the pressure on children to conform to inappropriate and outdated academic processes, and is critical of the overstimulation from an abundance of attention-grabbing media devices and permanent states of connectivity, all of which combined tends to have a somewhat anaesthetising effect, disengaging students from their own learning experiences.

To an outsider, contemporary Digital Humanities can sometimes seem little more than algorithm-testing or visualisation of text, place or historical simulation. However, philosophy of science and technology (and, perhaps in particular, cognitive science) has armed the Digital Humanities scholar with a variety of terms and approaches. These describe the sophisticated relationships we have with technology that enable people to develop coping strategies for our overstimulated, mediatised (and globalised) culture. These terms include: prosthetic memory; extended cognition; disembodied telepresence; interculturalism; even

Jaron Lanier's antiquated phrase, *Virtual Reality* (now resurrected in an extraordinary new lease of life, thanks in no small part to Google's Oculus Rift project and the HTC Vive home VR system, as well as augmented reality wearable tech such as the much-hyped Google Glass project). The maths found in these arguments is fairly common-sense; the human brain is simply not designed for the levels of mediated stimulation, the persistent connectivity, nor the sheer amount of information at our disposal. But in many ways, to leave things at this common-sense level is not enough. At a more fundamental existential level, we (in the most generalised, collective sense) are at a loss. And this is ironic, given that Web 2.0 connectivity was supposed to be the way *out* of our collective funk, not a means of accelerating it.

The plan of work

Broadly speaking, the structure of this book covers three interrelated themes which intersect at the levels of theory, philosophy and new media praxis, with which I aim to address this phenomenon of acceleration. It should be noted here that in Part I of the book I devote a substantial amount of space to a companion commentary relating to issues prevalent in Web 2.0, social technologies and social media interactions. Some of these issues (the libre/gratis distinction and political economy; ethics and recognition in social interaction; collaboration and neoliberal competition) are discussed very much with key thinkers in mind (respectively: Lawrence Lessig and Christian Fuchs; Charles Taylor and Axel Honneth; and Clay Shirky and Michael Sandel). This is to both set up the context for the non-specialist reader, but also perhaps to more fully prepare the ground for Part II, where I introduce innovations specific to recognition politics, psychological theory and social technologies. I also break new ground in the sense that I apply these innovations to currents in social media studies. It should also be noted that although I develop the themes throughout the book roughly in the order in which they provisionally appear in the following few paragraphs, variations of these themes appear in a number of chapters, and do not necessarily follow in neat order according to those chapters. This is to fully acknowledge the interrelatedness of themes, and also to underscore the fact that one theme doesn't necessarily proceed or follow in a causal relationship from the others. However, it is hoped that the reader will glean from the provisional order I outline here the kinds of interrelatedness occurring throughout the book.

The first theme is to outline an *ethics* of Web 2.0 literacy, following up on some of the issues described in this introduction. In Part I especially, I discuss various aspects of media literacy – policy, legislation, technological innovation, social anxieties and so forth – with a specific focus on the British context and discourses around the notion of the digital. The conditions arising from the regulatory environment in the UK, and the steer in education policy towards a more 'Digital Britain', are the backdrop for thinking about the role Web 2.0 has historically played. This is a role that has helped to shape the political, social and cultural life of Britain, the legacy for British people subject to these policies and the future for the children of the Web 2.0 phenomenon. The ethics approach I draw upon in order to think these problems through is indebted to the communitarian views of Charles Taylor and closely follows up on the work of Michael Sandel's interventions in the arena of global economics (2012). My modest suggestion is that, by following this work, one can discern that the right questions are not being asked of the Web (nor of education, for that matter). Perhaps we ought to do more to ensure not only that the ends justify the means, but that the means are of themselves understood for what they properly are; that is to say, that the technology ought to be used to enrich people's lives (rather than impoverish them, in several senses of that term). Furthermore, this enrichment ought to take a form more aspirational than training to facilitate more efficient consumption of digital goods and services. In addition, the discussion takes the view that the instrumentalism of the data economy is not an easy fit, nor is it a good fit, for human beings as both social beings and as individual agents.

The second theme of this book relates to this aspect of 'fit', as the discussion revolves around the psychosocial roles of agency in Web 2.0 cultures, and the way in which people find themselves 'locked-in' to the configurations of *connectivity*. More specifically, I wish to discuss the tensions inherent in the psychosocial roles of individual and collective agency in the digital realm, and indeed tensions emerging in the anxieties surrounding the maintenance of popular distinctions – online/ offline; public/private; individual/community; work/leisure and so on. Generally, when we assert these distinctions, we are enacting an anthropocentric agency for the expression of identities as individuals, as members of communities and societies and as subjects operating within institutions. This expression occurs within (or against the backdrop of) the confines of bounded systems of laws, regulations and conventional standards. My argument is that, in Web 2.0-dominated cultural shifts, these tensions take on specific appearance-forms, which manifest in two concepts.

The first of these concepts is *affordance* – a concept first outlined with clarity by the ecological psychologist James Gibson, in his final work, *The Ecological Approach to Visual Perception* (1979). As will be discussed, this concept is sometimes drawn upon to concretise mediating relationships between technology, human desire and behaviour. This is largely the sense in which I employ the term. It ought to be acknowledged, perhaps, that often in new media rhetoric, the concept is related to, but distinct from, notions of accessibility, of technological determinism and of 'effects' debates. The other concept in which these tensions manifest is that of *always-on*. As we shall see, this accounts for a number of behaviours and cultural phenomena in social media engagement today as a state of permanent or semi-permanent connectivity. It also relates to the burgeoning interest in communication studies and security studies concerning the intricate and complex way that panoptic technologies (the many seen by the few – CCTV, surveillance technologies, security and data intelligence measures etc.) and synoptic technologies (the few seen by the many – social media applications, microblogging sites, even Reality TV and parasocial practices of remote or public intimacy) come together in an intense, image- and optic-driven social institutionalism. The notion of always-on, particularly in what I see as its articulation with affordance, draws from a number of diverse fields and is influenced by the work of Foucault (1977), as well as Mathiesen (1997) and Doyle (2011). Always-on perhaps finds its most visible articulation in the work of Sherry Turkle (2008, 2011, 2015). I want to argue that these concepts provide insight into recurring cultural themes of recognition and reflection – fundamental psychosocial building blocks for identity mobilisation – in popular online activities, which activate through the various tensions outlined above.

The third theme in this book, and perhaps the most innovative in terms of theoretical engagement, is that of cultural complexes and how they constellate in Web 2.0 relations; if you like, the 'psyche' aspect of lock-in described above, and how the ethics of connectivity necessitate a new approach to recognitive political and psychological thinking. This theme is, in essence, a critical theory of *recognition*. In my discussion of various ethical, philosophical and political approaches to self-realisation in interpersonal communications, as well as the ways in which recognition and identity-mobilisation manifest in online communications practices, I draw ideas from a number of psychology traditions. In this way, I substantiate the conceptual and theoretical frames implied in the notion of psyche as a component of any notion of self, as we might understand it today. The existing political and psychological theories of recognition, drawn mainly from the philosophical anthropology of Axel Honneth (1995, 2002, 2012) and social psychology and self psychology (Smith 2012; Kohut 2011) are both synthesised and moved forward considerably, in order to meet the challenges presented by connectivity.

Towards the end of the book, I engage a specific derivation of the term 'complex' from Jungian depth psychology. The complex in this sense brings together the building blocks of the psyche, often experienced as partial personalities in the Jungian terminology. Jungian and post-Jungian thought uses the term to describe the constellation of affects, images, emotionally charged associations and collective psychic material. The notion of the 'cultural complex' is a development of the original term in post-Jungian thought and psychotherapy (e.g., Singer 2004; Kimbles 2000). It is used to describe the psychosocial, cultural and political effects of collective psychic material, as well as powerful moods and behaviours characterised by repetition, lived out at a cultural level as part of a *zeitgeist* of attitudes and behaviours – worldviews that tend to become internalised by individuals through identification or amplification processes. I prefer to lean towards the post-Jungian *cultural complex*, rather than what I feel is more limited in the mentally centred Jungian complex. For me, the cultural complex tends to offer a more materialist outlook, is phenomenological in its theoretical framing and is historical in its character. During the course of this book, I draw these ideas together to develop a framework for connectivity ethics, relating to a concept I have developed elsewhere called the cultural complex of 'negative affordance' (Singh 2014). This complex is developed in psychic life when people tend to misrecognise the relationships they have with other people. More specifically, this involves a misrecognition brought on through an amplification of pressure to engage in contemporary practices of 'connectivity', which itself in turn feeds into a congruent misrecognition in the civic and political spheres where merely participating in online discourse becomes a synoptic for political, transgressive or subversive action.

Web 1.0, Web 2.0? (3.0, 4.0, 5.0?)

It is in the light of this thematic framework that I will proceed with the work at hand. Before I begin that work, however, I would like to address the following questions in order to set up the discussion: what exactly is, or was, 'Web 2.0'? Further, in what ways does the term Web 2.0 relate to the term 'social media'? Or, the term 'Internet', for that matter? And, because Web 2.0 was such a visible, historical cultural moment, should we stop at version 2.0? What about subsequent 'versions'?

Let us begin with the last question. It ought to come as little surprise that there are a number of often contradictory definitions of Web 2.0, and many of these attempt to define it through its distinction from earlier instances of Web formats and architecture (sometimes simply described as Web 1.0). Some commentators have emphasised *discursive*, rather than material, characteristics which distinguish various approaches to the Web. Matthew Allen, for example, has explored the emergence of Web 2.0 as a discourse of *versions*, rather than as a specific technology or set of technologies. As such, Allen recognises that 'Web 2.0 is a contested term which, in practice, has come to have several legitimate operating definitions' (2012: 261). This suggests that by extending the versioning process into Web 3.0/Semantic Web/IoT/wearable technology, are we not simply reproducing this versioning discourse? Indeed, I think that there is an always-already supersession logic to this discourse that merely serves to mystify and obscure. Other scholarship has sought to recast perceived Web 1.0 and Web 2.0 distinctions in terms of *approach*. And whilst these perspectives tend to maintain the version discourse through insisting on a distinction, they also attempt to reconcile the two sides of the issue by acknowledging other forces as work which demand that distinctions are maintained.

For example, in his book *Making is Connecting* (2011), David Gauntlett describes the differences between Web 1.0 and Web 2.0 through a gardening allotment metaphor: Web 1.0 featured lots of people doing often complex, creative work, but this work took place on separate and individual plots. Each person tended their own plot, perhaps sometimes visiting the plots of others, but, ostensibly, the plots remained separate, and were maintained by a particular gardener. 'By contrast, Web 2.0 is like a collective allotment. Instead of individuals tending their own gardens, they come together to work collaboratively in a shared space' (2011: 5). Web 1.0 attitudes tended to see other users as 'out there', as an audience of sorts. Gauntlett suggests that the power of the network reveals the potential for collaboration, where the older broadcast models of media are broken down, and the 'audience' is actually invited to come in and play. Thus, there is an interactive shift, from search and read-only functionality towards a 'plug-in-and-play' mentality.

This is in sharp contrast to other commentators who have described the political and social processes embedded in technological change to be deeply reactionary and restrictive. From a legal perspective, Lawrence Lessig (2004) has offered a well-known description of these reactionary forces within the context of international copyright law. Just as Lessig argues that societies as we know them cannot properly exist without property law, he also acknowledges the corruptive interpretation and dispensation of that law to benefit the interests of those in power at the expense of those without. He describes this eventuality as the result of a shift in legal and political emphasis, from a 'free culture' to a 'permission culture'. In his book *Free Culture: How Big Media Uses Technology and the Law to Lock Down Culture and Control Creativity* (2004: 8), Lessig writes that:

> For the first time in our tradition, the ordinary ways in which individuals create and share culture fall within the reach of the regulation of the law, which has expanded to draw within its control a vast amount of culture and creativity that it never reached before. [. . .] The consequence is that we are less and less a free culture, more and more a permission culture.

And as we shall see in Chapters 1 and 2 especially, following through some of Lessig's arguments, I suggest that this shift plays a crucial role in the critique of Web 2.0 and its creative potential. Gauntlett's position, which makes the argument that we are shifting from a 'sit-back-and-be-told' culture to a more 'making-and-doing' culture is countered, or at least in some sense diluted, by Lessig's position, which suggests the cultural shift is running in the other direction and contradicts the more positivistic freedom aspects of Gauntlett's model.

Terry Flew (2008) suggests that we need to take the distinctions back a step further, by thinking through difference in terminology; terms used in so-called 'new media' scholarship are often confusingly interchangeable. Starting with a definition and description of the Internet, Flew maps two of its central defining characteristics: its indifference to the content of data that is digitally encoded (a central tenet of Net Neutrality) and its capacity for differently configured computer systems to communicate with each other through common protocols. Dewdney and Ride (2014) elaborate on this kind of Internet/WWW distinction; the Internet ought to be thought of as a 'network of networked computers, made up of high speed connectors, transmission services and the management and storage of large-scale data', whereas the Web is a 'system of hyperlinking documents through a web-browser and distributed via the Internet' (2014: 55–56).

Alternatively, the Web might be thought of as an archive or library of documents and files containing any permutation of text, moving and still images, and graphics. In an interview with Vint Cerf, a central figure in the historical development of Internet computing who worked specifically on the evolution of packet switching and IP protocols, Flew seeks to map ways in which the Web changed as it became popular, and how this architecture differentiated itself from Internet infrastructure as a pure data communications network of networks. Cerf suggests that the early days of the Web eventually triggered a vast amount of information contributed by users, whereby consumers became producers. He also states that the Web provided a 'stunningly good medium' for collaborative work and play, a support for new business models, and a platform to provide aggregation of thin markets into dense ones regardless of location (2008: 15–16). In relation to this aspect of collaboration, Web 2.0 as a term is, more often than not, applied to the notion of 'participatory culture'. For Jenkins et al. (2006), this involves relatively low barriers to artistic expression and civic engagement; strong support for creating and sharing one's creations; informal mentorship whereby what is known by the most experienced is passed along; where contributions matter; and some degree of social connection between participants takes place (2006: 5–6). Wikipedia would seem an ideal candidate here as an example of Web 2.0 in this context, and an example of 'collective intelligence' – working towards the mutual recognition and enrichment of individuals (Lévy 1999: 13).

On the specific phenomenon of Web 2.0, Cerf (cited in Flew 2008: 16) is even more telling:

> The term is more marketing hype than real but there is an underlying opportunity to use new Web services standards to allow the business processes of different companies to automatically interact – accounts payable interaction with accounts receivable; order entry interacting with inventory fulfilment, and so on. The protocols associated with Web 2.0 will support such innovations.

The language here is quite instructive. The gear towards favourable conditions for business accountability and commercial applications is immediately discernible, whilst at the same time there is an acknowledgement that there are some 'business-as-usual' aspects to Web 2.0. That is to say, new business models, but the underlying social and economic logics, including the need for business efficiencies as a baseline concern, remain resolutely intact. This therefore requires some thought as to whether Web 2.0 represents any real or lasting change to these systems (as well as, perhaps, Web 2.0's underlying purpose, what it is properly for). This 'business-as-usual' approach is summarised in more robust terms by James Curran in his description of the 'New Economy' (2012: 5). He writes:

> The internet provides, we are told, a new, more efficient means of connecting suppliers, producers and consumers that is increasing productivity and growth. The internet is a disruptive technology that is generating a [. . .] wave of innovation. And it is contributing to the growth of a new information economy that will replace heavy industry as the main source of wealth in de-industrialising, Western societies. At the heart of this theorising is a mystical core. This proclaims that the internet is changing the terms of competition by establishing a level playing field between corporate giants and new start-ups.

Of course, Curran is implying that just because we are told that the Internet provides its promised democratic function, it doesn't necessarily follow that we are more free or emancipated, or that our interests are represented equally within society and reflected through patterns of Web traffic and content, or that markets are more competitive. Web 2.0, the plug-in-and-play world of user-friendly graphical interfaces, intuitive experience design and free-to-access applications, is laid over the top of Web 1.0 architecture, and Internet infrastructure, and in my view certainly gives an appearance that playing fields have been levelled by virtue of indicators such as its immediacy and even its popularity. By accident or design, these technological systems contain, for Curran, the key to the mysteries of fulfilling a kind of democratic manifest destiny; we are bound by and for the rules of free trade and a competitive marketplace, but the means to acquire a level and just playing field have been gifted us, and we would do well, one assumes, to honour that gift by playing the game.

Of course, millions of us do play the game. Flew argues that the concept of Web 2.0 has caught on for two reasons in particular. First, embedded within it are a range of features long seen as central to the notion of the Web as a communications infrastructure: participation, interactivity, collaborative learning and social networking; positive networking effects from harnessing collective intelligence – 'the quality of participation increases as the numbers participating increase, and this in turn attracts more users to the sites' (2008: 17). Today, this can be seen in the institutionalised popularity of 'super-blog' sites such as the *Huffington Post*, which, as time goes by, comes to resemble more and more a newspaper (complete with its traditional masthead, internationally based correspondents and dense editorial hierarchies) or news content producer. Second, some of the fastest-growing websites are based on Web 2.0 principles and, we could also emphasise, they are built upon media production and archive technologies and practices, e.g., Flickr (photography); Wikipedia (encyclopaedia writing and knowledge repository); YouTube (video); the now-defunct Technorati (a vertical search engine – indexing blogging, writing and journalism activities); Facebook (networking, documenting). With regards to this rise in popularity of Web 2.0 applications, Dewdney and Ride emphasise that 'The term "web 2.0" registered a profound set of changes in which websites included software that gave users the ability and opportunity to generate their own content and to share that within designated online communities' (2014: 57).

This usability function of Web 2.0 is of crucial importance, and, as we shall see in Chapters 1 and 2, fulfils a prophecy to achieve its nominal function: a democratised access for anyone with the even most basic media literacy. However, I will argue that this functional capacity is impoverished. Flew's 'quality of participation' is, in the communitarian sense, an empirical matter rather than an ethical one; that is to say, the Web 2.0 participation involved at a popular level is playful, creative and even communal, but is rarely fully civic in functionality. And, where one can fully acknowledge such movements, as discussed at length in Gauntlett's work or in the work of Banaji and Buckingham (2013), the fully offline immersion of users at the popular level in terms of civic action and intervention has not materialised, and perhaps this is not, therefore, its popular function after all.

When, for example, Jill Walker Rettberg differentiates Web 2.0 as a collection of second-generation Web sites, shifting from publishing content to services that allow users to share their own content and to use the Web as a platform (2008: 9), it is not made clear what that platform might be *for*, exactly. Web 2.0, and presumably whatever is in store as the next stage in Web evolution, was made possible in the first place by a combination of more sophisticated but simpler to use and cheaper technologies for the production of media content, combined with graphical hyper-linking, greater storage capacity at both local and remote levels and distribution infrastructures. Perhaps, then, this is enough for most people to engage – at the level of use, or consumption, through accessibility. Perhaps this is what people clamour for (if they clamour for anything): the technological affordance to consume content more efficiently and share those consumption habits more proficiently through simple 'plug-in-and-play' production.

Although this take on affordance is fairly common in academic discourse on Web 2.0, much of it is celebratory. Less common (although appearing with growing frequency since Nicholas Carr's influential think-piece for *The Atlantic* (2008) and subsequent best-selling book, which is partly based upon it (2010)), are critiques of how these shifts in media consumption might be related in some ways to our sense of selves, and to the relationships we create and maintain. These are issues I focus on in Part II of this book in particular, where I emphasise the remarkably accelerative effect upon the affirmation status of the individual. This is particularly in the formation of online identities, the mythology of individualism and self-actualisation and the process of individuation and self-realisation within online (particularly always-on) contexts. In a world already hyper-focused upon the parasocial cult of personality and individualist notions of meritocracy, with so many of us locked in to 'optic' societies, this acceleration is a contrary force to the progression of democratic agency that it is often nominally assumed to engage.

In the lexicon of thinking on the Web, there is a deflective and mystifying shift, from that of business to that of self-fulfilment. The versioning aspects of the '2.0' part are uncomfortably implicated in commercial logic and language of software upgrades, suggesting a linear progression in teleologies which does not match reality; and this is perhaps why it makes little sense to reproduce such mystification in subsequent versioning discourse (Web 3.0, 4.0 etc.). There are some crucial interventions emerging, however, deviating sharply from the mythologising of the individuated, participatory Web 2.0, user, which might allow us to diverge from the versioning discourse. In an early intervention, David M. Berry (2008) describes a version of Web 2.0 which identifies the linguistic turn of the kind found in Curran's mystified centre as key to its deflection effects. He writes (2008: 203):

> Web 2.0 emerged as a slogan after a conference organised by O'Reilly Associates, a publisher of open source technical manuals. The conference asked delegates and speakers to imagine that if today's Web was considered a version 1.0 (usually considered a buggy, unfinished and chunky version of software) then what would the second generation of the Web, or 'Web 2.0'

look like. This has proved to be an extremely influential idea and has exciting many new software development companies to pursue new and challenging web technologies and platforms.

Whereas Gauntlett would argue that Web 2.0 is 'not simply a particular kind of technology, or a business model, and it certainly isn't a sequel to the Web as previously known. Web 2.0 describes a particular kind of ethos and approach' (2011: 5), for Meikle and Young, O'Reilly's model of Web 2.0 defined as a business revolution and an attempt to understand how success can be met in the shift to online platforms for businesses more generally is the important emphasis over and above the creative and participatory outcomes. In effect, this approach to Web 2.0 represents an academic shift in emphasis towards labour and work. They write (2012: 66) that:

> This is an important distinction because it places a much-needed emphasis on the corporate imperatives that drive Web 2.0 projects. [. . .] the users do the unpaid work of building and promoting the business, creating its content, and generating advertising material through using the service.

This relationship where digital labour is not paid for, or at best is solicited through the exchange of labour for goods and/or services, is a subject I touch upon in relation to different themes in Part I of this book. For Web 2.0, as a guiding principle of its Web 2.0-ness, this usually and exclusively entails services rather than goods; for example, Google revenue is partly based around advertising streams through renting online spaces for advertising purposes, but this is a relatively small part of a much bigger picture. Its revenues also, and mainly, accrue through search data produced by its users (that is to say, the users of their free-at-point-of-access services) and leveraged or sold on by the proprietors.

There are some significant exceptions to this. Notably, these are examples where digital and real-world labour supplement one another. For example, well-known high street chains require their store employees to act as social media 'brand ambassadors'; that is to say, in exchange for goods from the store either gratis or at a concessionary price, employees like and share products endorsed by the chains across their personal and professional social media streams. They therefore not only produce track-backs to the company and its goods and services, but also rich data about the company, the employee, their friends and even their friends' friends (depending on how far the initial posts are shared, tagged and otherwise treated) to be archived or sold on to third parties. In tandem with these movements of data, at an informational level, strict social media policies are enforced by corporations to protect reputation and branding. For example, an employee tagged in a photo uploaded to Facebook behaving in a way deemed unacceptable (say, on a drunken night out with friends) and also identifiable as an employee in the photo (for example, wearing a branded sweatshirt worn as uniform in their place of work) could be subject to gross-misconduct measures. Classroom discussions are rife with tales of

friends, and friends of friends, having to defend themselves in an employer disciplinary meeting as a result of these kinds of scenarios, and such discussions are typified
by an expression of anxieties as to how carefully one needs to operate impression
management on social media sites.

This brings us to a question that will help to shape the final chapters of this
book: the anxieties, both social and psychological, surrounding the fundamental status of social media users, and Web 2.0 participants more generally. Some
political scientists suggest from a political economy perspective (e.g., Fuchs 2013;
Allmer 2015) that users of services such as Google, or Facebook, are also its *de facto*
employees (with none of the remuneration or rights conventionally treated as a
given in employment contracts). If one is to be persuaded by this approach, then
it follows that the users of such services ought not to be regarded straightforwardly
as the customers either. Public anxiety surrounding the use of products such as
personal photo galleries and other images, information regarding one's identity and
the data trails generated through social media use are fairly widespread these days.
Given the massive uptake in Facebook as the cardinal example amongst many of
the more popular social media applications, this ought not to be a surprise. In the
last couple of years, I have observed a much warier attitude amongst my students
when discussing aspects of social media use, online presence and privacy, for example. Patterns in terms of anxiety have emerged along these lines, and I have heard
countless testimonies concerning young people's conscious decisions to reduce
their social media use in tandem with modifications to self-disclosure behaviour
and privacy settings. Some of these anxieties doubtless stem from the increasing
awareness of some of these issues via news coverage – there are several well-known
studies which conclude such findings (e.g., boyd and Hargittai 2010; Madden and
Smith 2010). This is certainly a concern. However, my main focus for Part II of
this book is much more interested in tracing the psychosocial aspects relating to
another of Meikle and Young's observations. They state (2012: 67 [emphasis in
original]) that

> Much of this coverage and anxiety starts from an implicit assumption that
> Facebook's 750 million users[1] are its customers and should be afforded the
> respect this suggests. *But Facebook's users are not its customers – the users are*
> *the product.*

At first, this might seem a rather disingenuous statement, and indeed Meikle has
somewhat distanced himself from these direct arguments since (2016). However,
I argue that we have heard this before – couched in other language, perhaps, and
from another time and context (almost entirely). To me, such a statement is highly
reminiscent of classical Marxist notions of the commodity fetish as outlined in his
book *Capital*, vol. 1. In particular, in the section entirely devoted to the idea that
our relationships to commodities (that is, goods and services in simple terms) may
at first appear straightforward. Marx wrote that, 'So far as it is a value in use, there
is nothing mysterious about it, whether we consider it from the point of view that

by its properties it is capable of satisfying human wants, or from the point that those properties are the product of human labour' (1999: 42). However, the complications arise when the relations of labour to commodities are distorted through capital. Use value (how the value of a thing relates to subsistence; made for the use to which it is put) and exchange value (what a thing may be sold for) are on the one hand articulated, one in the other such that its usefulness arises out of its exchangeability, and on the other hand are subordinated to surplus value (profit). There are a number of reasons why this is of particular relevance to user participation, particularly in social media contexts, and to my mind has direct relevance to what Meikle has recently described as the 'sharing industry' of Web 2.0 (2016). Data held in a database holds no exchangeable value for the average user, even though for appearances' sake the information which the data represents may in many ways come to represent the *interests* of the user (mobilisation of identity, for example; expression of an opinion; exchange of an idea; sentiment; user gratification). In other words, an identity profile of the user has a value beyond the user themselves – a value which in current popular media contexts is rarely if ever harnessed by the user.

An example might help to shed light on this. Consider a database made up of profile details (tied inexorably closely to a sense of identity expressed in social media forms) whose value is added every time a user posts, clicks through, likes or comments on a post. This is value-added even to the point where mouse hovering, keystroke and field form data for unpublished posts can be traced through user activity and added to a data profile. One of the important questions this book seeks to raise in light of this concerns the complexity of identification mechanisms in such technologized contexts: what if we, as users, are over-identifying with the profiles we generate online? If not self-identifying as such, then perhaps being identified that way by external entities such as recruitment agencies, employers, friends and family? Furthermore, what happens if we misrecognise the processes via which such data is generated and sold, when the process itself is so intimately tied to our sense of identity, to our means of expression and to our everyday social encounters? What kinds of anxieties emerge, and what psychic implications occur in response to such states of misrecognition?

There are, of course, recent interventions from neo-Marxist and political economy sectors of the media and cultural studies spectrum which seek to address at least some aspects of these questions in relation to a number of key themes. For example, to digital labour specifically (Fuchs 2014; Scholz (ed.) 2013), to alienated and estranged labour in social media contexts (Andrejevic 2013; Fuchs 2015; Terranova 2004 and 2013) and resultant perceived threats to privacy and other democratic rights (Fuchs, Boersma, Albrechtslund and Sandoval (eds) 2012; McChesney 2013). Some, including myself, would suggest that these interventions are long overdue, and demonstrate a willingness to think through such processes and phenomena critically; to give serious consideration to historical specificity and continuity; and to identify an urgency in needing to deal with emergent problems associated with such phenomena. Indeed, Jaron Lanier's recent books (*You Are Not a Gadget* (2010) and *Who Owns the Future?* (2013)) seek to explore vaguely similar ground in terms of identifying a clear and emerging crisis in the field of digital labour – although, as we shall see later in this book, his suggestions for solutions fall very far from Marxist and neo-Marxist perspectives. Lanier makes the bold statement that 'The Internet has destroyed more jobs than it has created' (2013: 15), which contravenes, to an extent, the conventional wisdom about digital wealth creation. As is somewhat evident from this, Lanier's matter-of-fact approach to the impending economic crisis brought on by deindustrialisation in the developed world, and global division of labour, is characterised by the idea that subsistence has become disaggregated from the means available to us to earn a living. Thus, I would contend, the importance of critical inquiry and theoretical intervention in this field is confirmed – critics from all sectors of the political spectrum seem to converge around this one urgency, even if they cannot agree on the particular nature of the problem (and the particular kinds of value represented by the problem) and potential solutions.

To add to the evidence that these questions are both far from straightforward, and indeed somewhat contradictory, in his book *Networks without a Cause: a critique of social media* (2011), Geert Lovink takes a slightly different perspective. Straddling the boundaries between a critique of estranged labour on the one hand, and a view of identity-formation and expression on social media platforms on the other, Lovink's perspective is eye-catchingly critical of the contemporary media landscape. For him, Web 2.0 is the latest manifestation of a long process of tension and conflict, where 'friction-free' alliances between various stakeholders who had very different vested interests in the way the early Web evolved (states, corporations, artists, NGOs) are splintering apart in the real world, and this fragmentation is a symptom reflected in the evolution of Web discourse and functionality. Web 2.0 is, for Lovink, a saga that has run its course (2011: 1). As such, 'it is no longer sufficient to complain about network society's dysfunctionalities in terms of usability, access, privacy or copyright infringements' (2011: 3) because that historical moment is, for all intents and purposes, over. These are discourses which are embedded in our consciousness of what the Web is, and what it ought to be: a safeguard for, and platform upon which, public sphere engagements can be nurtured. I return to these in Chapter 1, as on-going (if fragmentary) normative ends, for which the promises of the early Web, which laid down promising roots in the soil of democratic aspiration, bear sour fruit.

Theorising the declaration of death

But, hang on a moment – am I actually saying that Web 2.0 is dead? Surely we've only just begun to explore its potential? Judging by nearly all of the studies just cited (many of them fairly recent), Web 2.0 and its concomitant technologies are still very much a part of the academic discourse on media ecology. The relationships evidenced between the identification discourses outlined in the questions

I posed a moment ago, addressing modes of *sharing* in both Web 2.0 and social media, seem to have cross-pollinated to such a degree that it is difficult to imagine one without the other. As a matter of fact, from the vantage point of the time of writing, it appears from here that the term 'social media' has not only come to replace 'Web 2.0', but often seems to elide all senses of the term 'Internet' as well, at least as far as popular culture goes. Allen (2012) reimagines the relationships of these related terms as a sort of timeline or continuum. This is particularly useful in the context of finding adequate grounds for critiquing the kind of innovation rhetoric that usually accompanies technological transformation, or declarations of revolutionary change, which have a tendency to embed relations of power within them. Like many scholars conducting inquiry into innovation of new media technologies, Allen's approach invests in a sense of tension between continuity and change, and additionally a sense that there are no points of singularity from which media technologies emerge. For my tuppence-worth, I would suggest that this continuum approach necessarily takes into account an historical, material and cultural perspective on technology, its prehistory and its possible futures. For example, Allen (2012: 262) states that

> [. . .] behaviours and sensibilities now usually discussed in terms of Web 2.0 predate the term, and indeed were evident in online activity prior even to the World Wide Web. This culture of use involves several features, principally that users create content as well as read it; and that access to and participation in this endeavor [sic] is part of a conversational approach to information circulation, involving online sharing within friendship groups.

If Web 2.0 is indeed dead, or at least on its knees, then surely it does not make sense that educational establishments are dismantling established media courses and tooling themselves up for the push towards digital skills provision in specifically Web 2.0 technologies? That is to say, the shift away from studying and towards doing; away from generalised critical acquisition, and towards vocational emphasis, professionalization and 'employability'? Why the discrepancy between what we see happening in the politically oriented wings of Digital Humanities and how institutions are responding to demands for skills? The answer to this should hardly be surprising, and can partly be accounted for by the ways that educational establishments tend to take what seems like forever to do things. Higher-education institutions do attempt to respond to trends in technological development or the marketplace, but within the demanding environment of intensified bureaucracy and quality control, it can take years to bring an educational innovation online. This institutional lag is echoed through different rates of access, modes of participation and cultural practices – shaped by local conditions and material, historical peculiarities that govern an extremely uneven context for the awareness, adoption and use of so-called new media technologies. As Allen (2012: 263) points out,

> Web 2.0 also appears to be a questionable act of periodicity, given that many of its assumed tendencies or features were inherent in the use of the web at least as early as the 1990s. [. . .] even if Web 2.0 does in some way speak to a qualitative change in the internet, this change did not occur at the same time for everyone.

Within this context, then, it seems counter-intuitive to the point of madness to set up educational courses dedicated to Web 2.0 and its *enfant terrible* of frank discussion and self-disclosure – social media – when these phenomena are both very small parts of much wider socio-cultural shifts, and are more-or-less obsolete, critically speaking. One of the problems, of course, with declarations of death in any theoretical discourse stems from the fact that there are few people who would agree with such declarations or, at the very least, upon the conditions within which that death is set. Ideally, with any teleological mapping of technology and innovation, situations in which the death of one technology and the rise of another technology to replace it tend to be fairly unproblematic: in such histories, a technology is superseded by a superior technology; demands for one technology fall off as newer, more exciting technologies come online.

These kinds of histories would have us believe that, for example, the sound film replaced the silent film because, rather straightforwardly, the former is superior to the latter. The same goes for colour film replacing black and white, and for cinemascope replacing earlier screen ratios. CGI animation replaced cell and stop-motion animation for the same reasons, and so on. These arguments are defensible only in the sense that replacements happened and, in an empirical sense, the newer technologies satisfied a demand for newer products and services, not to mention newer consumer experiences.

However, death does not come as naturally to technologies as we would ordinarily like to think. Claims to return to an authentic root of creativity or artistry are common in the creative industries. For example, the rock supergroup Audioslave made a point of declaring in sleeve notes for all LP releases that 'All sounds made by guitar, bass, drums and vocals'. The emphasis in Audioslave's music draws attention to the fact that synthesis and technical gimmicks are often regarded in rock culture with suspicion, as inferior or inauthentic. It echoes older assertions which seemed to be predicated on similar grounds – for example, as early as 1973, the rock band Queen were claiming 'no synthesisers' in the making of their albums (although this changed later in their career). In the field of cinema, the paratextual marketing material for George Miller's *Mad Max: Fury Road* (Aus, 2015) emphasised the use of traditional stunts, effects and editing techniques over the use of CGI – the idea being that CGI somehow deadens the realism and authenticity of setting. This was a promotional tactic little changed from that used in *Minority Report* (Spielberg, US, 2002), which used special features in its DVD release to emphasise the spectacular use of CGI effects, *and* presented the spectacle of Tom Cruise performing his own wire work and stunts through behind-the-scenes footage. In all of these examples, older technology is prized for its ability to communicate a sense of the 'real', where newer technologies have been tarnished with a reputation for corrupting this sense (but are nevertheless sometimes used to 'fudge' or complement traditional effects methods).

Staying for the moment with the theme of cinematic evolution as a well-trodden pre-Web example, various critical approaches have accounted for change in cinema by looking specifically at technological innovation itself, and have tended to return to questions of the imperatives behind the development of (for example) sound technologies (Altman 1985) and colour (Branigan 1986, Buscombe 2004) in commercial cinema. This has been reflected in the critical discourse on innovation in cinema: moving towards the next step of evolution of narrative film in particular, as a superior cinematic storytelling form. Importantly, when employing the term 'evolution' here, I am making a distinction between 'progress' and 'improvement' in critical discourse. The former can sometimes intimate change without associated value, whilst the latter always implies value.

Both sound and colour (first introduced at either end of the 1930s in commercial cinema respectively) have seen recent evolution in the form of Dolby 5.1/7.1 and IMAX systems, both of which arguably lend themselves comfortably to the kinds of filmmaking that occur in Hollywood today. *The Jazz Singer* (Crosland, US, 1929) and *Gone with the Wind* (Fleming, US, 1939), whilst by no means the first examples of sound and colour film respectively, are generally considered to be the first films around which marketing and promotion of these technologies were ostensibly centred. However, one could argue persuasively that it was as much the review system as it was promotional material from the studios that helped to ignite the popular interest in these films and the technologies they employed as it was due to the technological innovations themselves. Of course, whether this is a directly causal relationship, and in which direction this relationship might go, is another question. It is worth bearing in mind, however, that several so-called 'determinist' theories have developed in media studies and elsewhere, often regarded as antitheses, which attempt to address this causality. Raymond Williams' approach, for example, in *Television: Technology and Cultural Form* (1990) is often regarded, somewhat incorrectly, as a pure form of cultural determinism – that is, cultural practice drives the technological development in a cause-effect relationship. By contrast (and commonly taken in opposition to Williams in cultural studies approaches), Marshall McLuhan's technological determinist approach (1964), seeks to illuminate the development of technology as a force behind both social relations and cultural practice. Brian Winston (1986, 1996, 1998) incorporates both determinist approaches in his model of 'supervening social necessity' – that is, a kind of social determinism, in which certain elements within the social sphere (such as mechanisms of capitalism, popular culture, government policy etc.) determine which inventions become mass-produced and, in their turn, enable future research and development. In Heath's words (1980), there is a high level of 'interrelatedness' between technological, social, ideological and economic instances in the historical development of the cinematic apparatus.

The reason for this desideratum into the world of cinematic innovation is that it gives us historical perspective on technologies and their deaths which is not yet afforded in the context of Web histories. The historical innovation of the Web, whilst highly visible, and a subject of this book, has not had enough time to culturally bed itself down to the point where one can make as clear assumptions of the interrelatedness of historical instances as is the case with cinema. However, one can quite clearly see that discourses around innovation, supersession and death are shared within cinematic histories and those of Web technologies. One means by which we might engage such questions is through an examination of the state of theoretical discourse in the academy, the casualization of academic media studies and the 'vocationally focused' shift in emphasis at a policy level throughout the university system in the UK. I touched upon some of these themes in *Feeling Film: Affect, Authenticity and Popular Cinema* (2014), and in this introduction have already mentioned my own experiences of teaching design-focused courses, in relation to what might be described as a shift from education to training.

In my view, there is absolutely nothing wrong with training. It has an important place in the learning experiences of ordinary working people, and provides some sort of chance for those people to keep up with the challenges of a fast-changing professional workplace. However, as I will go on to develop in a number of ways during the course of this book, there are several ethical dimensions for this shift (particularly in the arena of media and digital literacy) which such a focus tends to ignore and which we, as media educators, forget at our peril. At the most abstract level, perhaps, these ethical dimensions of a well-rounded media education towards full digital literacy take the form of subject knowledge. Perhaps more specifically, such digital literacy affords, in practice, the theories which help us to question why it is that such technological and cultural shifts take place, further to the questions relating to how one might go about using such technologies in the workplace. This issue brings us to another kind of death: the death of theory – particularly within the educational environment.

McQuillan et al., in their edited collection *Post-Theory: New Directions in Criticism* (1999: ix), state that 'The death of Theory is a persistent theme in Theory. Theory has been troubled by futures, ends and limits for some time. In effect, what is at stake is the right to write its own epitaph.' There is, it seems, nothing new in theory, in participating in the declaration of its death. By the same token, McQuillan et al. admit that, if anything, 'Nothing stimulates the production of Theory like the proclamation of its own death, regardless of who makes the proclamation'. The 'death of theory', therefore, is an ongoing meta-theme of theory, but I would also say that it is one of its motivations and is an object (worthy) of its study.

Further to the notion of the casualisation of media studies and its related disciplines, in her book *Thinking in Images*, Catherine Constable opens with an attack on a general dismissal of theory, by stating that 'Film theory is in crisis. This frequently made assertion can be seen as a reflection of a general concern about the status and value of theory and theorising' (2005: 1). This statement, by itself, reflects the state of film studies in general in the UK and, whilst perhaps not directly a concern of this book, if her claim may be upheld, then it has far-reaching consequences for how film and media theorists today work and disseminate their research in the university. This 'general concern', centred on the value of theory and theorising, is an observational remark regarding the problematics of educational policy; of what media studies should focus on in higher education (in the classroom, in scholarly publications, and in research funding bids and impact case studies), and why. As Constable (2005: 1) goes on to say:

> One such solution has been the suggestion that all theory should be abandoned because it is overly complex and ultimately unproductive. [. . .] I would argue that complexity is not an indication of lack of efficacy and the claim that all theory should be simple if it is to be useful is itself a problematic assumption.

What Constable finds objectionable in its focus on productivity is the fundamentally utilitarian view espoused by neoliberal educational policy, which does not engage with theory as work, necessarily; theory's place as a signifier of vocational value, and theorising as a transferable skill, have certainly come under scrutiny in recent years in institutional practice. My point here is that the provision for media literacy in general, and digital literacy in particular, has taken on a patina of empirical, rather than ethical, concerns. The danger here, is that we are entering an era where the use and consumption of the technologies available to us becomes the focus of education (the questions of what and 'how to'), at the expense of critical engagement, and knowledge of why our relationships with media technology are the way they are (the questions of why and 'how come'). An additional danger is that we are confronted with a problem that we are tempted to tackle whilst entrenched in divisions broadly drawn along the lines of disciplinary difference. The main challenge here is to recognise the ubiquity of the situation, and to accept the fact that meeting the challenges of empirically focused policy requires that recognition. Geert Lovink has written about these challenges extensively. On the question of the salience of Constable's ideas for digital media studies, as much for traditional film studies, I draw the reader's attention to a comment that Lovink makes in his book *Networks without a Cause* (2011: 77–78). He writes that

> Digital media studies rarely have been much of a critical intellectual project. The maniacally impulsive culture of pop has proven to be a black hole for theory talent. Instead of generating concepts at a Twitter pace, most 'new media' ideas are neutralized and flattened within a general atmosphere of budget cuts and slow change. [. . .] Theory is no longer a potpourri of living ideas but a fixed collection of twentieth-century canonical texts.

Within this quote one might find the seeds of both despair and hope. It seems that a flagrant disregard for the ethical dimensions of the learning experience, in favour of an altogether more instrumentally driven empirical model of customer service, is the order of the day – at least in the UK, if not elsewhere, and at least amongst the arts and humanities subjects and probably the 'softer' sciences. We might despair at the thought that older paradigms and ideas are not adequate to the challenges of the fast-paced changes associated with our media ecology. The curious mix of choices currently on offer for the academic, where research needs to be third-streamed and publishing is both slow to move but embraces the speed and finance of the open access market. This effectively means that theoretical consolidation is near-impossible. Yet the statement is also hopeful, in that we find ourselves in a position very similar to the brothers and sisters with whom we share our interdisciplinary departments; and as with any theory-building project, starting from collegial spirit is as good a place as any to proceed.

Note

1 As of March 2014, 1.13 billion users (or, more accurately, user accounts – these could include fake accounts, secondary and tertiary accounts for users or groups, and bot accounts), according to Facebook's own published statistics. To give a snapshot of the exponential rate of user increase, as of end of July 2015, 1.49 billion monthly active users were registered on the http://investor.fb.com/index.cfm site.

PART I
Connectivity and the spirit of conviviality

1

A COMMUNITARIAN DISQUISITION ON DIGITAL LITERACY

Geert Lovink (2011) usefully summarises early Web commentary as being comprised of four key themes or discourses. These discourses cover usability, access, privacy and copyright, discourses which underpinned some of the themes I addressed in the introductory chapter, and I continue that discussion here. Together, these ideas, and ways of communicating these ideas, constitute powerful freedoms of opinion, communication, expression, economy and creativity. These familiar freedoms are commonly thought of as key characteristics of modern democracies, as well as vehicles for the mobilisation of identities within such political frameworks. Indeed, in the popular sense, these ideas, communicating such freedoms, are key to understanding the principles driving the Web, particularly as kinds of promises made on the potential of the Web for democratic process. Of course, these promises for democracy were always far-fetched; and, indeed, as John Bellamy Foster and Robert McChesney state in an article for the *Monthly Review*, the far-reaching aspirations of the early commentators on Internet technology certainly had the highest hopes for its social and political impacts. They outline these hopes as 'more competitive markets and accountable businesses, open government, an end to corruption, and decreasing inequality', amounting to kinds of promises towards a better life (2011: para 5). Indeed, so stark and damning is their critique of Web discourse that it is worth repeating here at length.

> The Internet, or more broadly, the digital revolution is truly changing the world at multiple levels. But it has also failed to deliver on much of the promise that was once seen as implicit in its technology. If the Internet was expected to provide more competitive markets and accountable businesses, open government, an end to corruption, and decreasing inequality—or, to put it baldly, increased human happiness—it has been a disappointment. To put it another way, if the Internet actually improved the world over the past twenty years as much as its champions once predicted, we dread to think where the world would be if it had never existed.

Of course, many people would claim that their lives have indeed changed for the better, particularly in the realm of participatory cultures where the technology itself seems to afford ever-greater access to the means of production, and a sense of connection with others who also participate. In sum, for Foster and McChesney, the early Internet, and subsequently the Web, promised so much and seemed to deliver; and yet in some ways, we live in a world strangely uniform in its inequalities, suffering and corruption.

As we shall see in Chapter 2, several well-known thinkers on these issues, such as David Gauntlett (2011) and Henry Jenkins (1992, 2006, and with Green and Ford, 2013, and with Ito and boyd, 2015), have suggested that, in various ways, the very act of participating in media connectivity and creativity creates the conditions for a more democratic culture. This is connected to an older argument involving the importance of a literate public for the dissemination of democratic ideas and literacy in general as a mechanism for increasing political awareness and participation. For Lovink, commentators more generally have often concentrated on the relative functionality or dysfunctionality of these connectivity elements as a key indicator of the health of democracy at the turn of the millennium, and, indeed, one might think of this approach as sitting in the tradition of debates on the state of the public sphere.

In my view, we need to think through these issues within the specific cultural and political frameworks of digital literacy, as this feeds off both the aspirations of all four Web discourses Lovink mentions, and also provides us with material outcomes of these discourses in the formation of policy and legislation in the area of digital literacy. This is even the case in relation to Lovink's remarks in regarding Web 2.0 as having run its course, and therefore killed off the urgency of these questions in popular and academic criticism. As stated in the Introduction, for Lovink, Web 2.0 is 'no longer sufficient to complain about network society's dysfunctionalities in terms of usability, access, privacy or copyright infringements' (2011: 3) because that moment is, for all intents and purposes, over. However, I want to argue that the disappearance of these discourses (or at the very least, their reduced urgency) is something of a signifier for the ways in which the ideological contestation for the status and definition of digital literacy has tended to decouple from the civic (and, therefore, ethical) values which underpin it as a public educational project.

In the course of Chapters 2 and 3, I intend to take the reader through some of the concerns in defining and refocusing what we might take digital literacy to mean, particularly in light of some of the myths surrounding notions of creativity and connectivity – and, therefore, how we might proceed with an ethically focused media education in response to currents in Web 2.0 discourse. Before this, however, it will be necessary and useful to take a step back, asking some key questions regarding Web 2.0 discourse. In what ways might one start thinking ethically about how the death of Web 2.0 came about in the first place? Where does the notion of its death come from, and what specific moral forms does it take? How might one reconcile this with the current focus on Web 2.0 and digital skills, social media strategies, policy-making in the UK and shifts in emphasis within media education?

Four Web discourses on promises made and broken: usability, access, privacy and copyright

I would like to start by drawing from the field of information ethics in order to tease out some of the salient concerns for Web and Web 2.0. Here, one may begin by thinking through Richard Mason's (1986) seminal paper, 'Four Ethical Issues of the Information Age' in *Management Information Systems Quarterly*. In this paper, Mason outlines four main ethical issues for information thinking. These may be summarised (1986: 5) as follows.

- Privacy: 'What information about one's self or one's associations must a person reveal to others, under what conditions and with what safeguards? What things can people keep to themselves and not be forced to reveal to others?'
- Accuracy: 'Who is responsible for the authenticity, fidelity and accuracy of information? Similarly, who is to be held accountable for errors in information and how is the injured party to be made whole?'
- Property: 'Who owns information? What are the just and fair prices for its exchange? Who owns the channels, especially the airways, through which information is transmitted? How should access to this scarce resource be allocated?'
- Accessibility: 'What information does a person or an organization have a right or a privilege to obtain, under what conditions and with what safeguards?'

These ethical issues are useful to consider the more general ethical dilemmas with which we are confronted in the field of technology. They are also useful in thinking about how our digital lives overlap considerably with our political identities as individuals, as well as our social being, constituted as members of communities or as individual actors within institutional frameworks. In fact, these are issues to which I return, in various forms, within a variety of contexts throughout the remainder of this book.

Certainly, even the more practically oriented courses in the field of digital media studies have at their centres some sort of coverage of these themes or, at least, a combination of some of them. Indeed, those educators I have spoken to regarding the direction of digital content in media studies have managed to keep some of the more obvious principles intact. To my mind, especially when one takes into consideration the shifting definitions of such concepts, and the shifting emphasis in importance amongst these issues in the course of the last two or three decades in the field of information ethics, these issues remain remarkably salient. This salience has been tested out in the field.

For example, Freeman and Peace (2005) take the idea of 'justified hacking' as a test case, stating that the 'ethical nature of the hack depends on the actions being protested, the violation of another organization's property, and the resulting damage done' (2005: 10). This can be thought through in relation to wider ethical challenges where illegal acts may in some cases be deemed ethical. The classic case usually cited in legal studies is that it was illegal to hide Jews in Germany and certain occupied territories during World War II. Clearly there seems to be a humanitarian aspect to such an action which would make this an ethical thing to do, but this activity historically took place as an illegal activity. In terms of justified hacking, therefore, Mason's terms remain salient.

As an aspect of digital literacy and ethics which will be the focus of discussion later on, the notion of 'accuracy' is an interesting one here. Ordinarily, and certainly in the wider field of media studies, one might assume that accuracy of information is important in dealing with problems associated with anonymity, grooming, data protection and security, misrepresentation, input- or system-error – in fact, a whole host of familiar and newsworthy problems. Indeed, an empirical view might assume that, in order to pay for the services or applications of a company – services which, in the case of many popular social media applications on the market today are free to access – they would (and ought to) have the right to data on you, yielded from your use of the service or application. However, to take a properly ethical view, there may be reasonable exceptions to this. In falsifying data in a hack, one might be, say, the victim of domestic abuse and in hiding from an abuser. It is therefore entirely understandable that one might wish to protect or falsify data on location, shopping habits, visual information such as photographs, surreptitious webcam snapshots and so on to protect oneself. So many everyday technologies run background location-based data in popular applications. In this scenario, it is reasonably justifiable that the victim would seek to mitigate against location-based data being used to track them down by an abusive party through a malicious hack. This would particularly be the case where options to alter privacy settings or switch off location-based data within the parameters of the applications themselves have failed. The automation of such services, as well as the connectivity between programmes (e.g., Facebook Connect- and Slingshot-type processes; Instagram one-touch upload functionality; Google+, Instagram and YouTube interconnectivity etc.), and the default settings of many of these applications set to publicly viewable, means that although such openness of information is arguably unintentional, the outcomes often tell a different story. It is also worth noting that this kind of hack to protect oneself from harm might contravene the terms and conditions of the use of both the mobile hardware (and any associated contract) and the applications running on that hardware, but in this scenario such behaviour might be reasonably and ethically justified as steps toward protection from real harm.

This is also closely linked to the idea of privacy. In recent years, major news events covering cases such as the newspaper hacking scandal and the subsequent Leveson inquiry in the UK, the Wikileaks scandal and the Snowden/NSA case all fed off anxieties surrounding security and privacy. Certain questions have emerged: what is public knowledge, what ought to be kept as private matters or matters of national security and what is in the public interest to know? Indeed, in such extreme hypothetical cases similar to the one mentioned above concerning a victim of domestic abuse in hiding from their abuser, the notion of privacy extends to security (being fearful for one's own life) and the very real harm that might ensue if one's identity and location are exposed. However, these ethical considerations ought properly to also apply to less-extreme cases. Leveson was not only particularly instructive in opening up such questions, but also instrumental in exposing the limitations of relying on a public inquiry to mobilise policy at an administration level. Indeed, the UK's historical digital literacy policy and e-security legacy in the light of recommendations as set out in the 'Byron Report' (2008), which examined aspects of children's safety online, and offered some reasonable and realistic recommendations for policy (most of which were never enacted) seems to evidence this limitation.

In relation to accessibility, this issue is closely related to both property and accuracy issues – for example, how much access should an individual have to information stored about him or her in another entity's system? Again, relating to data mining as a consensual practice in exchange for free-to-use and free-at-the-point-of-access applications and services, there are serious questions that perhaps ought to be raised with regards to exactly how much people understand concerning how information and data about them is used, stored, secured and sold on to third parties. The extent to which the importance of this comes to light revolves around a growing public awareness of the encroachment of such intrusive and open practices and how this has quietly eroded yet another facet of privacy in modern democracies. I discuss the implications of such erosion and encroachment in relation to the psychological dimensions of connectivity, identity and alienation throughout Part II of this book.

Once again there are intersections with other ethical issues and, in particular, with the notion of digital property – and, specifically for Freeman and Peace, intellectual property (2005: 14). They ask questions that address aspects of ownership of information, storage and security of data and if that data is representative of someone specifically. Current examples might include their consumption habits, their Snapchat stories, photo galleries on Facebook where they have been tagged and identified etc., and whether or not that person has the right to access and alter that data.

Of particular salience here is the usual prevalence of news stories to create moral panics around the uses of technology and the perceived safety (and indeed, wildness) of children and youths. The fact that location-based data is often embedded at a meta-level in photo and video galleries in many social media applications is a cause for anxiety, particularly in cases where parents may have, in an entirely innocuous everyday act, posted snaps or video clips of their children. The stories go something like this: what's to stop a sexual predator from tracking these children down using the metadata found online, and the visual information represented by the photograph? The anxieties caused through such attention to these phenomena are real enough – and typical parents' responses might include removing photos and content relating to their children and/or changing privacy settings retrospectively. My view, however, is that this is not the end of the story. Tagged photographs or video clips of this sort present us with a specific problem. Again, similar anxieties might be caused and similar questions raised concerning the online safety of children, and the subsequent potential abuse of information and data gleaned online (in this case, information-rich identity tags linking, potentially, to other social media profiles as well as providing real-world names and details). However, in addition to this dimension, a more general ethical question ought to be raised regarding the practice of tagging and how data might be generated about other users without their direct knowledge or consent. For minors (and especially children who do not meet the minimum age requirements to hold their own social media accounts) the question of consent seems to have been disavowed altogether, because they are not of majority age to provide any such consent. This practice of being tagged without consent (and, sometimes, without knowledge on the part of the 'tagged') can be examined, for example, in the following hypothetical scenario.

'Jared' is tagged by 'Phil' in a photograph (taken in 2012 and posted on Facebook in 2013) on a night out at his student union bar. At the time he was snapped, Jared was drinking alcoholic cocktails featuring a well-known energy drink during a drinks promotion-themed night, of the kind prevalent in student union bars throughout the UK, with the logo of the energy drink clearly made out in a canvas banner in the background of the photograph. Jared had been working at the local branch of a well-known electronics retailer during the day, and went straight to the union bar to join his friends, still wearing his branded staff uniform. He is unaware that he has been tagged because he hasn't examined his timeline with close scrutiny and has not checked his privacy settings since an automated update happened the week previous to the night of the photograph. Besides this, he is unaware that Phil has the ability to tag him in photos. Jared graduates in 2013 and wishes to put his wild student days behind him, and so quits drinking and enjoys a healthy lifestyle. He is also not a particularly heavy user of Facebook, preferring outdoor activities, and after graduation leaves his account almost completely inactive. In 2015, Jared applies to work at an accountancy firm, but despite being the most capable applicant, fails to make the interview round thanks to the recruitment policies of the firm, who employ specific social media sweeps of applicants' profiles. The photo Phil took of Jared incriminates him in dubious night-time behaviour of the sort that the firm would disapprove of in their employees. The firm have a policy of not providing feedback to candidates who do not make the final interview round for job applications. Jared therefore remains unaware of the incriminating photo. Forward to 2017, and Jared receives a written notice threatening legal action from the retailer he worked for as a student for contravening his employer's social media policy. He tracks down the photograph in question, removes the tag and asks Phil to remove the picture. Phil complies. However, during 2019 Jared receives several marketing calls from an energy drinks company, several marketing emails from a dating site and from an electronics retailer and marketing texts from low-cost insurance companies. These companies all have data files on Jared's consumer habits, which include, nominally, all of the practices which may be inferred from the data gleaned from his social media profiles.

These are, of course, over-simplified and fairly extreme hypothetical possibilities that recent 'opt-out by default' initiatives such as GDPR are set up to mitigate. However, it is perfectly within the realms of possibility that any of these eventualities might occur, purely beyond Jared's control but within the bounds of legality.

Ethically speaking, the question of agency is of particular importance. Jared appears to have little in his defence here, because this has all occurred within the legal bounds of the terms and conditions of Facebook use, to which he agreed, and within the rights of the institutions which have decided to take umbrage. The fact that he, along with millions of other users, hadn't paid any attention to the terms and conditions policies of his social media accounts is of no concern in the legal sense. Neither is his ignorance of his former employer's social media policies – nor, it would seem, is there a moral right to protection from marketing spam.

As you can see, via this hypothetical case, the questions around the right to access and alter personal data (as well as clarity on the terms of its use) are questions which extend well beyond the realm of social media applications, and ought to be of concern to the knowledge economy and those working within it. A fairly well-known example of this problem can be found in Jaron Lanier's essay for *Edge*, titled 'Digital Maoism: The Hazards of the New Online Collectivism' (2006). In this essay, Lanier outlines specific problems relating to the privileging of the wisdom of crowd-thinking on wikis, and Wikipedia specifically. He even goes as far as describing it as a form of online collectivism or reminiscent of a Maoist rationalism, where each addition of grassroots thinking leads inexorably to a fundamental proletarian truth of some kind. This is the notion that the group-think is more wise and accurate than any one single mind could be. Lanier's position clearly is something of a criticism against some of the more anti-elitist (and, one could say, anti-intellectualist) leanings of the Wikipedia ethos. He cites that fact that, every so often, Wikipedia describes him as, amongst other things, a 'filmmaker', a fact that he disputes. In fact, he has attempted to change this attribution many times; but in each instance of change, the article reverts back to the previous version (the current version of the article at time of writing omits this fact, but cites the 'Digital Maoism' essay itself).

The fundamental difference between Wikipedia and frozen encyclopaedias is often thought to revolve around the fact that Wikipedia has the ability to constantly evolve and adapt to changes in knowledge bases. This is true, although one might also say that this deflects from another truth which has been associated with Web 2.0 cultures. This truth asserts that elite knowledges, and assertions of individual ownership of knowledge, are often discouraged in favour of widening participation and the virtues of collective thinking, an extreme application of what James Surowiecki (2004) has described as the 'wisdom of crowds'. Clearly in this case, however, Lanier surely knows whether or not he really ought to be considered a filmmaker, given by his own admission that he made a single, poorly produced amateur film during the 1980s, and has not really showed interest in following this career path since.

There are some well-known critics of this group-think tendency aside from Lanier. For example, in his best-selling book *The Cult of the Amateur* (2007), Andrew Keen seems to express an understandable, though flawed, defence of specialism against a perceived insidious growth of amateurism and a general banality in participatory media of the kind found in Web 2.0 cultures and technologies. His position is understandable in that these user-generated interventions into art, intellectual life and social dynamics seem to have indiscriminately devalued specialist knowledges and instead champion a species of relativist, levelled knowledge. Conversely, however dangerous it is to overplay the hand of political engagement in Web 2.0, Keen's rather reactionary response to such challenges does not, to my mind, place *enough* emphasis on the political challenges such practices present to hierarchical structures of elitism, and to inequality in cultural and social capital.

Both Lanier's umbrage and Keen's reaction to this breaking down of traditional knowledge bases raise some important considerations with regards to ownership of face-value information, which lies on top of (although in concert with) the data layer in Web architecture. Lanier's oft-communicated anti-Marxism is equally visible in his recent work *Who Owns the Future?* (2013), a work to which I devote some discussion in Chapters 2 and 3. As we shall see, in that book, Lanier is both vehemently anti-corporate and anti-Marxist in his approach to what he perceives as an inevitable economic crisis in the information sphere, and the global data economy in general. Whatever the evaluation of his position in relation to the relative merits and flaws of political economy or corporate-driven entrepreneurial cultures, one might find a sharp perceptiveness in Lanier's observations regarding immediate ownership of and control over the information representing oneself. It feeds into a cultural anxiety of the ability to express one's identity and to keep oneself out of harm's way. This is not just in terms of pure physical harm, although this is certainly a consideration, but also from unwanted negative attention and online abuse. It also feeds an anxiety around being able to engage others in digital environments, using these remarkable tools at our disposal without having to compulsorily remain connected by social, institutional and economic pressures.

What is telling in Lanier's position is that he embodies a number of striking contradictions as a commentator, a professional, a scientist and an artist. Indeed, in many of his online talks (found readily via Vimeo, YouTube and a host of other video streaming sites) he seems to fully acknowledge and appreciate the contradictory position he occupies in digital cultures. The following question that Freeman and Peace posit in their review of Richard Mason's work could just as easily have fallen from the typing hands of Lanier himself: 'Is it best for society to allow one company to consistently maintain a dominant market position in an industry that impacts our lives on such an everyday basis?' (2005: 14). It is, granted, entirely possible that Lanier would feel compelled to qualify this kind of question with a remark on his current employment status. He has occupied numerous corporate positions and worked on a number of high-profile development projects; at the time of writing, one of his current occupations is as a computer science consultant at Microsoft. However, the kinds of 'one company' to which Freeman and Peace hypothetically refer, Lanier has drawn out in specific examples as 'siren servers' (2013). These are a small and shrinking group of super-successful companies (such as Microsoft, Google, Apple, Amazon and so on) who have cornered the data market, and are increasingly the only players equipped to deal with the masses of Big Data that exist today. To put it simply, this is *media concentration*; accelerated, amplified and intensified to the point of virtual monopoly.

Although he may well balk at the comparison because of his critical stance towards the political Left, in my view, Lanier's position on this bears a remarkable resemblance to Noam Chomsky's view of concentration strategies in traditional corporate media contexts (with Herman 1988). The modest solutions to current situations are very distinct in both thinkers. However, the basic structures regarding access to information, the ownership of its production, dissemination and interpretational use that Chomsky identified as characterising multinational media corporate practices, in collusion with various nation states and power interests, are similar in Lanier's worrying analysis of information flows. To draw from Freeman and Peace's humble conclusions regarding the ethics of information, 'These monopolistic situations gained through legal practices could, in coming years, find themselves in conflict with the best interests of society' (2005: 14–15). As we shall see in Chapter 2, this certainly seems to have come to pass. For now, to set up the ethical parameters of this kind of conflict, I wish to outline a distinction in communitarian moral philosophy as a model for thinking through the properly ethical dimensions of any digital literacy project.

Digital literacy: the ethical and the empirical

A moment ago, I briefly touched upon what might be described as an empirical view of free-to-use and free-to-access services and applications. In this view, one might assume that at some stage in the creative or product development process someone has given up their time, their labour and their considerable knowledge in order that the development proceed at all. Therefore, it seems to follow that in order to pay for the labour and overhead costs involved in providing the gratis services or applications of a company, a user could reasonably be asked to give up the rights to the data streams they generate through their use. Regularly, in social media applications and services, media companies assert their right to collect, accumulate, store and sell data that the user generates. I also intimated, however, that to take a properly ethical view, there may be reasonable exceptions to this right. In what follows, I wish to outline exactly what I mean by this.

In order to proceed with this work, I would like to draw out a speculative methodology for an ethics of Web 2.0, from the writings of communitarian moral philosopher Charles Taylor. In his book *The Ethics of Authenticity*, he outlines a 'culture of authenticity', and in the face of the challenges presented to us in such a culture, Taylor suggests (1991: 72) that we need to

> [. . .] undertake a work of retrieval, that we identify and articulate the higher ideal behind the more or less debased practices, and then criticize these practices from the standpoint of their own motivating ideal. In other words, instead of dismissing this culture altogether, or just endorsing it as it is, we ought to attempt to raise its practice by making more palpable to its participants what the ethic they subscribe to really involves.

Taylor's language is quite specific here. He is making explicit an approach to thinking ethically as in some ways flying in the face of corrosive practices ('debased', as he describes them) and the motivations behind the choices that people make in the face of pressure to slide into such debasement. We need to, effectively, rise above the kinds of ideals that cause more harm than good, to think about what we would want, what good we would want to achieve in the world and what right choice could we wish to make to the benefit of the most people. In my view, this could be put in other words: to rise above the pedestrian, uncritical and impoverished ambitions of material acquisition for its own sake, and the twin cults of sustainability and (individual) personality. In the context of this current study, this would be applied to developing (digital, amongst other) literacies in the service of public projects, perhaps exclusively (though not necessarily so), rather than the current exclusive appearance form of servicing a consumer culture and a self-serving and somewhat narcissistic individualism. This ultimately involves taking a real ethical position – taking a stand. Taylor clearly sought to do this in much of his career, and we can see influences of this kind of position in recent work into digital media ethics (van Dijk 2005; Ess 2009; Kieran 1999), economic philosophy and anthropology (e.g., Graeber 2013; Foster and McChesney 2011), and in Lanier's recent interventions (2010, 2013). I will go on to discuss some of these specific positions in the following chapters. For now, this kind of standpoint might be used as a beginning to inquire into the poverty of ambition laid out for digital literacy policies in the UK, and ways that we might begin to raise the bar in terms of what goods we might aspire to.

Here, specifically, I would like to draw from Michael Sandel – a moral philosopher whose own work clearly owes a debt to Taylor, and indeed whose positions on policy (particularly in relation to the economy) might be described in communitarian terms (although Sandel himself might object to the label as such). I use Sandel's work because it seems to me that his views on the economy are helpful in thinking through how current impoverished policies on digital literacy, and the limitations of Web 2.0 culture, come to pass in the first place. To generalise, one might describe his recent book *What Money Can't Buy: The Moral Limits of Markets* (2012) as a study in how the dogmatic and popular insistence on monetisation as an ideological principle of efficiency and fairness for all spheres of life is a clear example of plain wrong-headedness. He sums up his position eloquently in an interview with Decca Aitkenhead in the *Guardian* (2012).

> My point is that the debate, or the argument, with someone who held that view of the purpose of the hospital would be a moral argument about how properly to understand the purpose of a hospital or school. And, yes, there would be disagreement – but that disagreement, about purpose, would be, at the same time, a moral disagreement. I'd say 'moral disagreement' because it's not just an empirical question: How did this hospital define its mission? It's: What are hospitals properly for? What is a good hospital?

My view here is that his distinction between the empirical (as a mission statement of the sort dominant in corporate culture – 'you said. . . we did') view of purpose, and an ethical view of purpose (the proper; the good) is a normative principle that is pregnant with potential in its application to a number of relevant fields. Taking his last clause ('What are hospitals properly for? What is a good hospital?'), one might substitute the term 'Web' (What is the Web properly for? What is a good Web?), or 'digital literacy' ('What is digital literacy properly for? What is good digital literacy? Indeed, what makes for good digital literacy?'), and the moral outcomes are quite clearly similar, if not the same. I shall repeat these propositions frequently, as they provide the starting point for reflecting on the current state of Web 2.0 and the current focus of digital literacy policies. The phrase, 'What is a good Web?' is rarely spoken aloud, possibly due to the popular myth that we have found the answers already. As a matter of fact, such a question actually underpins much of Web and Web 2.0 evolution, particularly in relation to the aforementioned four historical discourses. The nub of applying Sandel's argument, however, is fairly simple: the arguments surrounding digital literacy and Web 2.0 are generally not just utility arguments; they should take in ends too.

I want to argue, in line with much of what Sandel has to say, that this is primarily due to a radical (or, more precisely, reactionary) disengagement from the implications of getting involved, taking a moral stand and asking questions concerning what good education can do in a world where markets tend to dominate thinking, policy and, ultimately, choice. As a corollary to this, one might also tender the question of the domination of education provision itself by market-led thinking. Sandel has described this domination as a kind of 'moral tawdriness'. Clearly, markets not only tend to spare us from public engagement, particularly public argument about the meaning of goods (i.e., what is considered good, as well as 'goods' traded in the marketplace), but also, markets enable us to be non-judgemental about values, which still allows choice, but within the moral boundaries of what might be described as illusory neutrality. It is this illusory neutrality that Sandel would describe as a double disengagement – from duty, on the one hand, and from responsibility, on the other. Certainly, in this regard the rhetoric of the Coalition administration in the UK (2010–15) in their flagship policies ('Compassionate Conservativism'; the Big Society etc.) have since proved red herrings of the worst political order – what Slavoj Žižek (2008: 118) would call the *objective violence* of liberal communism.

> The justification of liberal communists is that in order to really help people, you must have the means to do it, and, as experience of the dismal failure of all centralised statist and collectivist approaches teaches, private initiative is the efficient way. So if the state wants to regulate their business, to tax them excessively, is it aware that in this way it is effectively undermining the stated goal of its activity – that is, to make life better for the large majority, to really help those in need?

Whenever one reads Žižek, of course, there is the deep temptation to view his proclamations as some sort of sophisticated, cynical joke. However, if this state of affairs concerning the background of systemic, objective violence is at all persuasive, then what he is describing is a particularly sick joke (much like his own example of the laxative chocolate which helps you lose more weight, the more you eat); and we perhaps ought not shoot the messenger for delivering the message as written. There is good reason for this cynicism – Žižek is not alone, and there seems to be a common voice in articulating such views (even so, from wildly differing political standpoints, and disciplinary fields). It is worth pointing out that in this statement from his book *Violence*, he is not advocating a return to statism. Ironically, such a position might in fact be gleaned from the opposite direction; that statist collusion with big business is embedded in such 'liberal communist' gestures. My view is that we read Žižek in what we can only assume to be the spirit he may well have intended, and that the objective violence visited upon the world is largely driven through a market psychosis. I draw psychosocial equivalents much closer towards the end of this book, but here, by 'market psychosis' what I really mean is that the dominant view is hell-bent on letting the market decide the fate of policies for which it might not be an easy, nor a good, fit, and quite regardless of the material consequences. Sandel puts this much better in his *Guardian* interview (2012):

> So letting markets decide seems to be a non-judgemental, neutral way. And that's the deepest part of the allure; that it seems to provide a value-neutral, non-judgemental way of determining the value of all goods. But the folly of that promise is – though it may seem to be true enough for toasters and flat-screen televisions – it's not true for kidneys.

Nor, would I argue, does the market provide a value-neutral way of determining what good might come from the Web, particularly in light of the early promises to engage, empower and fulfil user-potential in the democratic senses. And this is aside from the question on how best to promulgate a robust and critical digital literacy policy that does not necessarily follow from market-based decisions. In fact, a market-driven digital literacy could more precisely do without elements of criticism and self-awareness in order to best operate according to its own drives. At the most superficial level of this, how can one even decide what is best for Web 2.0 culture, if one is not equipped with the critical tools to ask the questions that will give truly meaningful answers?

Sandel's ultimate position, which may be summed up in the question 'What should be the role of money and markets in our society (in a good society)?' seeks to reappraise the use of a market incentive to try to solve social problems. He gives several examples, such as paid sterilisation for drug-addicted women, or the incentivisation for American elementary schoolchildren to read a book, free McDonald's Happy Meals for children receiving A's and B's in their (McDonald's-sponsored) report cards and cash rewards for grade school children who achieve good grades.

In the first case, one can see a problem that is swept under the carpet – instead of finding and addressing root causes of addiction embedded in socio-economic arrangements and addictive behaviours in consumer-driven cultures, a more discernibly punitive, and altogether dehumanising, measure is offered. In the second educational case, tried out in several major cities in the US at the suggestion of influential economists at the neoliberal end of the spectrum of thought, the initial evaluation might be to say that it is worth a try. However, according to Sandel (2013), what emerge from a serious consideration of these incentivised strategies in education are the following questions.

> Will the cash incentive drive out or corrupt or crowd out the higher motivation, the intrinsic lesson that we hope to convey, which is to learn to love to learn and to read for their own sakes? And people disagree about what the effect will be, but that seems to be the question, that somehow a market mechanism or a cash incentive teaches the wrong lesson, and if it does, what will become of these children later?

His conclusions follow the results of such experiments in education policy.

> The cash for good grades has had very mixed results, for the most part has not resulted in higher grades. The two dollars for each book did lead those kids to read more books. It also led them to read shorter books.

It led them to read shorter books. The instrumentalist take on the task at hand seems to have bypassed the activity of reading itself and short-circuited towards the specific end involving economic reward – as with Žižek's chocolate laxative weight-loss programme, in which less exercise but more chocolate produces the desired results, the children start to read *less* in order to gain more money (an incentivised, desired result).

This mechanism can be found in a number of fields. One such field, and an arena with clear political and ethical implications, is that of green consumerism. A large part of green consumerism centres on the drive towards reducing carbon emissions and waste, and one could say that any programme which seeks measures to help prevent an entire planet from dying is probably a step in the right direction. However, the discourses emerging through (especially big) business economics reduces this question to the practice of carbon off-setting. Following Sandel, and following Žižek's chocolate laxative example, one might regard this as ethically dubious at best. It lends the practitioner something of a licence to pollute; by paying someone else to reduce their carbon emissions, this is tantamount to absolving oneself of responsibility, through a financial exchange.

There are specific case studies that apply general principles of creativity and collaboration to Web 2.0 contexts, and the rhetoric of digital ways of being. In his book *Cognitive Surplus: Creativity and Generosity in a Connected Age* (2010), Clay Shirky cites a study of the impacts of fines for tardiness on parents who picked up their children late from kindergarten. The study by Gneezy and Rustichini (2000), conducted in ten Israeli kindergartens, attempted to assess the deterrence hypothesis: that 'the introduction of a penalty that leaves everything else unchanged will reduce the occurrence of the behavior subject to the fine' (2000: 1). Their study found that the imposition of a small 10-shekel fine in six of those institutions had a disastrous effect on the goodwill of the relationships between the institution and the patrons. Shirky states (2010 [emphasis in original]) that 'The new rule was imposed at the six centers the following week, and its effect on the parents' behaviour was immediate: their lateness *increased*' in direct contravention of the deterrence hypothesis, about three-fold. This was not the end of the matter, however. The lasting (arguably, tragic) outcome of the study's findings came after the institutions reverted back to the pre-study conditions where no fines were imposed. The researchers found, contrary to the expectation that behaviours might revert to their pre-study patterns, the parents *continued* to be late at almost triple the rate of pre-study levels. Shirky comments that

> The pre-fine bargain between parents and teachers was what Gneezy and Rustichini labelled an 'incomplete contract' – a set of relations that took place partly in the market but left considerable room for the interpretation of certain behavioral norms, including those around pick-up time. [. . .] Once the fine was instituted, however, that ambiguity collapsed, along with behavioral norms that had been established. The fine turned the day care from a shared enterprise into a simple fee-for-service transaction, allowing the parents to regard the workers' time as a commodity, and a cheap one at that.

The fact that reverting to a non-fine state made no difference to this attitude of reduced responsibility and consequence suggests that the goodwill in the relationship between the institutions and the patrons had gone. The *culture of trust was broken* and the difference here is that the reduction of a civic service to a monetary transaction suggests that markets can indeed irreversibly taint the social relationships they touch. Reduction of social relationships to exchange forms may be considered, *de facto et intrinsecus*, corrosive. In Sandel's approach, this is a corrosive influence on our sense of communities and the democracies within which they operate. It is also widespread in neoliberal economies.

Incentivisation is a question that lies largely outside of the scope of this book. However, it is clearly central in its terms of the motivation not only for the users to engage with their social media practices and the production of their own content (if it brings the rewards of being able to make a living – visible examples of this being celebrities operating as part of the YouTuber phenomenon). It is also worth mentioning in relation to how the employability agenda of many digital media studies courses in HEIs across the UK seem to focus on jobs in the 'creative industries', and a focus on design and management skills for the creative economy, at (arguably) the expense of an education. I take such an extreme view of this, because it has become fairly clear that the neoliberal view on the functions and purposes of education are a crucial indicator of neoliberal encroachment into every sphere of life. It is a kind of totalism. Sandel takes a surprisingly moderate view on this, eschewing the political perspective in favour of a more measured ethical distinction between market economy and market society. A market *economy* may be thought of as a tool for organising productive activity, whereas a market *society* is a way of life where everything is for sale, and there appear to be no limits. However, it is in this second statement arguing against this social norm that Sandel's work begins to take on a robust political shape; and it is against this development of a market society that I wish to develop politicised objection.

'Spaces for rent': neoliberal impacts on digital literacy, and the ethical perspective

To help outline that political shape and the form of that politicised objection, I would like to briefly detour into the arena of neoliberal policy in the UK, as it has had some visible and lasting impacts on the popular notion of what digital literacy is for and, specifically, the ideal functions of a good Web 2.0. More generally, I suggest, it has had a lasting impact on the psychic and social imaginary, in terms of agency and political action, because the predominant world-view of neoliberal societies tends to flatten the grounds upon which objections and contributions can be made from individuals as agents, and communities and societies as collective movements. Political geographer David Harvey's perspective on the legacy of neoliberal policy is particularly instructive and influential in this regard. In his book *A Brief History of Neoliberalism* (2005), Harvey describes neoliberalism in the first instance as 'a theory of political economic practices that proposes that human well-being can best be advanced by liberating individual entrepreneurial freedoms and skills within an institutional framework characterized by strong private property rights, free markets, and free trade' (2005: 2). As we shall see in Chapter 2, one of the key freedoms associated with the discourse of access and usability (key to the contemporary understanding of individual entrepreneurial freedoms) comes in the form of participatory culture. The very notion embodied by Web 2.0 technologies about the ease of plug-in-and-play interfaces and the democratising effects this may or may not have for users and their creativity is explicitly connected in the neoliberal form to the creation of economic and technological conditions for entrepreneurial activity.

Andrew Hurrell and Laura Gomez-Mera note of neoliberalism that there are two principle meanings of the term (2003). First, in the sense of market, liberal economic policies have historically been coupled with Thatcherism and opposed to Keynesianism in accordance with a number of measures. Such measures include systematic privatization and deregulation, liberalization of trade and finance, the shrinking role of the state and the encouragement of direct foreign investment (especially through favourable tariffs for like-minded neoliberal regimes). Hurrell and Gomez-Mera link neoliberalism in this sense to the structural adjustment programmes promoted by the IMF and the World Bank, especially in describing the character of the economic ideology behind globalisation. The move into a pro-longed period of strong austerism in the UK since the 2008 economic crisis is certainly related to these adjustment programmes; the slightly more moderate aus-terism found in the EU and that institution's perspective on the recent economic disasters is also driven by this aspect of neoliberal logic. Second, in international relations, neoliberalism denotes a theoretical approach to the study of institutions, where international cooperation is made possible 'namely that states are rational, unitary actors which seek to maximize their utility in an anarchic international system' (2003: 368).

This is not the end of the story, however. For Steve Reilly (2000), neoliberalism is '[. . .] more a label attached to a package of politically expedient positions than any important revision of liberal thought' (2000: 572). In this sense, then, the term is characterised by the following attributes: a rejection of some of the orthodoxies found in the historical American liberal traditions of Roosevelt's New Deal and Johnson's Great Society; a rejection of Keynesian state intervention whereby heavy regulation and intervention may leverage markets towards civic or public func-tions; a conservative critique of the welfare state; an opposition to trade unionism and organised labour; a concern for social pluralism and tolerance (in a continuance of later liberal traditions), particularly in relation to the championing of individual rights; and a reliance on emergent technology. It is through these characteristics that neoliberalism has become hegemonic in its dominance as a discourse through multiple spheres of life. In its heady and alluring mix of individualism, flexible eco-nomic conditions and suspicion of state authority encroaching on such rights, in neoliberal logic there seems to be a conflation of individual freedoms and freedom of the market, each articulated in the other.

Returning to the work of Sandel, one is tempted to assume that his moderate standpoint, in making his distinction between market economy and market soci-ety, lets neoliberalism off the political hook. However, in my view, Sandel's work in the ethics of markets and specifically in the flow of market reasoning extend-ing to all spheres of public, civic and moral life opens the door to a full political critique of the neoliberal form in much the same way that Harvey and others have attempted. Sandel suggests that many economists assume that markets are inert, and that markets tend not to touch or taint the goods they exchange. Whereas this may be good enough for material goods, the same may not be true for social practices informed by values we care about. It is the difference between toasters and kidneys.

For Sandel, in common with many of Charles Taylor's views regarding a sense of belonging, the sense of commonality and community is eroded by marketisation, and this seems particularly short-sighted and unjust. This is especially so in the era of austerity and austerism, at a time of rising inequality and social immobility, exorbitant rising costs of living and when people of affluence lead fundamentally different lives to those lived by people of more modest means, and in different spaces. The impor-tant element here stands quite apart from the regular Marxist critique of inequality: for Sandel, democracy doesn't require perfect equality; however, what it does require is a shared common experience in the course of everyday life across society. This is, essentially, the mechanism via which we come to value common goods, and through which we come to view others with some sense of recognition and compassion. It is, in short, a pathway to convivial understanding – a possibility dealt with in some detail in Chapter 2 – and provides a signpost towards what I describe in Part II of this book, as a 'Principle of Mutuality' at the level of both the psychic and the social imaginary, in a connected world.

So, in the scheme of this moral critique, one needs to ask fundamental questions regarding the totalising influence of the market: where do markets belong? Where do markets not belong? What are markets properly for? For Sandel, it is fairly clear that markets might function properly when it is fully acknowledged that although they may make for economic efficiency, markets ought to have moral limits. In other words, instrumental efficiency is not necessarily a universally applied good; and extending market logic into spheres outside of the economy would neglect what markets are properly for.

In conversation with the historian A.C. Grayling (2013), Sandel outlines the origins of economics, going back to Adam Smith, as a branch of moral and political philosophy, claiming that it was only during the twentieth century that economics emerged as an autonomous discipline – regarded as a value-neutral, scientific way of measuring the efficiency of markets. In common with Harvey, Sandel suggests that in recent decades, economics expanded its remit to explain and inform all branches of human life through economic reasoning. The market incentive changes the meaning of the activity and crowds-out attitudes and norms that we care about (i.e., ideas of 'intrinsic' or common goods) central to these practices – again, the example of schoolchildren reading books for a cash incentive, leading children to read shorter books, serves to outline the idea that markets taint what they touch. Sandel draws on an example to illustrate this further: getting paid to have an advert tattooed on one's forehead may be a rational economic choice. However, there is an argument here that some sort of fundamental coercion by economic circumstances would lead a person to do this where in other circumstances they would see the tattoo advert as fundamentally degrading, and therefore morally objectionable. This is an argument often waged against prostitution or sex work; the transactions involved may be freely entered into, nominally, but these kinds of transactions may be described as degrading. Ultimately, of course, this ethical dimension is governed through an Aristotlean ethos, whereby the credibility of sex workers as moral agents is called into question. We see this in the laws governing sex work, in the misrepresentation of sex workers in news reports and television programmes and also in the reduction of sex workers to the status of commodities in the trafficking industry. The 'legitimisation' of such work by bringing it under the aegis of corporate business, as is the case in some German cities today with their relatively recent liberalisation of the adult industries, for example, merely serves to underline the power of market thinking in altering the discourses of such activity, and the subsequent treatment of those involved.

In terms of 'spaces for rent', in my classroom discussions with students, many of whom work in entry-level jobs in the retail or hospitality industries to pay their way through their studies, a common phenomenon young people experience in such circumstances is the compulsion to act as a brand ambassador for the company that employs them. Certain very well-known retail chains in the UK practice such insistence: the young people employed to assist customers on the shop floor are required to act as ambassadors for that company through their personal social media presence. This involves the ambassador regularly updating their social media status to feature the latest products that have entered the shop, and to endorse products through a mix of text, images and personal appearances (for example, holding a bath bomb or tub of hair gel, and smiling to camera, wearing the store t-shirt with the company logo visibly in shot etc.). In return, the ambassador often receives no *extra* remuneration, but instead often receives gratis goods or discounts, and gets to keep the t-shirt. A clear code of conduct is implemented by the company for those employees on social media platforms, whereby, wearing the t-shirt, the ambassador is bound to uniform and restrictive rules of behaviour (and in my hypothetical case earlier, 'Jared' was subject to legal action for his own negative association in a social media setting). Therefore, the employee becomes a kind of shop window through which, products, goods and services are displayed for social media users (their 'friends') to browse. They become spaces for rent. In this instance, friendship networks on SNSs, therefore, are reduced to relations between products, goods and services, and consumers. The ambassadors, meanwhile, act as, in Jameson's terms, 'vanishing mediators' (1989). It is a postmodern instance of what Benjamin described as a 'space for rent' (1986), where subjects are inculcated into their total-ised environment, stripped of objectivity (and therefore critical agency) through financial coercion and reduced to a reflective surface off which surplus value may be reflected. In an insightful show of prescience, (1986: 85), Benjamin described the prominence of market value in modernity.

> Today the most real, the mercantile gaze into the heart of things is the adver-tisement. It abolishes the space where contemplation moved and all but hits us between the eyes with things as a car, growing in gigantic proportions, careens at us out of a film screen.

As we shall see in the following chapter, many thinkers have put forward the argu-ment that social media applications open up channels for participation through creative enterprise (i.e., especially David Gauntlett's 'making is connecting' model). However, as is the case in relation to the practice of social media ambas-sadors where brand data is channelled through social media presence, if the market incentive changes the meaning of an activity such as Web creativity in social media contexts, then we therefore have to ask the question: what is Web creativity and connectivity properly for? Indeed, some current thinking on this has attempted to tackle the contradictions inherent in asking such a question.

The direction of development of Web 2.0 technologies certainly points to a system geared up for monetisation. Lanier (2013), points towards the specif-ics of monetisation in the context of the corporate monopolisation of Big Data.

An empirical view of this arrangement focuses on its obviousness; only entities with the resources and processing power necessary to engage with such massive data sets can truly engage with them. But this view says little about the ethics of such a situation, where datasets are aggregated from millions upon millions of origin points, and where many of these millions are actual people, generating actual data about their actual lives, in real-time. Lanier's particular engagement with this aspect of Big Data argues that general survival of modern democracies may hang in the balance, and that new micro-economics models need to be considered seriously in order that people can earn a living through the data they generate. It also feeds back into the argument I outlined in the introduction to this book, concerning an emphasis on plug-in-and-play approaches at the expense of bottom-up creativity, and incompatible with rounded educational approaches in the university. I would also suggest that it is intertwined with Shirky's example concerning the corrosive influence of markets upon goodwill within communities, and the rather serious implications this has when cultures get broken, and are not easily fixable afterwards.

Further to the idea of community, and a sense of the individual agency of moral actors within communities, Sandel gives the example of the ways in which application of market logic to the sphere of political engagement and participatory democracy ignores what such engagement is for. Clearly, rather than the instrumental view, which would have it that an efficient political engagement would get us what we want, properly-speaking, political engagement is a good thing precisely because it helps to make us better than we might otherwise be. He describes this quite colourfully, in terms of a 'reciprocally constitutive' relation, articulating a very old problem in moral philosophy: the tension between the individual and the society, and the tension between what constitutes the good according to the needs of one, the other, or the many. The relative conviviality of such connectivity between individuals, and the relationships between individuals and their communities (particularly online communities), is the subject for discussion in Chapter 2.

2

PSYCHOSOCIAL DIMENSIONS OF RECOGNITION IN CONNECTIVITY ETHICS

In a critical piece posted on his blog, Christian Fuchs (2011) takes aim at the notion of spreadable media, at Henry Jenkins in particular, in response to a keynote Jenkins delivered at the 2011 conference of the ICA on the subject. In this piece, Fuchs states that

> Jenkins simply constructs a dualistic 'both. . .and'-argument based on the logic: 'Web 2.0 is both . . . and . . .': both pleasure and exploitation, both a space of participation and a space of commodification. He wants to focus on the aspects of pleasure and creativity and wants to leave the topic of exploitation to others and does thereby not grasp the dialectics at work and the relations of dominance we find on web 2.0.

Of course, Jenkins must be empirically correct in his assertion. For, surely, the logics of Web 2.0 closely mirror the cultural and socio-economic contexts within which such technologies are built and used? Late capitalist, neoliberal societies tend to operate in the tensions between pleasure and exploitation, between participation and commodification; in this way the desiring subject of capital is directly *recognised* as an *agent* of consumption, as well as its product. The flow of convenient stuff, the blurring of work and leisure time through the advanced bureaucratisation of Web activities (processes of pointing, clicking, swiping, sharing etc. are after all staple acts of both contemporary office work and social media activity), and the relative ease and immediacy of Web-based products and productivity mean that there is, until a last instance of resistance or sedition, no need to revert to coercive or repressive apparatus. It is a trade-off relationship freely entered into.

Furthermore, there is no need to doubt that Web 2.0 users are creative when they generate and diffuse user-generated content. Creative acts and processes such as meme production, vlogging or Twitch TV broadcasting explore the creative imagination of content producers. But in some aspects at least, this is beside the point. It is the matrix within which creativity is leveraged which seems to be the issue here, because 'Creativity is a force that enables Internet prosumer com- modification, the commodification and exploitation of the users' activities and the data they generate. Creativity is not outside of or dual to exploitation on web 2.0, it is its very foundation' (Fuchs 2011). Web 2.0 creativity is, in other words, the means by which the material commodification of the user is realised. The user is the product.

As already discussed in Chapter 1, the ways in which application of market logic to the sphere of political engagement and participatory democracy ignores what such engagement is for. If creativity, as a political act in itself (with the potential for political and civic value), is administered as an enabling mechanism to further intensify commodification processes in Web 2.0 and social media contexts, then surely this reframing of creativity would place its political functionality – its very ability to enable counterhegemonic or subversive acts – in jeopardy? I find myself departing from Fuchs on this particular issue, at least to some extent. Creativity – in its various forms as concept, process and act – does not necessarily need to be framed in this way. Indeed, one ought to apply an ethical, rather than empirical, description of creativity to examine what it is properly for and how it may provide a conceptual frame for progressive civic life beyond commodity-identity. As a political idea, process or act, creative gesture is a good thing, precisely because it helps to make us better than we might otherwise be. It sits in precisely this frame because as far as it embodies a political engagement of some kind, it embodies what Sandel has termed a 'reciprocally-constitutive' relation that in some ways, mirrors Gauntlett's sentiment of connecting through making. This, as I indicated at the end of Chapter 1, articulates a perennial problem in moral philosophy: the tension between the individual and the society, and the tension between what constitutes the good according to the needs of one or the other.

In the context of Web 2.0, creativity both enables community *and* exploita- tion, and therefore represents the tension between the rituals of creative freedom and expression on the one hand, and the commodification of users on the other. Therefore, Web 2.0 creativity embodies the dialectic between the two forms of recognition outlined by Taylor, mentioned previously. On the one hand, the social and communal bonds of recognition upon which communities rely to function properly; and on the other, the systematic recognition of the consumer-subject as an aggregate of data and the result of sophisticated and automated data profiling, generated through ostensibly and perceptibly creative acts.

In Chapter 1, I discussed various ways in which market logic has been appro- priated for and applied to a whole host of social and cultural practices, including those associated with Web 2.0. To the observation that we appear to be living in a market society, I would add that the generality of such practices of applying market logic necessitates the urgency of critical inquiry into the moral forms that govern Web 2.0 as technology, as practice and as a concept. There have been occa- sional interventions from progressive cultural studies scholars on the subject of the 'wrong-ness' of Web 2.0. However, these tend to suggest (as does the influential recent example of this – Jenkins, Ford and Green's *Spreadable Media*, 2013), that the nature of the wrong-ness or failure should be attributed to the disconnects between producer logics (characterised by profit drives and commodification) and consumer logics (characterised by gift culture). This is instead of rethinking the ongoing dialectical struggle within the frame of neoliberal contexts and the accumulative needs of capital to sustain desiring consumer-subjects and commodity-identities. I have tried to argue how objectionable this disconnect can seem in the light of ethical frameworks which seek to ask what such practices are properly for, and how the influence of monetisation and market logic is a corrosive force on the proper functionality of those practices, in an ethical sense.

This discussion included aspects of digital literacy, a subject to which I return in subsequent chapters. Digital literacy is essentially a public educational project that has been to an extent co-opted in its most impoverished plug-in-and-play mode, mainly for the purposes of generating revenue at low/no cost for large service providers. Occasionally, distance-learning tools have been relied upon to shore up gaps in resources, funding and expertise left by financial systems geared towards marketing and recruitment to tertiary educational programmes (as featured to illuminating effect, for example, in the investigative documentary feature, *Ivory Tower* (Rossi, US, 2014). Service provision, in its broadest market sense, is dominated by corporate entities such as Facebook, Google, MOOC providers (e.g., Coursera) in the educational context and open source publishing facilitators in the context of content distribution. It is also, to an extent, governed by a system of gatekeeping in terms of modes of openness and access available to the publishing distribution industry, for which there is a mass of concentration of rights in the hands of a few very large corporate players, and a fair few more medium and small competitors at regional levels. Therefore, service provision for any digital literacy programme has to negotiate, either with or as alternative from, concentrated interests of ownership and possession of resources represented by media giants, who Jaron Lanier (2013) has described as 'siren servers'.

In the current chapter, I will examine the notion of consumer-subject as located through a complex matrix of recognition. In relation to this, I also begin considering Web 2.0 functionality in relation to a number of key dimensions: creativity, connectivity, agency, individual identity and, perhaps most visible in social media studies, the 'trade-off argument' concerning personal data, digital rights and digital labour. I move on to examine how the notions of demonstrable consumption and competitive self-interest are embedded in market societies. I also discuss the tension between this market society logic and contrary notions of mutuality in ethics debates. Finally, I discuss how these ethics debates shape a distinction between utilitarian interest-as-advantage and ludic interest-as-curiosity. To set this narrative up, I begin by examining the processes by which the desiring consumer-subject, as a node of creative expression in Web 2.0 cultures, is located through recognition. I work with the understanding of recognition in moral philosophy, and in particular Charles Taylor's description found in his book *The Ethics of Authenticity* (1991).

There, Taylor writes of the universal acknowledgement of recognition as an important aspect of social identity relations (1991: 49):

> [. . .] on an intimate plane, we are all aware of how identity can be formed or malformed in our contact with significant others. On the social plane, we have a continuing politics of equal recognition. Both have been shaped by the growing ideal of authenticity, and recognition plays an essential role in the culture that has arisen around it.

The present chapter's discussion informs understanding of the background logic of Web 2.0 creativity rhetoric, and necessarily seeks to incorporate a more 'affirmative' dimension of the debate in respect of social identity relations. In this light, I draw upon those thinkers for whom Web 2.0 functionality provides a crucible for creativity and connectivity, agency and individual identity, and for whom, ultimately, the price of giving up one's personal data to pursue such meaningful creative enterprise is sometimes worth paying.

Making, connecting and trading-off

In his book *Making is Connecting* (2011) David Gauntlett sought to outline a suite of communal and civic activities of creativity, DIY ethics and Web 2.0 technology-appropriation as fundamentally political and politicised practices of connectivity.[1] However, for all of his championing of Web 2.0 and 'convivial' creativity and sharing practices, Gauntlett fully acknowledges the allure of capital as an underpinning of the development, marketisation and use of these technologies. Following the Frankfurt School of thought on this, Gauntlett (2011: 11) states that

> [. . .] modern capitalism succeeds not by menacing us, or dramatically crushing our will on the industrial wheel, but by encouraging us to enjoy a flow of convenient, cheerful stuff, purchased from shops which gives us a feeling of satisfaction, if not happiness.

Transferring this seductive state of satisfaction to the context of social media applications and the world of Web 2.0 takes no leap of imagination. There seems to be an increasing awareness of the darker, unethical side to the terms and conditions of the use of such technologies amongst its user base (the Netflix hit *Terms and Conditions May Apply* (Hoback, US, 2013) seems to be an indication of the popularity of this cynicism). However, it is nowhere near enough to offset the fact that users seem happy (enough) to pay the data price in exchange for the use of what should be acknowledged as convenient, user-friendly, highly entertaining and useful tools. Users and consumers are, after all, desiring subjects – and consumers desire, amongst other things, satisfaction.[2]

In the field of marketing theory, Markos, Labrecque and Milne (2012) conducted research into the expression of authenticity as a desirable drive in online communications. They noted (2012: 160) that such is the ubiquity of this trade-off or exchange that people generally and occasionally tend to let impression management lapse where they feel it is to an advantage for relationship maintenance:

> [. . .] the modern marketplace creates an atmosphere of casual information sharing, even as it fosters an air of uncertainty about transactions involving information. Most research also finds that consumers do not use the privacy tools available to them, such as clearing out needless cookies, reading privacy policies [. . .] or paying attention to privacy seals on Web sites.

In other words, social media users are generally aware of the inherent problems associated with disclosure, information sharing and data terms and conditions, but there are nevertheless commonly held practices and browsing habits which mitigate self-protection, including the desire for different levels of social interaction at different times. These are practices and habits which social media companies have exploited for some time, and which can lead to inadvertent consequences. The bottom line here is that there is a growing awareness of, and a *laissez-faire* attitude towards, the fact that the Internet tends not to forget what information human actors easily forget. A minimal aggregation of personal data can identify specific individuals and their online history, through tracking how many social media accounts one has, what cookies have been stored on personal computers and devices, meta-data on shared content and location history through the triangulation of IP addresses, geolocative applications and other information cues from status and notification histories.

Counter to this perceptibly lax attitude, Gauntlett's critique of the 'sit-back' model of rather passive media consumption and his championing of 'making and doing culture' is admirable. After all, he is attempting to emphasise the proper and popularly imagined functions of Web 2.0 technologies as being means to engage political debate, to participate in communities, to make and share in the spirit of connectivity that such technologies afford. He does this through thinking about what everyday creativity means, how meaning is created and shared in a more general culture of 'making and doing', with emphasis on how Web 2.0 technologies have the potential to afford such practices. He therefore tentatively suggests that creativity is political in nature, because making is connecting, and connecting facilitates relationships of various kinds, including collective, communal and civic relationships.

In response to his own assertion that scholars on the 'critical' or 'political' end of the new media spectrum might find his work, at best, some sort of sweet side show, I would agree to an extent. However, for the record, I personally don't see his work like this in the strictest sense; I see it as an important acknowledgement of the place and value of creativity as a way in which people connect, build communities, build trust and generally share experiences. To do this is to both *recognise* and *be recognised* in social contexts. I've seen this happen in a number of contexts – as an educator, as a practising musician and as a social media user. Recognition, in this sense, is very much part of the fabric of everyday life. I argue that the social cohesion function of creativity forms part of the communitarian approach I bring to the normative potentials of Web 2.0 technologies.

However, the problem that I see in Gauntlett's position is that he may have overplayed his 'affirmative' hand. Since the publication of the first edition of his book in 2011, and despite (or perhaps exacerbated by) the discernible 'trade-off' mechanism in social media use outlined above, there are growing anxieties surrounding these social technologies. Certainly, there is also a growing awareness about how state and corporate collusion has begun to transform the meaning and functionality of such technologies. Perhaps, this is particularly in light of a number of highly visible public scandals such as Wikileaks, Prism and Cambridge Analytica, the rise of 'fake news' and 'post-truth' discourses, allegations of political manipulation of social media feeds in the run-up to general elections or referenda and so on. Such anxieties have come to the fore in the popular imagination and in mainstream news. I touched upon this in the previous chapter. I now wish to add to that discussion here the notion that the normative functionality of Web 2.0 is moving increasingly towards a place that, following Sandel and Taylor, allows neither the proper ethical dimensions of digital literacy to function, nor the creative, convivial aspects of connectivity (as espoused by Gauntlett and others) to thrive. Indeed, even by Gauntlett's own admission, all is 'not rosy' with Web 2.0.

This is principally due to the way that market logic is applied in a general and totalising way to participation and creativity. In an echo of Sandel's viewpoint on the corrosive influence of this totalisation, for David Harvey (2005: 165):

> To presume that markets and market signals can best determine all allocative decisions is to presume that everything can in principle be treated as a commodity. Commodification presumes the existence of property rights over processes, things and social relations, that a price can be put on them, and that they can be traded subject to legal contract.

This observation seems to both underpin and directly contradict the models of political creativity guaranteed by Web 2.0 technologies and cultures that Gauntlett describes in his book. It also seems to support his notion that, although Web 2.0 incorporates a participatory culture, it can also be described with some confidence in the traditional media studies sense, as a culture industry: quite literally, an industry manufacturing aspects of creative culture to satisfy (but importantly and accurately, commercially exploit) the desire for creating and connecting. Above all else, the product being manufactured is the desiring consumer-subject in an inexorable drive towards a totalising commodity-identity. For Christian Fuchs (2011), this aspect of Web 2.0 cultures seems unconscionable as an affirmative structuring presence in societies. He saves his most venomous critique for Henry Jenkins in what follows, but here we might infer that a more general target would include any notion that participatory culture fully lives out its political promises. Fuchs writes at length (2011 [my emphasis]) that

[s]ocial media culture is a culture industry. Jenkins' notion of 'participatory culture' is about expressions, engagement, creation, sharing, experience, contributions and feelings and *not also* about how these practices are enabled by and antagonistically entangled into capital accumulation. Jenkins has a reductionistic understanding of culture that ignores contemporary culture's political economy. Furthermore he reduces the notion of participation to a cultural dimension, ignoring the broad notion of participatory democracy and its implications for the Internet. An Internet that is dominated by corporations that accumulate capital by exploiting and commodifying users can in the theory of participatory democracy never be participatory and the cultural expressions on it cannot be an expression of participation.

As mentioned at the beginning of this chapter, Jenkins, Green and Ford (2013) have suggested that, in various ways, the very act of participating in media connectivity and creativity creates the conditions for a more democratic culture. This approach is connected to an older argument involving the importance of a literate public for the dissemination of democratic ideas and literacy in general as a mechanism for increasing political awareness and participation. However, in their book this political functionality tends to read as an afterthought. It was possibly not the authors' intention, but there are tensions in the tone and framing of their argument which strongly suggest that this was a work published with culture industry interests in mind every bit as much as the progression of media scholarship.

Before I turn to the political implications of recognition in the context of these tensions in Chapter 3, I wish to expand on the relative conviviality of connectivity between individuals and the relationships between individuals and their communities, particularly online communities, in order to tease out 'creativity' in this political frame. This is because, for all of the amplified language of commodity-identity I have used thus far, one's intuition as a social media user (or a Web 2.0 creative) is strongly affirmed as free.

'Free', as famously outlined by Richard Stallman (2001), ought to be understood in both the *libre* political sense of free movement, expression and so forth, and *gratis*, that is to say for a bewildering array of Web 2.0 applications, in the civic sense, free at the point of access.[3] This intuition not only stems from the plug-in-and-play view of Web 2.0 applications and processes alluded to in the Introduction to this book; but also, the residual utopian promises of early Web discourse as a democratising cultural effect, and the prospects of activism afforded through Web 2.0 community action. From there, conjoining this chapter and the beginning of the next, I wish to discuss how alternative models of creativity can be argued to potentially provide the very foundations of an alternative politics to those of a market society, which brings the kind of purpose that Sandel would describe as striving to make ourselves better than we might otherwise be. In this sense, we may start to tease out precisely what reciprocally constitutive relations might look like in Web 2.0 contexts, how they have been conceptualised and how they might apply to the contexts of online life. In addition, we will begin to explore a dialectical exfoliation within relations of capital, myth and cultural complex as aspects of a recuperative total system, where the reciprocally constitutive is jettisoned in favour of an 'always-on' cultural worldview.

Conviviality, esteem, the 'demonstration effect' and debt

In his public conversation with the historian A. C. Grayling (2013), Sandel points to a number of virtues of social institutions which help to create and maintain a sense of social cohesion. They lend for us several layers of community, encourage fellow-feeling, allow a measure of self-governance and, it may be persuasively argued, add to both the scope and to the quality of public deliberation. Above all, Sandel argues that social institutions have within their functionality the ability to foster the conditions of justice and, more precisely, a value concept of being just. That is to say, 'being just' is an attitude and action valued within society, espoused and supported through certain social institutions, and allows people to bridge some of the nagging tensions between individuals and the society within which they live. Web petition movements such as 38 Degrees and Web-RL crossover movements such as Occupy have, as their central logic, a drive towards civic projects which might ease some of those tensions and lead to a *transformation* or accommodation of some kind, through other-regarding. Just as important perhaps, as we shall see, in this sense such movements are, by most measures of the research, inherently creative.

Of course, within Sandel's particular approach, we see that the notions involved in 'being just' associate themselves with the specific notion of social contract, and the even-more-focused notion of fairness in relation to equal individual rights for those actors who subscribe to the value system inherent in such a social contract. In the context of the subject matter of the current study, this takes shape within the specific debates already mentioned on immaterial commons and intellectual property. I shall return to this aspect later in the chapter. However, I would first like to apply to the notion of creativity, particularly in its potential framing as a political concept, process and act, beyond the limits of the social contract and the pure apprehension of contractual obligation. I will approach this, however, with the caveat that a tension between consensus and challenge be necessarily retained in this vision of political agency.

Frank Adloff, a key figure in the sociology of philanthropy, offers an alternative approach to political participation as part of the 'Convivialist Manifesto' – a document of consensus amongst several European intellectuals and thinkers from an array of disciplines and political alignments published in 2014 and sponsored by the German Federal Ministry of Education and Research. Here I would like to outline some of the salient aspects of that document, as part of what I see to be fundamental to a renewed understanding of creativity in participatory and social media. Adloff writes (2014: 11) of Mauss's well-known and influential 1924 anthropology essay *The Gift*:

According to Mauss, although the gifts thus offered appear at first sight to be voluntary, they actually have a highly binding character and are cyclically dependent on one another. The nature of gift, says Mauss, is ambivalent, since gift-exchange oscillates between voluntariness and spontaneity at one end and social obligation at the other. The giving of a gift is a deeply ambiguous process and one which Mauss sees neither in economistic terms, as self-interest, nor in moralistic terms, as purely altruistic. Instead, Mauss stresses the essentially competitive side of giving: we cannot ignore a gift; we have to react to it as we would to a challenge – which we either respond to or decline to respond to (also tantamount to a response, only a negative one).

This reveals in the thinking of Mauss, a third principle of social bonding through gift-exchange; in addition to those forms of recognition associated with voluntariness and spontaneity, and with social obligation, is a recognition secured by the exchange of gifts and founded on social ties and mutual 'endebtedness'. It is important here to emphasise the linguistic distinction: the term used in the convivialist manifesto is translated as 'endebtedness', and not 'indebtedness'. It may be a mistranslation. However, it would seem a fortuitous error if it were indeed the case. To my mind, the latter, conventional spelling would imply economic or moral debt, and also a serious social obligation that is not necessarily founded upon principles of voluntariness and spontaneity. Indeed, debt in this sense has a financial legal status, for which debtors are obliged to pay lenders what they owe. It has a binding character which, although in place to provide a reasonable level of security for lenders, also has in the current era of austerism, the psychological effect of subjecting the debtor to a state of semi-permanent financial anxiety. Indeed, surely it was ever thus in times of financial insecurity. In 'indebtedness', the ambiguity and tension between social obligation and voluntariness – a dialectic central to the nature of the gift – is lost, replaced by legal contracts, financial coercion and debt-anxiety. It is also accompanied by culturally laden feelings of *shame*. By contrast, it appears that to be 'endebted' is to recognise the communion between individual actors or groups, and how the constitution of such may be reciprocated. The binding character here is undoubtedly affirmative, is mutual to all parties and avoids institutional obligation.

Of course, this reading of mutuality is by no means a new realisation. In his book *The Affluent Society*, the influential economist J. K. Galbraith wrote at length about consumer indebtedness and the financial products invented to facilitate the satisfaction of what he saw were the twin sources of desire in late capital – advertising and emulation (1962: 167):

> It would be surprising indeed if a society that is prepared to spend thousands of millions to persuade people of their wants were to fail to take the further step of financing these wants, and were it not then to go on to persuade people of the ease and desirability of incurring debt to make these wants effective. This has happened.

Whilst this perhaps flies in the face of intuition – to suggest perhaps that we are not, as consumers, rational agents capable of making our own choices – I would point out here what I think to be the most important factor in Galbraith's general observation: desirability of incurring debt to satisfy *wants*. Again, *satisfaction*, rather than happiness (or indeed subsistence), is the emotive drive. In fact, the prospect of happiness doesn't necessarily factor at all, it seems, because the act of participation itself is enough to stimulate a vested interest for individuals in a market society. And once again, to be clear: when I use the term market society, what I mean by that is the market as a total system. Economists working in the twentieth century, and from all parts of the political spectrum, sought to engage this as a phenomenon of *conspicuous consumption*. According to Ken McCormick (1983: 1125–6), influential key economists in the early to mid-twentieth century and, in particular, James Duesenberry:

> [. . .] maintained that the attainment of a materially high standard of living has become a 'generally recognized social goal'. Thus, our culture defines success as accumulation of material goods, with the result that we have converted 'the drive for self-esteem into a drive to get high quality goods'.

The interesting addendum to this was that, in fact, in these models of consumer culture, even as early as the postwar period, conspicuous (absolute) consumption, though important, was found to be secondary to *relative* consumption – and, therefore, *competitive* consumption. In other words, my consumption is demonstrably greater than yours. The logic here was that consumer-subjects who felt *relatively* less successful suffered from a loss of self-esteem. Therefore, another way to see this is that the drive for self-esteem (and the recognition associated with its social momentum) and the drive for competitive consumption have, in some sense, elided in the logic of satisfaction. Furthermore, as McCormick writes, '[. . .] frequent exposure to higher quality goods than one usually consumes will cause an increase in one's consumption expenditures' (1983: 1126). This is something that Duesenberry labelled the 'demonstration effect'.

These aspects of conviviality, creativity, consumption, self-esteem and recognition all form part of the cultural complex that I have elsewhere called 'negative affordance' (Singh 2014: 129) which seems to be intertwined with the demonstration effect and the to-be-looked-at-ness aspects of everyday online social documentation. This is something that I will discuss further towards the end of this book, specifically in relation to the cultural complex as a post-Jungian depth form. However, it is worth a pre-emptive exploration here in its specifically economic psychosocial form. The demonstration effect is apparent in Web 2.0 contexts in the practices that evolved – creative practices such as meme production and replication, blogging and vlogging as modes of opinion-sharing and the artistry of microblogging, especially on the massively popular Twitter, where the platform demands a form of expression in 140/280 characters or fewer. All of these practices can be regarded creative in the sense that they form social collaborations and interactions between individuals, domains and fields. They also all rely upon connection with other users and with audiences, as well as upon a recognition through feedback mechanisms in order to maximise reputation ratings, through-traffic and, in the world of professionalised Web entrepreneurship, therefore, revenue. However, it must be said that on the Web, fields of recognition are diffuse and somewhat nebulous, and that quality judgement relies on reputation algorithms as much as human gatekeeping. To see and be seen in the 'right places' on the Web seems to be related to both exposure to endorsed practices of quality content, and also to the ways such content is reproduced and replicated through sharing and viral practices, as well as conditions of data automation.

To see and be seen, even at this superficial level, should be regarded as a recognition of sorts – but a recognition governed through consumer relations rather than civic or convivial relations. The distinction is, I hope, of clear importance to the reader – in Duesenberry's demonstration effect, there is an emphasis upon the need to eliminate feelings of inferiority that result from others' consumption of perceptibly superior goods (and indeed, others' superior consumption-as-lifestyle). This model downplays the notion of a more-conscious 'conspicuous consumption' in favour of a less-conscious imperative towards self-esteem (and the psychic image of esteem in the sense of social relationships, emulation and relative life stage) as a *recognised* relative consumption.

In Web 2.0 cultures, there are many ways to perceive this superiority (or inferiority) relative to one's peers, as examples of the demonstration effect. The first is technical superiority. One can demonstrate possession of the latest version of hardware and software on the market (a factor traditionally associated with conspicuous consumption), but also demonstrable through the use of technology in creative production and use in a shared online community. The opportunities to showcase one's dexterity in the demonstrable use of new technologies, applications and fads are mixt and evidenced through the instantaneous nature of information that flows through one's social media feeds. The second is aesthetic superiority. It assumes a technical ability and standard, which pushes towards the increasing professionalisation of the Web, as well as the increased emphasis on technical skills and training in digital literacy programmes, as previously discussed. The third factor encompasses newness or novelty of contribution. For example, a novel user experience or interaction design for a website, or a new way to demonstrate leverage for smart city data such as interactive street lighting, or sustainable energy waste management in public buildings via app developments. Thus, newness or novelty build upon the first two factors.

Contributions are recognisable in a Web field, largely based upon the aesthetic and technical use of the latest technology, without which it might be considered difficult to make a significant novel contribution in the first place. This is largely where the art of persuasion comes into focus. Such creative uses of technology are likely to function as advertising space for a technology, a practice, a specialised training for which aspiring Web 2.0 entrepreneurs are likely to want in order to emulate a successful creative intervention. Interestingly, in this aspect of demonstration effect, where technology, aesthetics and creativity intersect, we may make a connection to Thorstein Veblen, whose sociologically inflected work emphasised the role of taste, novelty and newness in his influential contribution to the understanding of consumer markets in the early twentieth century.

In his book *The Theory of the Leisure Class: An Economic Study of Institutions*, originally published in 1899, Veblen writes (2007: 17) that

> So soon as the possession of property becomes the basis of popular esteem, therefore, it becomes also a requisite to that complacency which we call self-respect. In any community where goods are held in severalty it is necessary, in order to insure his own peace of mind, that an individual should possess as large a portion of goods as others with whom he is accustomed to class himself.

Here we can see that, for Veblen at least, the two modes of esteem – a social, 'popular' esteem and the privatised mode of 'self-respect' – hold clear links to property as indicators of both what we might call wealth and freedom. It is a strange twist of fate that the mode of accumulation in Web 2.0 was through *gratis* forms of freedom that for Lanier (2013) have thinned development markets to the point of being unsustainable. The monetisation that he describes where data production should be paid for, directly to the producers (i.e., users) rather than to the owners (i.e., the 'siren serves') is not permissible. This is precisely because the goods 'held in severalty' (data) are immaterial goods, and practically useless to those users who do not have the means (digital literacy) to exchange them, and thus extract meaningful value.

And yet, users subscribe to the free-to-access services *en masse*, in what I would describe as a psychosocial imperative to both conspicuously perform the role of consumer to *demonstrate* one's participation, and to recognise the relative status of others (*esteem*) as they perform their own roles in online communities. This return of the importance of participation is crucial as a psychosocial imperative – precisely because it engages the spark of recognition that one is part of a community. This dependence upon consumption in order to facilitate participation has been noted in the field of political science. For example, as Amitava Krishna Dutt (2008: 532 [my emphasis]) notes:

> When others buy some things with network externalities – such as cellphones and internet connections – one is left out of the loop when one does not have these things. When many people have something, social norms require others to have it as well, and *not having it can result in a loss of dignity*; Adam Smith's example of leather shoes makes this point well.

This simple observation masks a deep psychosocial mechanism which defines self-esteem and popular esteem in equal measure. For it is supposable, therefore, that a loss of dignity resulting from a lack of recognition of high relative consumption is aligned with an increased sense of shame; dignity and shame are dialectical bedfellows in the dialogue between deep psychological motivations and tensions.[4] Commodity-identity is such a powerful identification mechanism that it shapes the social norm requirement for material acquisition, amplified through the popular acquisition of technologies of connectivity.

It both constructs and reinforces the lock-in phenomenon which Lanier (2010, 2013) has described in detail, where technological lock-in means that non-acquisition may lead to social 'lock-out' for those not already in. Commodity-identity in Web 2.0 contexts, therefore, may be regarded as a powerful means for understanding one's sense of self and of others in the social fabric. It is not just about persuaders creating wants, as wants are also created through emulation. Galbraith, as did other influential economic thinkers such as Keynes, Duesenberry and so forth, noticed this race to consume.

In sum, therefore, mainstream twentieth-century economics anticipated the emotive and psychological aspects of recognition in consumer culture at a time roughly contemporary with, or subsequent to, the publication of Mauss's classic observation in *The Gift*. What is significant here is, I believe, that the mechanism of competitive consumption negates the best possibilities of gift exchange as a creative civic project in a market society because recognition and esteem are here reduced to the status of mutual competition. It is an opportunity, in other words, to outdo one another – a problem for moral philosophy that runs deep – is central to the modern critique of fully rounded, autonomous agency, and dates back to Tocqueville and his notion of egoism (cited in Taylor 1991). And, as Charles Taylor notes, 'The result of all of this has been to thicken the darkness around the moral ideal of authenticity' (1991: 21). The intellectual challenge, and the challenge of praxis, then, is how to accommodate, or at least mitigate, the worst of these reductionist and instrumental tendencies, through critical inquiry.

In another discussion predating and anticipating the convivialists, but drawing upon this Tocqueville tradition (*Don, intérêt et désintéressement: Bourdieu, Mauss, Platon et quelques autres*), Caillé (1994) traces the misconceptions that have arisen in regard to the interpretation of Mauss's theory of gift back to the fact that often no clear theoretical distinction was made between utilitarian interest-as-advantage and ludic interest-as-curiosity. Caillé argues that this led to precipitate conclusions about the (egoistic) advantage-oriented stance of those taking part in gift-exchange. Similarly, in analysis of gift-exchange, emphasis is often placed on the (Kantian) moral obligation to do something (e.g., the popular narrative of 'giving something back' to a community), with no notion that this obligation also has a playful element of voluntariness and spontaneity connected with it. Influential interpreters of Mauss such as Claude Lévi-Strauss and Pierre Bourdieu have tended to overlook this multi-dimensional aspect of gift. It is also systematically ignored in approaches that mirror the dichotomy in social theory and either trace interrelated and reciprocal action back to instrumental rationality (Blau 1964; Coleman 1994) or see it as compliance with normative rules (Gouldner 1960). This blind spot is one of the very reasons why, according to Caillé, we need to develop a third paradigm (see also Adloff/Mau 2006). This third paradigm, which may be called *convivialism*, is a crucial development in the ethical understanding of social bonds as mutual recognition. In the manifesto, Adloff (2014: 13) states that

> [p]eople are not only interested in themselves; they are also interested in others; they can act spontaneously and empathetically on behalf of others. And the quintessential organizational embodiment of this type of action is the autonomous civil-society association, in which the principle of gratuitousness, of mutual giving and taking, operates to full effect.

Elsewhere, Caillé (2011) has stressed that the principle of voluntary association is dependent on intrinsic motives. If quantifying yardsticks and monetary incentives are introduced, this can lead to the erosion of these motives – an erosion that, in Sandel's terms, would wear away the reciprocally constitutive relation of recognition that exists between individuals, and between individuals and communities. Ultimately, then, this thread leads back to the moral, rather than empirical, descriptions of purpose and the good life. This is revealed through the etymology of the term 'convivial', and how it is understood in different cultures which have the mutual recognition of (and struggle between) individuals in common. It is worth marking down here at some length the manner in which the Convivialist Manifesto describes this approach to conviviality.

> By convivialism we mean a mode of living together (*con-vivere*) that values human relationships and cooperation and enables us to challenge one another without resorting to mutual slaughter and in a way that ensures consideration for others and for nature. We talk of challenging one another because to try to build a society where there is no conflict between groups and individuals would be not just delusory but disastrous. Conflict is a necessary and natural part of every society, not only because interests and opinions constantly differ [. . .] A healthy society is one that manages on the one hand to satisfy each individual's desire for recognition, and accommodate the element of rivalry – of wanting permanently to reach beyond oneself, and of opening up to the risks this entails – and on the other hand to prevent that desire from degenerating into excess and hubris and instead foster an attitude of cooperative openness to the other.

In psychosocial and existential terms, we might describe this, after Laing's framework of the authentic self, as a 'creative relationship with the other', in which there is a mutual enrichment of the self and of the other. It is for Laing, as he describes in his influential book *The Divided Self* (1965), a benign circle. This benign circle is a good in itself because it promotes well-being and accommodates difference, without resorting to a sterile relation between anonymous and equal entities; indifferent and disinterested individuals driven by rational, and primarily economic, self-interest. The model importantly retains a diversity which, whilst it might be thought of as a radical relativism of a sort, can more accurately and productively be described as a creative, reciprocally constitutive and convivial way of being which at the very least recognises the possibility of passionate, non-rationalised thinking and doing. I return to this reading of the benign circle of recognition in Chapter 3, where I follow up by discussing the politics of recognition and the state of relativism and other myths of connectivity (indeed, connectivity itself as a kind of myth) in online interpersonal communication. To begin that discussion, I will signpost the psychological dimensions of the problem of recognition – a theme taken up at length in Part II of this book. I wish to begin do so by establishing in a little more detail what I mean by describing creativity as a concept, process and act, and how creative freedoms establish affirmative senses of community (even online) which are subject to exploitation in Web 2.0 contexts.

Notes

1 At time of writing, Gauntlett is preparing a second edition of his book for publication.
2 A number of positions have emerged that, whilst outside of the scope of this book, have nevertheless gained traction in the fields of business intelligence, social media marketing and strategic communications. Such positions draw from classic game theory to think through co-operation and competition, consumer attention and satisfaction and payoff matrix. Examples from this perspective include Anderson (2010) and Asikomurwa and Mohaisen (2015).
3 Although, it ought to be noted that Stallman has on several occasions publicly outlined the need to maintain this distinction because, in common with Lanier, he sees the importance of the ability for programmers to be able to make a living, and so *gratis* software applications present a serious issue for the continued evolution of creative programming (see Stallman 2001 and 2004, for examples).
4 I explore this dialogue further in Part II of this book.

3

CONNECTIVITY, CREATIVITY AND OTHER WEB 2.0 MYTHS

The previous chapter examined processes by which the desiring consumer-subject is located through a complex matrix of recognition, working with the understanding of recognition in moral philosophy, and in particular Charles Taylor's description of the universal acknowledgement of recognition in social identity relations (1991). In this light, I also began the work of considering Web 2.0 functionality in relation to creativity and connectivity, agency and individual identity and the 'trade-off argument' concerning personal data, digital rights and digital labour. At the other end of the production-consumption nexus, I examined how the notions of demonstrable consumption and competitive self-interest are embedded in what Michael Sandel has described as market societies, and that this rubs up against contrary notions of mutuality found in convivialist notions of other-regarding. We saw how this tension seems to be exacerbated through the social, economic and cultural practices intertwined in social media communications, and how that intertwining has reinforced tensions between a social, 'popular' esteem and the privatised mode of 'self-respect'. I discussed the Veblenian idea of utilitarian interest-as-advantage and how convivialist ideas tend to de-emphasise this in favour of what might be described as ludic interest-as-curiosity. The notion of 'ludic' is useful because it emphasises a playful, creative aspect at work in social relations and the social imaginary, in the convivialist approach. And it is this aspect that I turn towards now – Web 2.0 is, after all, predicated on models of user-generated content, the crowdsourcing of individual creative talent and the playful creative economies that emerge through those collaborative models in semi-permanent conditions of connectivity.

In sum, I think that my own approach to creativity is grounded in its place as a crucible of and for social relations and the social imaginary. It is also important, however, to recognise that the tensions embedded in the struggle for a sense of the *ownership* of creativity in Web 2.0 legacy cultures (in the recognitive, ethical and existential, as well as economic senses) is inherently a political tension. I return to this towards the end of the chapter, but it is worth noting something remarked by the political economist Christian Fuchs in response to Henry Jenkins' notion of 'spreadable media' in a blog post written in 2011. Fuchs wrote that, 'Creativity is a force that enables Internet prosumer commodification, the commodification and exploitation of the users' activities and the data they generate. Creativity is not outside of or dual to exploitation on web 2.0, it is its very foundation' (2011).

In what follows, and somewhat in parallel with the critical tone set here by Fuchs, I seek to acknowledge the roles of creativity as normative psychosocial expressions of desire and recognition, overlaid with emerging exploitative relations of production in creative economies. In order to do this, I will discuss various models of creativity to consider its roles (in its various political forms) as a concept, a process and an act. I wish also to re-engage the political theories of recognition in the work of Charles Taylor (1995) and Axel Honneth (1995, 2012). I will do this through a critical discussion of creativity, evaluating the salience of a number of key thinkers (including Claxton 2003; Csikszentmihalyi 1992, 1997, 2006; Gauntlett 2011; Runco and Jaeger 2012; Stein 1953). Additionally, I will discuss the phenomena associated with accelerated and automated echo chambers and 'filter bubbles' of opinion in social media feeds (Pariser 2011; Shirky 2008; Lovink 2011, 2016), which tend to simultaneously polarise and depoliticise creativity in social media contexts. This is especially the case, perhaps, within online communities that privilege entrepreneurial-competitive species of creativity over entrepreneurial-collaborative creativity. The competitive species runs contrary to popular discourse and, I argue, tends to result in more impoverished forms of creative deliberation (such as flaming, trolling and so on). In this way, I will address how collaborative creative freedoms can establish affirmative senses of community (both online and RL, as well as fulfilling aesthetic and civic motivations) and benign circles of self- and other-regarding in semi-permanent conditions of connectivity – circles which are threatened by exploitation and degradation in Web 2.0 contexts, as well as toxic interest-as-advantage psychosocial competition.

Creativity as concept, process and act

In the vast literature on creativity, there are few areas where agreement can be reached as to its definition. One area where there is some consensus is in acknowledging the *popular* conception of creativity and what it involves. In the most general sense, creativity theorists, often working in the fields of social psychology and education, have identified that most people would conceive of creativity as belonging to creative *people*. It is, in other words, an attribute of personality or genetics and is accorded somewhat mystical properties of certain people who have a propensity for creativity – the 'X factor', to use a familiar term. This is perfectly understandable. When one thinks of celebrities and other public figures, for example, it is sometimes with a sense in which they are endowed with a mystique or an aura of otherness;

and it is often accompanied by a sense that these are people who have gained their status through talent, innovation and creativity; and, occasionally, through hard work. Guildford (1950 [cited in Runco and Jaeger 2012]), for example, acknowledges this meritocratic, popularly held definition of creativity thus:

> In its narrow sense, creativity refers to the abilities that are most characteristic of creative people. Creative abilities determine whether the individual has the power to exhibit creative behaviour to a noteworthy degree. Whether or not the individual who has the requisite abilities will actually produce results of a creative nature will depend upon his motivational and temperamental traits.

This definition of creativity assumes that the cultural capital of 'creative individuals', the power to express their creativity in whatever context, is attributed to ability. These kinds of attributes are generally associated with 'deserved' celebrity status. The contrary nature of celebrity means that the opposite is also true and just as widespread in the popular imagination: the denigration of certain people in the public eye who display no discernible marks of creativity, talent, or effort and yet are still agreed to hold some measure of celebrity status. Reality TV participants and YouTubers are typical of such cultural manoeuvres – indeed, elsewhere I have written about this contrary aspect of un/worthiness and celebrity at length (see Singh 2015, 2017).

Celebrity notions aside, these are rather general observations of the popular definition of creativity; for which, an aspect of recognition in the field as contributing to, transforming or changing culture in some way complicates the idea that creativity is merely associated with personality. Other general conceptual definitions of creativity include aspects of production (i.e., making something, or transforming cultural understanding), and embodying the dynamics of the new and the innovative with a process that is very old, and very human. As David Gauntlett (2011: 17) writes:

> Because we are human beings, creativity is something we do rather a lot, and understood in this broad sense it includes everyday ideas we have about how to do things, many of the things we write and produce, acts of management or self-presentation, and even, of course, witty or insightful speech.

In this sense, then, creativity is not only something profound and linked to mysterious persons of genius (or indeed imbued with an aura of the mystique of misunderstood genius), but can be thought of as an everyday, personal experience. It can be a very intimate way of communicating not only ideas, but feelings and worldviews – expressed in ways that are not reducible to formal or institutionally recognised modes of creation. So, it may be true that many people might not think of themselves as creative, and may think that creative acts are done more-or-less exclusively by those gifted with an intuitive ability to create. However, there is also a dialectical sense at which this somewhat magical property of creative ability (or one that is mastered through years of practice, craft and endeavour) is also a very ordinary set of acts and experiences for which we all have the potential to fulfil. Moreover, we do so every day, and in any number of cultural domains – perhaps especially in interpersonal communications. More specifically, we might say that, because creativity is most often experienced as a profoundly personal process, and at the same time is one that is shared sociably and collaboratively, it holds close similarities to Taylor's dialogical notion of recognition, other-regarding and the social contract with significant others. Therefore, it can be said to be a highly emotive experience bound up with what one might describe as the formation and mobilisation of social identity. Such mobilisation would be, in Sandel's terms, a somewhat profound, 'reciprocally constitutive' process.

What seems to be the case for most thinkers in creativity theory is that there is a sense of newness in the act of creation, but that, in sharing the products of that creation, one is counting on the recognition of others that something about the world (or one's experience of the world) has somehow been transformed, or contributed towards. For Mihaly Csikszentmihalyi, creativity is more specifically '[. . .] a process by which a symbolic domain in the culture is changed. New songs, new ideas, new machines are what creativity is all about' (1996: 8). Csikszentmihalyi's work on creativity is most influential in two related and crucial interventions in the field of creativity: first, his 'Systems Model of Creativity' (1996, 2006) and, second, his concept of 'flow' (1992).

More recently, Hsu-Chan Kuo (2011) has used Csikszentmihalyi's Systems Model of Creativity to map a conceptual framework for the study of creativity, in which a synthesised field of interaction processes govern creative choices at a personal or local level. I argue that a more detailed and considered approach to this synthesised field of interaction is required in order to fully engage the cultural contexts (and, in particular, the notion of cultural capital as reflective of power relations) within which creativity emerges, is recognised and is harnessed. To my mind, a fully synthesised field of interaction is comprised of a number of dimensions. These would include: material conditions; Althusserian 'problematics' as the context-specific system of questions commanding the answers given from an ideology (1977); and something approaching Brian Winston's 'supervening social necessities' (1986, 1996, 1998) model of the social sphere – necessities which can perform roles in both accelerating and disabling ideation, prototyping and dissemination. Examples of this might include profit-motive, risk, social taboo, political expediency or a whole host of social norms and values governing the sanction of innovative ideas and processes. Such dimensions, whilst implied, are generally de-emphasised in Csikszentmihalyi's work, and almost invisible in Kuo's reading. However, both scholars maintain that the interaction of the personal and social is of crucial concern as a crucible for creativity. I argue that this interaction needs to be more fully acknowledged in relation to the dimensions just outlined. Where Kuo does revisit the interaction of the personal and social in creativity theory, he writes (2011: 67) that some investigators advocate the study of creativity *primarily* in the social context:

[. . .] regardless of whether creativity is considered as personal traits, creative behaviour, a cognitive process, or either something that can be trained, creativity should be linked to social contexts, and be understood by the interaction processes.

In Csikszentmihalyi's well-documented system, 'Creativity is a process that can be observed only at the intersection where individuals, domains, and fields interact' (2006: 3). To clarify, in this context the domain is comprised of a set of rules and practices; the creative individual can be understood as contributing a novel variation in the contents of the domain. The field, for Kuo, is 'held by various gatekeepers, such as experts and scholars, who have the rights to choose which variations can be reserved in the domains' (2011: 68). Creativity, therefore, can be understood as a confluence of the three subsystems of domain, individual and field within social context; additionally, I argue a subset of both problematics and of supervening social necessity. Interestingly, Kuo uses the term 'sanction' as a way to describe the somewhat institutional recognition processes whereby a group (a field of gatekeepers) is entitled to make decisions as to what should and should not be incorporated into the domain. It is therefore impossible to sustain a robust definition of creativity without fully acknowledging the interaction of these subsystems, and the dialectical tensions inherent in their social arrangement. For Csikszentmihalyi (2006: 3):

> [. . .] what we call creativity is not the product of single individuals, but of social systems making judgements about individual's products. Any definition of creativity [. . .] will have to recognise the fact that the audience is as important to its constitution as the individual to whom it is credited.

Here, of course, Csikszentmihalyi is using the term 'audience' to refer to the institutional levels of gate-keeping, expertise and authority. But we might also recognise, particularly within popular cultural contexts and the reputation and rewards systems constituted through Web 2.0 interactions, that the role of audiences (as in, consumers, end-users, producers etc.) is crucial here. Gauntlett identifies that the problem with Csikszentmihalyi's approach is that he tends to emphasise the end product and the judgement of others, particularly of experts and gatekeepers (2011). Although one might say that audience almost always plays an important role in the distribution of creative products, as we have seen in Web 2.0 contexts the 'sit-back-and-consume' nature of mass broadcast media has been superseded by the more interactive and collaborative context of DIY creativity online. Gauntlett states that 'it might be considered strange that we are unable to say if creativity has happened or not, without turning to subject experts' (2011: 74), going on to venture that Csikszentmihalyi's model seems to deny that creativity is centred on experience, feeling and process. And this is the case even when he discusses 'flow' – the term Csikszentmihalyi uses to describe the experience wherein a person is fully and joyfully immersed in their actions, and the work they do is satisfactorily challenging to the extent that they would probably do it for free if they weren't paid to do it in the first place (1992).

This is well within the context of his main point, which is to say that creativity is central to our relations of connection and recognition. Gauntlett's work, focusing as it does on everyday creativity, challenges the professionalised aspect of Csikszentmihalyi's model. He insists that, in separating feelings and experiences from a more definable or quantifiable reality of high-end creativity, this might involve, for example, a value-status of creative work, in the sense of global or national recognition of the sort found in Nobel Prize-winning physics, say, or the kind that is written up in a scientific journal. In this way, Csikszentmihalyi often privileges authoritative creativity over common experience. Csikszentmihalyi's vast interview sample for the number of studies published took in this sort of high-level creative participant as much as ordinary professionals, and so his focus is understandable. However, by contrast, Gauntlett recognises that 'Creativity might be better understood as a process, and a feeling. In this way of looking at it, creativity is about breaking new ground, but internally: the sense of going somewhere, doing something that you've not done before' (2011: 17). There is, therefore, a sense of purpose in creativity, which fulfils development of esteem and furnishes individuals with an experience of both self- and other-regarding that has cultural (and potentially civic) value.

As mentioned in previous chapters, I have sympathy with this democratising view of creativity, and recognise it as part of the discourse on the Free Web that has dominated in the past. Gauntlett's critique of the 'sit-back' model of passive media consumption and his championing of 'making and doing culture' is particularly relevant in this context. For Gauntlett, Web 2.0 is about 'harnessing the collective abilities of the members of an online network, to make an especially powerful resource or service. [. . .] any collective activity which is enabled by people's passions and becomes something greater than the sum of its parts' (2011: 7). Therefore, for him at least, Web 2.0 practice has political and civic value.

As discussed briefly in Chapter 1, Clay Shirky's work addressed the corrosive influence that incentivisation has on civic projects. Shirky's work on 'cognitive surplus' (2010) also argues that the actions of groups add up to much more than the aggregated acts of individuals, and that if we could harness this in some way then changes could be made in the checks and balances within market societies, to mitigate incentivisation's more extreme effects – intense privatisation of experience amongst them. For example, he argues that the massive amounts of free time in modern democratic societies spent on watching TV could be harnessed and better spent on civic collaboration and creative endeavour. At the time of his writing, the total sum of hours of human thought spent on Wikipedia – every edit made to every article, in every language, and every argument about those edits – would represent something like 100 million hours.[1] Shirky suggests that Wikipedians find the time to do this largely through avoiding traditional twentieth-century mass media entertainments; by *producing* rather than just consuming. He writes (2010: 10) that:

Americans watch approximately two hundred billion hours of TV every year. That represents about two thousand Wikipedias' projects' worth of free time annually. Even tiny subsets of this time are enormous: we spend roughly a hundred million hours every weekend just watching commercials.

Admittedly, that is a massive surplus of aggregate time; time that, Shirky argues, could be put to better use – i.e., thinking and sharing. Even if we take into account the more recent evidence from Nielsen and BARB surveys in the US and UK respectively, where on-demand and streamed content (timeshifted content) have surpassed traditional broadcast media consumption in the total audience (Bury and Li 2015), the aggregate consumption time in front of televisual screens is staggering. So, the question remains, if we are to take Shirky seriously on his premise: why don't we? Why don't we put our time to better use? Shirky attempts to answer these questions by suggesting that we tend to spend the surplus of time consuming TV because we judge it to be a better use of time than the available alternatives, whatever these might be. It is worth quoting him in full on this (2010: 11).

> Life in the developed world includes a lot of passive participation: at work we're like office drones, at home we're couch potatoes. The pattern is easy enough to explain by assuming we've wanted to be passive participants more than we wanted other things. This story has been, in the last several decades, pretty plausible; a lot of evidence certainly supported this view, and not a lot contradicted it. But now, for the first time in the history of television, some cohorts of young people are watching TV less than their elders. [. . .] young populations with access to fast, interactive media are shifting their behavior away from media that presupposes pure consumption.

He explains this in a number of key ways: for example, that some people are surprised that individual members of society would actually *want* to voluntarily create and share things *gratis*; and surprising, perhaps especially, when compared with previous generations' supposed characterisation of passive participation in consumption. Gauntlett's argument seems to revolve around the notion that 'we' (whoever 'we' are) pursue more active engagement with media, and this does seem to chime with Shirky's account of a recent shift. There are ways in which these two commentators differ markedly, however. There are a number of assumptions in Shirky's thinking – primarily down to the way that he seems to be addressing a popular audience in his book, and attempting to paint rather broad strokes in an effort to explain his position. Another version of events would be to say that the passive forms of consumption he is attempting to identify are natural products of a market society. Time, and the experience of time, are privatised resources and this is internalised to such an extent that it is rather difficult to see an alternative. What is worse is that the common perceptions of effort involved in the creative use of resources are circumscribed by the problematic association of creativity and knowledge creation with either persons of special ability, or through hard-won recognition in the field. So, whereas people may have recently shifted away from TV as a major media pastime (and whereas there does seem to be a lot of productivity on social media, wiki and Web 2.0 services requiring a specifically active role), for most of us, we might say that consumption patterns have merely moved on to the next media platform, rather than having been revolutionised outright.

Wiki∗edia² as creative civic project, and the dialectics of authority

One reason for this could be that, although we tend to periodise technological evolution, the reality is nowhere near as neat. This is as much to do with significant crossovers in technological and leisure time evolution, where institutional arrangements tend to be remediated through new technologies, rather than overturned. To reiterate a point Gauntlett makes, many influential definitions of creativity, including Csikszentmihalyi's, rely upon gate-keepers, experts and authorities to say if creativity has happened or not. Gate-keeping in this sense occurs in institutional forms all over the creative industries. Amongst the reasons as to why this happens, we might say that this turns upon a habit learned in the liberal arts which proves tenacious and most difficult to shake off: placing value in the author and in authority and granting those in the field the status of the authentic. This is particularly the case in the creation and dissemination of new knowledge and is wrapped in the psychosocial recognition institutions of esteem and self-esteem.³ Clearly, however, the disruption that Wikipedia (as the most obvious example, but also by far the most popular example amongst a whole host of other wikis and open knowledge-building platforms) contributes to that traditional sense of field, and its diffuse collaborative appearance-form presents a challenge to this view of authority. This is far from a straightforward challenge, however. To my mind, once again, this is identifiable as a dialectical relation existing in the status of authority, which platforms such as wikis expose. It is not merely the case that all voices are equal, are heard at the same volume or are granted the same privilege – that is a relativism indicative of critiques levelled (and quite incorrectly applied, in my opinion) against the blogosphere, a slightly different case which I discuss at various points in Part II of this book. Yet, at the same time, one cannot say that traditional forms of knowledge are left untouched by the challenge to which they are presented.

For all of Jaron Lanier's posturing (2006) against the collective aspects of knowledge-building accomplished through wiki-like platforms (some aspects with which I find myself in agreement) there is a sense that wikis have afforded a space in which we cannot assume that traditional knowledge formations still hold the same allure as in the pre-Web era. I use the term *affordance* here in both the purely (and incomplete) technological sense, and also in the sense of providing context for economic relations of knowledge: that the plenitude of information leads to an abundance of competing knowledges which are no longer exclusive and scarce. How do wikis illustrate this?

In his 'Digital Maoism' essay (2006), Lanier uses Wikipedia as a case that represents a more general trend towards seeing the collective as all-wise. Although both Gauntlett and Shirky's approaches to Web 2.0 are attractive, they are as much problematic for the relativistic reasons one might associate with group-think or the descent into mob mentality in the Twittersphere; the kind of collectivism which Lanier critiques so venomously. Part of this issue is the belief that problems in wikis will be incrementally solved, and information incrementally corrected as the process unfolds through discussion and talk page activity. This belief has a similar logic to that found in James Surowiecki's book, *The Wisdom of Crowds* (2004). In common with other conceptions of collaborative knowledge-building or creative co-operation (such as Pierre Levy's 'collective intelligence' concept (1997), or the populist conception of the 'hive mind'), Surowiecki suggests that diversity of opinion, independence from other people's opinions and specialist local knowledge expressed in a modal averaging-out of collective opinion, are fundamental to success in terms of any collective, creative enterprise. He offers a number of real-world examples to support his argument. These individual dimensions to collective decision-making also seem fundamental to our ideas of what a modern democracy should look like in terms of recognising the needs of individual opportunity and common good. He writes (2004: xiii–xiv) that

> [u]nder the right circumstances, groups are remarkably intelligent, and are often smarter than the smartest people in them. [. . .] Even if most of the people within a group are not especially well-informed or rational, it can still reach a collectively wise decision. This is a good thing, since human beings are not perfectly designed decision makers.

One might be tempted to sympathise with the idea of common good embodied in wise decisions of a collective. However, although collective and deliberative actions are embedded to an extent in the architecture of wiki administration, this argument tends to sidestep the rather messy business of *recognition* as a tension and struggle between persons and communities as proposed by Taylor, and by other key recognition theorists (e.g., Honneth 1995; Honneth with Fraser 2002; Petherbridge 2011, 2013). It also sidesteps the confluence of the three subsystems of *creativity* – domain, individual and field in Csikszentmihalyi's Systems Model, particularly where the synthesised field of interaction processes that govern creative choices takes on a political character. Finally, it sidesteps the issues described at length in Chapter 2: that reasonable conflict inherent in the notion of 'endebtedness' is a form of social recognition, and in the convivialist approach is desirable as a factor of social cohesion and an expression of the social imaginary. These are articulations of the politics of recognition towards which I have so far been building, and towards which I have begun to apply to the field of connectivity ethics. To this set of articulations, I would like to develop the discussion, noting the important contribution that Wikipedia has played in making visible the dialectical tensions involved in collective decision-making and creative enterprise.

In his book *Wikipedia U: Knowledge, Authority, and Liberal Education in the Digital Age* (2014), Thomas Leitch discusses several interconnected ways in which the challenge to knowledge formation is contested in Wikipedia; often with contradictions as a work-in-progress fully in play. The first centres on moral and epistemic authority where Wikipedia's well-known claim on democratic, consensus-seeking article-generation competes with a sophisticated hierarchical system of administration, automated correction and trust committees. It therefore embodies 'one central value of liberal education, the need for constant critical attention and review, onto another equally central value, the need to preserve and respect the authority of the past' (2014: 19). In other words, what Wikipedia seems to want to do is to take its moral authority from the fact that it both adheres to and respects the knowledge of the past, and also from the freshness of approach that an appeal to absolute peer-reviewed neutrality and *opera aperta* can afford. It wants to take its epistemic authority from both the 'hive-mind' collective model of consensus on the one hand, where the wisdom of crowds prevails, as well as, on the other, a corrective system (and a punitive system against vandalism where it is deemed necessary) automated and calibrated to ensure consistency and order. One might say, therefore, that there is a dialectical tension between *vox populi* and *vox dei* which Wikipedia has kept in play, and from which it claims its ultimate moral and epistemic authority.

In this sense at least, what is important to remember about Wikipedia is that not only does it embody a sense of Web 1.0 mass readership/audience, and Web 2.0 collaborative contribution; it also partly as a result embodies an elision of sorts between information, knowledge and wisdom as distinct epistemic categories. On one aspect of this (2014: 30), Leitch writes that

> [a]ll encyclopedias, print or online, are by their nature secondary or tertiary sources whose authority is not based on any original research their contributors have done but on their synoptic range and organization. [. . .] The attenuation of central editorial control, widely noted in both attacks and defenses of Wikipedia, merely emphasizes paradoxes already unavoidably present in print encyclopedias.

This is to say, contributors know a large amount of information on very specific topics, where to find it, how to aggregate that information and how best to represent it. Taken in sum, contributors know a lot about a lot of subjects (in a realisation, of sorts, of collective intelligence theories such as Levy 1999). Editorial intervention however, most often comes in the form of systemic consistency and correction of style issues, ensuring order, curating the information. Editors and the editorial process also lend to the body of work a patina of credibility and, thus, reliability, through standardisation. It is this editorial aspect of the Wikipedia paradox which differentiates it from a perceived banality used by some commentators to characterise the blogosphere and certain aspects of independent citizen journalism, where many voices compete for attention in an increasingly accelerated media ecosystem.

For example, in *Zero Comments*, Geert Lovink (2008) notes that citizen journalism helps erode top-down models of 'truth' and 'authority', but only to break down into nihilism and banality. This is popularly known as an 'echo chamber' or 'filter bubble' effect in writing for the Web, in which a plurality of viewpoints and banalities compete with funnelled news feeds based on data profiling, to clutter the big picture of power relations in social structures. Filter bubbles have the secondary effect of merely reinforcing the real-life prejudices of those whose fact-checking habits only reach as far as the first three Wikipedia pages they see. This is a far cry from the kinds of creative freedoms to which I eluded in Chapter 2, which, pre-dating the Web, now stand as uneasy claims of political empowerment in Web 2.0 creativity more generally.

In his more recent work, *Social Media Abyss* (2016), Lovink takes this a step further by noting the historical importance of the term 'platform' to capture a middle ground of 'contradictory activities of online services as a neutral ground for DIY users and major media producers, while enabling the collision of privacy and surveillance efforts, community and advertising investments' (2016: 3). This is something of a tandem with Sandel's already-discussed notion of 'market society', where a society governed by market forces and market fundamentalism is a society that eludes its moral purpose, even when it empirically fulfils mission statements such as the implementation of social inclusion policy, or of equal-pay legislation in a sort of 'you said. . . we did' gesture. Lovink suggests a 'platform society' term as the basis for a critique of network culture which is in the beginning stages of burnout. Of click-through strategies such as clickbait for amassing online revenue, Lovink is especially critical: 'Recently, we've seen a cultural shift away from the active, self-conscious user towards the subject as docile, ignorant servant' (2016: 5). In this, he is referring to the manner in which ordinary users, whilst perhaps aware of the uses and governances of their data, as well as perhaps a limited perception of user status as digital labourer, are content to surrender the fate of their data to governance beyond their control in the trade-off for goods and services *gratis*. I would argue that it is not so much the notion that users are unthinking on this, but there seems to be a patina of compliance in such practices generally, where users are more than ready to surrender their data as long as access to free online services continues, relatively 'ad-free'. At more specific levels, Lovink suggests that the effects of docility are regulated and amplified through regimes of distraction in the attention economy of social media activity. In a critical manoeuvre echoing ideas of Frankfurt School alumni such as Kracauer, and in similarities to Foucault's notion of technologies of the self, Lovink assumes that the underlying function of such distractive technological practices is to act as a disciplinary force (2016: 28).

Of course, this is not so much a case of assuming a conspiratorial effort on the part of multinationals to extort time from users. Nonetheless, one can see a collective psychic image of control looming large in this arrangement, and it is something that I return to in some depth in Part II of this book, particularly in relation to my notion of social media as a *false-self system*. The point here is that even in such positivist accounts as Shirky's, where he attempts to persuade us that the assumption of a passivity and docility in mass media consumption is passé, there is an element in contemporary popular media cultures where participation in aspects of creativity in Web 2.0 and social media contexts can extend freedoms and express authorship only so far. The mechanism of commandeering such activity into the service of monetisation is more than enough to offset admirable civic, creative and socially rewarding projects such as Wiki*edia.

To my mind, this brings us full-circle back to moral philosophy arguments, and especially to Charles Taylor and his take on authenticity (1991). Taylor illustrates the importance of contact with others in the formation of identity, and how recognition plays a central role in dealing with authenticity. This is foundational to our knowledge concerning what is true about ourselves, our world and those with whom we share it. Much of contemporary life, as we know, is mediated through platforms which embody everyday expressions of identity and connection between individuals and groups. Additionally, some of the promises of the early Web (as discussed at length in Chapter 1) were predicated upon discourses of free movement of information, increasing access and participation and the flexibility of identity-formation and active agency. As we saw, these were promises that, in their historic forms at least, seem to have been abandoned, replaced by a much more passive, in Lovink's terms 'docile', form of engagement.

I argue that this cultural shift is mythic in character, because the new forms are transparently overlaid on the historic forms, as if the historic forms of access, usability, privacy and copyright were still predominant in the *motivations and drives* behind Web technologies and their uses today. This is particularly evident in the way that default creativity and connectivity is assumed in Web 2.0 discourse. If the principle modes of connectivity, and our sense of connectivity, are shaped by the technologies of social communication and information sharing, then this connectivity is, from a psychosocial sense at least, surely an impoverished and inauthentic one. 'Inauthentic', in the sense of not being true to itself, to its purpose. In this sense, then, although Lovink's work is firmly in the technological, political economy school of critique, he also joins the ethics level of debate on social media connectivity. He does this on the basis that his work addresses the obliqueness through which the promises of the early Web have transformed into vehicles for what he describes as 'platform-capitalism', and the problematic immaterial labour governed through platform interactivity. Usability, access, privacy and copyright, those most salient of early Web promises, are no longer serving a self-evident purpose. These terms merely signify activities which serve oblique economic purposes, untrue to themselves.

There are avenues of affirmative practice, use and demonstrable applicability to sustaining contact and co-operation in some popular online civic projects, as I hope to have illustrated in this chapter so far. However, there are fundamental problems associated with leaving the argument on connectivity there. The key to this lies in the perceptible discrepancy between purpose and use. There is a false dichotomy lying between purpose and use, entrenched in policy-making on digital literacy (especially, perhaps, in the UK), which fails to acknowledge their dialectical relationship; and, knowledge of both purpose and use of communications practices in our creative relationships with one another, in the existential and psychosocial senses of connectivity. In what follows, I explore this negative aspect of connectivity further, discussing assumptions regarding creativity and connectivity as myths of our time. This will then form the basis for discussion in Part II, where the focus will centre on recognition theory, self-realisation and the principle of mutuality in persistent, always-on contexts of connectivity.

Connectivity (and the conventional wisdom of connectivity) as myth

As has been the subject of discussion so far in this book, one of the defining characteristics in popular perceptions of Web 2.0 is its promotion and affordance of creative freedoms. This democratic and democratising mode of cultural practice is encountered in many forms. The following discussion takes place within a broader context that includes notions of creative freedoms, as well as freedom of movement within spaces, both physical and virtual. Its main focus, however, revolves around a perceived disintermediation of information flows. This is a context incorporating freedom of expression and opinion-formation, particularly within the public sphere, but also incorporates the popular perceptions around the ways Web connectivity has eliminated intermediaries in the traditional sense. Discourses around disintermediation include getting away from the gate-keepers, editors, paternalism and the kinds of 'authorities' brought into disrepute through publicised corruption or self-interest. In the former senses, this has much in common with the discourses associated with creativity and knowledge-building discussed earlier in relation to Wiki*edia. The latter senses concerning authority are related to popular notions of free speech and the expression of rights and the responsibilities (or, indeed, lack of intuited responsibilities) associated with those rights in those popular notions, in online communications contexts. This seems particularly acute when applied to contexts of deliberation, current affairs and news production and consumption; all of these dimensions of freedom are predicated on the assumption, characteristic of modern democracies, of an authentic individual (and rational) agency at the heart of choosing to act or not act on information, beliefs or provocation. They are encountered in both benign and toxic modes in everyday communications. Indeed, so familiar are we with these sentiments that in general terms we have internalised them as self-evident principles in the history of developed democracies. However, as has often been the case so far in this study, it is only when one begins to examine the tensions and contradictions at play between the interests of individuals and the interests of communities that the mythic content of such assumptions truly becomes apparent.

A. C. Grayling has noted two general positions that have been historically taken towards perceived asymmetry between individual and community (2013). The first is the libertarian conception, where the best kind of society is a minimal society. The second is a position often taken by both liberal and socialist perspectives – in that a good society compensates for the failings of the individuals in it, and the state or other entities intervene in a gesture towards common good. Indeed, this second conception is a remarkably similar mechanism to the 'consensus' model found in Wiki*edia, outlined earlier, and has a long tradition in the debates on the relationship between the conception of a public, and a general, understanding of modern democracy, based on the dissemination, acquisition and communication of information about the world. For example, John Dewey, in *The Public and Its Problems* (originally published in 1927), argued that 'To learn to be human is to develop through the give and take of communication and effective sense of being an individually distinctive member of a community' (2008: 332). This 'effective sense' is a form of recognition that takes seriously the relation between individual and community, the tensions between the interests of individuals and their communities as a whole, and their articulation, one in the other, with respect to the building and transference of knowledge. Dewey's take on public knowledge and opinion-making had far-reaching implications for how journalism as a practice developed during the twentieth century, and to this day has immediate relevance to the ways in which connectivity is transforming conceptions of the public sphere, and how knowledge is developed and shared in democratic societies.

The positions outlined above by Grayling are particularly relevant to both freedom of speech and the rights and responsibilities afforded by such freedom in this 'effective sense'. Indeed, in his response to Grayling, Sandel argues that freedom of speech deserves special protections for two reasons, neither of which depends on an assumption that the speech was freely chosen by an autonomous agent. First, there is a civic virtue that respecting freedom of speech is essential to democratic life (where democratic life matters not just because it satisfies individual preferences but because it makes us *better*). Second, Sandel broadly appropriates the Aristotelian virtue of the 'good life', where we are free when we participate in public deliberation and develop the full range of our human faculties. So, there is a position owed to the Aristotelian tradition – a virtuous circle where a good society leads to the flourishing of good individuals, without the need to rely on an assumed agency of freely choosing selves. This accords individuals liberties so that a society can be a good one. However, once again, Sandel's position goes in both directions: the reciprocally constitutive or mutually dependent, implying that individuals and their rights to freedom of speech are somewhat co-dependent upon others, and upon functional institutions, in social arrangements. However, it also should be noted here that free speech in this sense needs to be recognised as performing that particular Aristotelian function, where deliberation leads to the flourishing of individuals in a fully functioning society with the rights and responsibilities for that deliberation resting in the actors.

What I would like to concentrate on here is how this deliberative function is overlaid with the aforementioned newer forms of passivity, enabled through discourses of what we might call the 'conventional wisdom' that technology directly affords behaviours of freedom leading towards fulfilling, enriched, 'good' lives. The term 'conventional wisdom', in the sense that I am using it, is borrowed from the influential economist J. K. Galbraith, and his seminal work, *The Affluent Society* (1962). On one aspect of the notion of conventional wisdom (1962: 20), Galbraith notes that

> There are many reasons why people like to hear articulated that which they approve. It serves the ego: the individual has the satisfaction of knowing that other and more famous people share his conclusions. To hear what he believes is also a source of assurance.

Galbraith appears to be remarkably prescient here. His position on conventional wisdom has some quite striking parallels with the notion of the 'filter bubble' often referred to in popular contexts and written about most extensively in Eli Pariser's work (2011a and 2011b). This term refers to the customisation of Web experience through the use of personalisation filters, found in search engines and other ubiquitous products associated with Web browsing. These customisations, put crudely, change the way we experience the Web, altering the answers to queries by adapting them to our search histories. This is the beginning of what Pariser means by 'filter bubble' – but its implications are far deeper, and I discuss some of the image-driven psychological aspects of this in relation to social interactions on Instagram, amongst other platforms, in Part II.

Although still ostensibly a search aid, since 2011, the Google algorithm also functions as a mechanism to establish the *intent* behind asking what one has asked for, and gives results based on how it perceives you, derived from a bewildering set of variables relating to one's browsing history. As Pariser (2011b: 6) puts it,

> Every time we seek out some new bit of information, we leave a digital trail that reveals a lot about us, our interests, our politics, our level of education, our dietary preferences, our movie likes and dislikes, and even our dating interests or history.

The most obvious application for this is commercial – the optimisation of consumer experience is a highly marketable enterprise, which enables the targeting of individual users through personalisation. But of course, customisation of search experience is not merely about advertising and commercialisation alone; whereas it may be true that personalisation is shaping what we buy, our consumer choices and so on, there are other ways in which it shapes our everyday lives. For example, personalised newsfeeds have quickly become a primary news source for (potentially) billions of people: 'Personalization is shaping how information flows far beyond Facebook, as Web sites [. . .] cater their headlines to our particular interests and desires.' They are *prediction engines*, rather than mere search engines, which 'create a unique universe of information for each of us [. . .] which fundamentally alters the way we encounter ideas and information' (Pariser 2011a: 9). It is this 'unique universe' aspect of the Web experience that gives a more complete sense to the term filter bubble, because, at its extreme, Pariser implies a more totalised form, where personalisation is changing the way people *think* in social terms. Perhaps the more worrying aspect of this relates to the lack of awareness for the everyday user, and the implications of misplaced trust in personalisation systems. Pariser states (2011a: 3) that

> In polls, the huge majority of us assume search engines are unbiased. But they may be just because they're increasingly biased to share our own views. More and more, your computer monitor is a kind of one-way mirror, reflecting your own interests while algorithmic observers watch what you click.

The approach that Pariser has taken towards search engine bias and its relation to the psychology underpinning human emotional bias is part of a tradition, represented in significant corpus of work. This work is dedicated to the politics of search and its relationship with modern democracies (see, for example, Becker, K. and F. Stalder, eds 2009; Gates 2011; Gehring, ed. 2004 Segev 2010; Spink and Zimmer eds 2008). In my view, this 'politics of search' is a politics of recognition in the broadest sense. Referring back to Gabraith's words, to hear what one believes is a source of assurance and, frankly, something of a relief in a world where recognition is at a premium. This may not be a problem for most people. Indeed, this seems more or less a reiteration of the trade-off argument discussed in the previous chapter: 'While Gmail and Facebook may be helpful, free tools, they are also extremely effective and voracious extraction engines into which we pour the most intimate details of our lives' (2011a: 6–7).

However, the socio-political implications of this are apparent and, since the time of Pariser's writing, increasingly so. Indeed, this has been noted in various fields. For example, in personalisation design, the role of smart technologies in the personalisation design of clothes and other wearable technologies tends to make for flexible and increasingly individualised relationships between humans and machines. Whereas this might be considered a boon from a designer's perspective, simultaneously, the development of intelligent software agents such as Siri has led to arguments suggesting that projection of morally accountable agency to machines may have the effect of placing far more autonomy onto machines than they are designed to have (Kuksa and Fisher 2017; Oberlander 2017). Other fields of research, such as in user interface design, have for some time now engaged with the transformation of information flows following the development of adaptive systems and networks, and adaptive behaviour studies have been developed to engage the on-size-fits-all approach of interface automation in the processes of personalised information retrieval (Mourlas and Germanakos eds 2009). Further research fields, such as in bio computing design, engage with the role of automated detection technologies involving machines with smart vision and predictive analytics capabilities for a number of purposes, including surveillance and security in public and retail spaces (Gates 2011); enhanced medical diagnoses; or student learning styles (Hemanth and Smys eds 2018). The field of computational vision further extends this intelligent agency and smart vision by charting the rapid development of such technology from early theoretical interventions (Wechsler 1990) to fully realised applications in everyday life (Jenkin and Harris 2007; Hemanth and Smys eds 2018).

In my approach, drawing from ethical media studies, in exchange for personalisation filtering one must hand the rights to an enormous amount of personal data to large companies. The trust involved here is truly staggering, not least because most of the data handed over would be information we would not even dream of entrusting our dearest friends with. The ramifications of this range far beyond the merely personal, and impinge upon what is commonly thought of as a bedrock of advanced societies: democracy itself. Pariser writes that 'Democracy requires citizens to see things from one another's point of view', in what might be considered a fully realised socio-political recognition, 'but instead we're more and more enclosed in our own bubbles. Democracy requires a reliance on shared facts; instead we're being offered parallel but separate universes' (2011a: 5).

This separateness can satisfy individual desires, perhaps, but places those desires at a remove from social life. It diverts from any communitarian notion of civic virtue in democratic life where one's individual preferences align with the betterment of individuals *in societies*, as mentioned a moment ago. It is also a diversion from the Aristotelian notion of deliberation and the development of the full range of human faculties, both individual and community-based. For Pariser, opinion-making is now fully automated, following user data trails and targeting users directly, through whichever sites they access, and the era where it was necessary to develop premium content to get premium audiences has drawn to a close (2011a: 49).

News feeds reflect the trails of data generated by individual users, governed through algorithms to produce an overall picture fed back to the user that anticipates that user's worldview with remarkable accuracy. As a growing body of scholarship has shown (e.g., Lovink 2011, 2016; Meikle 2016; Pariser 2011a, 2011b; Shirky 2008), echo chambers of opinion in social media feeds tend to simultaneously polarise and depoliticise creativity in social media contexts. Additionally, within the accelerated media ecosystem of today, the saturation of celebrity news and gossip within traditional and social mass media platforms (in a discernible turn from paternalistic approaches to news content, and towards what tends to generate the most hits) tends to amplify these filter bubble effects. In turn (as I will develop more fully in the argument in Part II), this impacts upon the parasocial apparatus more generally. The emotional and affective investments made by fans in their efforts to engage with the social media feeds of their favourite celebrities and the professionalised PR and strategic communications involvement in branding strategies, enables ever-tighter circles of reference – in a counter-direction to Aristotelian virtuous functionality.

Although this situation might not necessarily present us with a working model of the reciprocally constitutive, it does seem to provide an indication of the tenacity of discourse on individual agency in relation to interpersonal interaction. People like to be affirmed through their choices, as much as they like to have the choices they make recognised as the 'correct' choices; they tend to be willing to put up with much that in other circumstances they would not countenance, to ensure they are not marked as different. Conversely, to stand out from the crowd is to be recognised and accorded social value in a championing of individualism. The phenomenon of self-disclosure online is a case in point here, and such practices are the subject of a range of scholarly approaches to social media behaviours (Baym 2010; boyd 2014; boyd and Donath 2004; Papacharissi 2010; Walker Rettberg 2008 and 2014). Through practices such as self-disclosure, users seek to acquire a sense of belonging, at the same time as expressing individual concerns or circumstances. Additionally, whereas this might run counter to our intuitive feeling that we are free agents with opinions and responsibilities that are independently and autonomously ours to govern, a feeling of belonging is a powerful psychological motivation for acting, particularly where one recognises others who are willing to share openly as much as oneself.

Indeed, in the contemporary accelerated media ecosystem, distinction as part of a social grouping or community has become a sort of currency; certainly, having a USP in one's identity as a professional online entrepreneur (as a YouTuber, vlogger or brand ambassador, for example) might be considered a marked advantage in a saturated marketplace. Entrepreneurial branding is, after all, a stock-in-trade commodity which tends to drive the market for social media applications in the professional sense, if not in the everyday general sense. At the very least, professional creatives are aware of some of these issues, and are more than willing to exploit this sense of ego-individuality-as-belonging – being as ordinary as the subscribers who adhere to the social media programme, but at the same time, distinct and extra-ordinary. However, this version of conventional wisdom goes some way to describing the manner in which users of social media seem satisfied with the kinds of trade-off arguments discussed in Chapter 2. Why? Security could play a major role in this attitude, as consumers seem to have been fairly happy to go along with this arrangement, exchanging fundamental (actual) freedoms for increased access and choice in their online consumer habits.

This consumer satisfaction is more important to the continued success of social media connectivity in monopolising our time than it first appears. It is also fundamentally tied into notions of creativity in interpersonal communication. Again, turning to Csikszentmihalyi (2006), we might say that satisfaction with the status quo puts a brake on desire to disengage with social media as a popular pastime. Novel uses of online action would be, according to his Systems Theory, driven through dissatisfaction rather than creative curiosity. Csikszentmihalyi writes that 'Greater sensitivity, naivety, arrogance, impatience, and higher intellectual standards have all been adduced as reasons why some people are unable to accept the conventional wisdom in a domain and feel the need to break out of it' (2006: 15). I would say that the opposite also holds true in the context of social media. In a system where sensitivity, naivety, arrogance and impatience are relied upon to generate the user data to feed off, the conventional wisdom takes a specific character: agency. To *feel* in control of what one surveys as an apparent open horizon of information (one's news feed) is to attain satisfaction. Indeed, it is an affirmation of one's will, and an expression of one's identity in a community environment. Even a growing awareness that social media is only showing you what you want to see to affirm a particular worldview is nowhere near as strong as the affirmation itself – 'to hear what one believes is a source of assurance'.

This discrepancy is mythic in character because it makes invisible its own contradictory nature. Even the thought of losing connectivity in its current form is therefore unconscionable. Whilst social media connectivity, thought of as a system, is particularly efficient in this regard, it is merely an accelerated version of systems that have existed in the past. If one considers connectivity to be a self-evident good without taking into consideration its mythic contents, then one is playing into the hands of conventional wisdom as one might a cult. Galbraith is especially radical in this regard. He writes (1962: 20) that

> In some measure the articulation of the conventional wisdom is a religious rite. It is an act of affirmation like reading aloud from the Scriptures or going to church. [. . .] Yet it is not a negligible rite, for its purpose is not to convey knowledge but to beatify learning and the learned.

Social media connectivity has become academicised in the sense that its meanings and functionality are self-evidently apparent for all to see; space and time are compressed, information flows are unimpeded, access is *gratis* and it is a convenient and expedient way to keep in touch. It is also ubiquitous, and the apparent universal uptake of one platform or another would support the idea that its use fits its purpose, for some utility approaches. Conventional wisdom would tell us as much, at least. But the elision is deeper than that. In considering this in relation to its psychological dimension, any anxiety produced through momentary glimpses of the discrepancy between what social media is for (connectivity, free expression, sharing) and what it does (presents a specific automated worldview and expresses a specific identity influenced by data and algorithm processing) is allayed through what might be described as a myth-making psychic architecture of affirmation. In post-Jungian terminology, it is a *numinosity*, pregnant with the power of the symbolic, freely choosing agent. This deep structural presence is important because it provides us with a psychological framework for thinking about the unconscious motivations behind the compelling case for social media connectivity in the first place. In other words, people really *want* it to work this way, and to argue *against* this would be to somehow leave an onion in the ointment. Conventional wisdom is, I contend, the psychosocial ointment that sooths over the wounds of social media connectivity.

I fully accept that this analogue might read a little too polemical, not to mention fancy. But it has a direct line of precedent on individual agency dating back to at least Galbraith. The discrepancy facing the critique of social technologies, that makes such a difficulty out of critiquing the deliberative, freeing, virtuous functions of social media connectivity, is once again an aspect of conventional wisdom which seeks to draw a veil over the actual relations built through social media data production. As Galbraith wrote, the 'conventional wisdom accommodates itself not to the world that it is meant to interpret, but to the audience's view of the world' (1962: 22). In other words, and to mirror Pariser's comments, it reflects the consumer back to themselves through the data they produce.

To put it another way, it feeds back to the user that which is *not dissimilar* – other users with similar worldviews and outlooks; content reflecting immediate or local concerns most associated with one's one social strata; and, at worst, a confirmation of the biases and prejudices of a user through likeminded feedback and automated content suggestions. As Pariser points out, whereas there have always been aspects of this in public and relational life in the modern world, the introduction of Web connectivity has amplified the impacts of bias exponentially, and added further layers of complexity specific to the modes of connectivity afforded communications in the Web era. One of the most problematic impacts is a systematic narrowing of sources of factual information through personalisation algorithms – ironic and somewhat alarming because the predominant discourses (those promises of the early Web discussed earlier in this book) still maintain an abundance of information at everyone's fingertips. Where intermediaries do exist (friends on social networks sharing news stories, being the common example of amateur curation) there are severe limitations to relying on the broadness of subject matter and opinion. Pariser's approach to this is similar to my own, where an impoverished version of 'informed public' is emerging. He writes (2011a: 66) that

> [. . .] the average person's Facebook friends will be much more like that person than a general-interest news source. This is especially true because our physical communities are becoming more homogeneous as well [. . .] and thus it's less likely we'll come into contact with different points of view. Second, personalization filters will get better and better at overlaying themselves on individuals' recommendations.

In fact, we can take these arguments right back to Mill, and his work *The Principles of Political Economy* (2000), originally published in 1848. In an eerily prescient echo of Sandel's 'market society', where physical, cultural and intellectual spaces are no longer shared across social strata, homogenising one's experiences of the world, one's self and other people, Mill writes (2000: 677) that

> It is hardy possible to overrate the value, in the present low state of human improvement, of placing human beings in contact with persons dissimilar to themselves, and with modes of thought and action unlike those with which they are familiar.

This observation remains crucial to the health of democracies more generally, and to the health of our social, political and interpersonal relationships. It is an ethical view of connectedness, which sidesteps the notion of connectivity for its own sake, to allow the possibility that one might see the myth for what it is. Pariser phrases the narrowing of dissimilar experience as a sort of 'autopropaganda', which amplifies the desire for the familiar and, importantly, does not allow us to experience for ourselves the sense of danger and power that exist in equal measure in the realm of the unknown. In other words, through persistent connectivity governed by personalisation, we are increasingly, and simply, being deprived of that most essential of human learning experiences: otherness. As Pariser (2011a: 15) puts it:

> In the filter bubble, there's less room for the chance encounters that bring insight and learning. Creativity is often sparked by the collision of ideas from different disciplines and cultures. [. . .] By definition, a world constructed from the familiar is a world in which there's nothing to learn. [. . .] If personalization is too acute, it could prevent us from coming into contact with the mind-blowing, preconception-shattering experiences and ideas that change how we think about the world and ourselves.

This remarkable feedback loop suppresses contrariness and otherness, shutting us off from the wider experiences somewhat necessary to learn about ourselves, the world and each other. Once more, one might find a precedent in Mill, this time from his later work, *On Liberty* (1974 [1859]). On suppression of opinion (a phenomenon seen with venomous regularity on social media exchanges), Mill writes (1974: 77 [emphasis in original]) that

> First, the opinion which it is attempted to suppress by authority may possibly be true. Those who desire to suppress [it], of course, deny its truth; but they are not infallible. They have no authority to decide the question for all mankind and exclude every other person from the means of judging. To refuse a hearing to an opinion because they are sure that it is false is to assume that *their* certainty is the same thing as *absolute* certainty. All silencing of discussion is an assumption of infallibility.

Everyone would like to hear feedback that accords with that which one believes, as this provides, as Galbraith describes it, an assurance. However, this is essentially how myth operates more generally; it makes silent and invisible all that dissents from that which is apparently true and eternal and, in turn, this has the effect of making the mythic status of the myth invisible. At a micro level, and immediate to the visible ways deliberation is curtailed online, this is also very close to the ways trolling works too. This is particularly in relation to those situations in which the troll defends his or her right to freedom of speech, whilst at the same time denying that same freedom to others within the discussion. This essentially dismisses the suggestion that anyone's right to freedom of speech necessarily entails obligations such as equitable access to those freedoms or the ethical use of those freedoms to reduce harms. This suppressive manoeuvre, disguised through the mythic content of the defence of freedoms, is ostensibly a reactionary mechanism against dissent from one's own worldview. Amplified through the compelling structural presence of the open-horizon news feed, which reflects a *close-enough* picture of one's own worldview, any dissenting voice runs the risk of being shut down with force, through public shame, ridicule or worse. Without a regular and meaningful exposure to dissenting voices, in other worlds, we become over-sensitised to them.

Often this is shaped by the moment, as much as through any consistency of worldview. Galbraith discusses aspects of this structuring compulsion in depth throughout *The Affluent Society*. He addresses, amongst other things, the mechanisms through which conventional wisdom tends to breed a short memory in economists, such that the myth of sustainable economic growth is reproduced time and again in economic thought, despite several cycles of boom and bust in any given generation's lifespan. For Harvie, Layng and Milburn (2014), this short memory extends across society, to draw people in and make us all, in some sense, economists. They describe this as a sort of privatisation of communication experiences; where an ongoing process of the privatisation of communal spaces, institutions and acts grows apace in neoliberal societies. They write that, in the context of ubiquitous digital communications and the digitalisation of the creative industries, some of the key traditional industries that would have given voice to protest for generations of disenfranchised young people in the past (popular music being their prime example) have experienced a hollowing-out in the process of digitalisation:

> We have come to view ourselves as human capital, as privatised enterprises locked in competition with others. Thirty years of training for competitive markets has shredded our sense of collectivity. The result is a much more precarious existence, a retreat from civic life into a private, atomised realm.

This is gamification at its most politically adept, and least ludic. It takes us back to the idea of the market society, and the totalising cultural image of interest-as-advantage. Harvie, Layng and Milburn go on to discuss that the precariousness through which this cultural image prepares us for competition in every aspect of our lives subsumes our self-belief in the most general sense. They paraphrase David Graeber, when they state that '[. . .] ideology isn't about what we believe. It's about what we believe the other believes. So [for example,] it's not important that we really believe austerity is the best available option; but it is important that we act as if we do – and we do that because we think everyone else believes in austerity' (2014).

The 'retreat from civic life into a private, atomised realm' noted above may seem a little far-fetched. However, it seems to speak of something which is lost, or at least missing. Both the collective and shared sense in which people tend to collaborate and create has been radically transformed through some of the contexts discussed in this current chapter. And, in the Aristotelian sense of 'making things better' that Michael Sandel so often draws from, a civic sense of creative discussion as the basis for consensus, reciprocal-constitution and mutual benefit seems to have been abandoned. There may be something lost through the specific character that Web 2.0 has taken on in recent years, where the negotiation of ideas, events and things is filtered through a different kind of creativity. As mentioned earlier in this chapter, Csikszentmihalyi observes that 'Creativity is a process that can be observed only at the intersection where individuals, domains, and fields interact'

(2006: 3). If that is indeed the case, then what shape does that intersection take when the individuals, domains and fields all rely so heavily on the mythic character of conventional wisdom?

At the beginning of this chapter I noted the remarks made by Christian Fuchs in response to Henry Jenkins' notion of 'spreadable media', that 'Creativity is a force that enables Internet prosumer commodification, the commodification and exploitation of the users' activities and the data they generate. Creativity is not outside of or dual to exploitation on web 2.0, it is its very foundation' (2011). This rather tainted summary of creativity is perhaps one interpretation of its character within the specificities of social media interaction, but, as I have attempted to describe during the course of this chapter, there are precedents and future directions that seem to corroborate such a position. It is, to return once more to Charles Taylor's moral philosophy, a 'narrowing and flattening of our lives' brought forth through virtuous consumption, technological dominance and a collective turning-away from political engagement. What remains intact of social institutions seems moribund in this light. The early promises of the Web, although still ideals that one might strive for, revolve around pre-Web concessions to human subjectivity, and the powerful image of emancipatory potential in freedom of information, deliberation and abundance. However, to turn once more to Eli Pariser, 'Many Internet watchers [. . .] cheered the development of "people-powered news" – a more democratic, participatory form of cultural storytelling. But the future may be more machine-powered than people-powered' (2011a: 52). In Part II of this book, I explore in more detail the cultural, ethical and, especially, psychosocial implications of this shift towards machine power, in an age of persistent connectivity, and what this means for 'people-powered', or person-centred, ideals. I will attempt to unpack this technology-consumption-depoliticisation arrangement, to develop a recognition theory that not only accounts for the transformed character of deliberative social interaction in Web 2.0, but also offers theoretical directions to reignite deliberation as a connective principle in the twenty-first century.

Notes

1 Shirky admits that this is a ballpark figure, but even if a generous estimate, today this figure has increased exponentially. The official statistics page for Wikimedia projects houses a bewildering set of tools for the calculation and visualisation of figures on edits, discussions and hits. At time of access, the opening paragraph stated that: 'While you read this, Wikipedia and its sister projects develop at a rate of over 10 edits per second, performed by editors from all over the world. Currently, the English Wikipedia includes 5,254,528 articles and it averages 800 new articles per day.' See https://en.wikipedia.org/wiki/Wikipedia:Statistics [accessed 04/10/2016].

2 The use of the term Wiki*edia here is to denote a number of variations on Wikipedia, Wikimedia and other Wikimedia sister projects. Its use is fairly common in Wikimedia circles.

3 It also happens in popular broadcast media: it is the nominal reason television shows such as *X Factor* (ITV 2004–present) and *Strictly Come Dancing* (BBC1 2004–present) have a panel of judges, experts in their field who often provide reasons for their evaluation such as the contestants making the song or dance 'their own'.

PART II

Recognition, self-realisation and the principle of mutuality

4

TOWARDS A RECOGNITION THEORY FOR SOCIAL MEDIA INTERACTION

In the early to mid-1990s in the UK, a high-concept advertising campaign for British Telecom broadcast nationwide. Featuring the actor Bob Hoskins, and with the memorable strap line, 'it's good to talk', the series of adverts were premised on the idea that we *are* our relationships. Our sense of being an individual character, our sense of home, family and friends, our sense of feeling connected to all of those things that seem to make up who we are, in fact, are all hinged upon being able to express ourselves, and have others express themselves to us. In other words, it really is 'good to talk'.

It seems a rather mainstream notion now – pedestrian, even. However, according to Robert Bean, writing retrospectively for *Campaign*, a trade publication for the advertising and planning industry, this was a revolutionary idea in marketing. To endorse the notion that connectivity is about a specific technology (in British Telecom's case, telephony), or even insinuate that connectivity is predicated on an ultra-modern telecommunications and IT infrastructure, was only ever a partial story. And that story was a narrative left over from the previous decade, where rampant deregulation of media and communications industries and infrastructures was part of a more general, publicly visible shift in the socio-cultural and political landscape, in an era of large-scale privatisation of state-owned industry during the Thatcher administration (and the Major administration which followed with more of the same). The real innovation from BT's marketing team was that the campaign focused upon what Bean describes as 'Reciprocated Confidences', the basis of which was that 'the exchange of "confidences" between human beings leads to better communications and, in turn, deeper relationships' (Bean 2009). In other words, BT were claiming to be about improving relationships, and the campaign sought to change attitudes of the ordinary consumer towards communications as a continuous or semi-permanent condition of connected exchange.

Indeed, there may well be a kernel of truth in what the BT campaign was all about. As we have seen in various contexts in Part I of this book, connectivity as a principle is culturally understood as more than just the machinery used to facilitate it. Even as, fundamentally, the mythic content of that notion foregrounds the technology's ability to enable connectivity where there is none, and, indeed, in ways that are simply not possible without it. The contents of this myth are perhaps, in practical terms, empirically true. The fact that an advertising campaign exploits this empirical state of connectivity (in turn engendering further mythic content about the status and nature of connectivity) says more about general shifts in attitudes than the technological aspects of connectivity. This idea of 'reciprocated confidences' is much more than a cool-sounding, one-shot deal. It speaks to a number of deeper understandings about the nature of human sociality and relationships and is reminiscent of entire bodies of work from several traditions of thinking on the subject. Little wonder, then, that the campaign was so successful and memorable. The BT campaign was more a continuity than a revolution, in these respects. Ultimately, from the positions of continental philosophy, of ethics and of social, depth and developmental psychology, 'reciprocated confidences' is really just another term for 'recognition' – a tenacious idea that has lasted since antiquity.

My argument here is that in recent years such empirical notions of recognition have been circulated as values within the popular culture, as some sort of equivalency around what it might mean to be connected. Recognition is already embedded in the interior logic of the popular understanding of connectivity, in its sense as a means to maintain relationships on a number of different levels. In its neoliberal turn, familial and individual relationships are prioritised here (as well as the globalised potential for business, which emerged with greater emphasis in later advertising campaigns for BT). But in online cultures we can also see the presence of other reciprocated confidences which circulate around community, and political awareness, and in the remaindered stock of state institutional arrangements in areas such as education, welfare and health provision as public goods. Reciprocated confidences, then, might be best understood not only in the gossipy sense of personal exchange on social media platforms, but in the related sense of *mutual trust* or *consensus*, at a larger, community scale. I argue, therefore, that there is a need for a recognition theory of always-on connectivity, at two related but distinct levels, to glean a more rounded understanding.

The first is at the level of the personal, the interpersonal and, in particular, in relation to both the formation and the mobilisation of identity. There is an abundance of discourse relating to the notion of online identity, particularly around the online-offline distinctions made in popular culture, as well as its dialectical counterpart, which focuses on the perceptibly blurred boundaries of virtual and real identities. These are arenas within which, according to commentators including Andrew Keen, pathological aspects of so-called 'digital narcissism' emerge (2007: xiii). One can understand the reasons why these discourses abound, although they tend not to be productive, and often end up in circular arguments concerning online echo chambers of opinion, or fears of addiction to social media use.

Such arguments are superficial, thin and self-perpetuating in folk psychology and popular media commentary – I have no desire to repeat them here. Instead, we need to consider thicker descriptions of the ways in which identities are mobilised online (and, by proxy, the ways of offline identity mobilisation), and how this sheds light on the praxes, behaviours and regulatory regimes that arise from such mobilisation. However, building a recognition theory to deal exclusively with identity can only go so far in describing the psychosocial implications of a semi-permanent condition of connectivity. A recognition theory which acknowledges and gives due weight to a psychology of self, in describing both the structures and the structuring presence underlying and influencing identity formation and mobilisation, is necessary to establish a fuller description at this level.

The second level of a recognition theory of social media connectivity establishes the grounds for describing how an accelerated media ecosystem challenges traditional social relations, particularly with regard to political and ethical issues around rights (in the senses of responsibility, property and freedoms), fairness (justice) and equity (commons). I covered aspects of these issues in Part I, but in the current chapter and beyond I aim to tease these out in relation to recognition theory's illumination of what we might describe as 'self-realisation', in the formation of both self and identity.

Of course, one needs to bear in mind the interaction here between the personal and political levels, particularly when constructing a critical treatment of agency, which operates as the interface between both. Whereas I will address this interaction in relation to connectivity ethics in my closing remarks in this book, my treatment of this will necessarily be brief due to space available here. It is certainly a matter that would benefit from a lengthier discussion, and I leave that task for another time.

An ethics of connectivity would necessarily need to establish both practical and moral reasons why connectivity is desirable, in an empirical sense and in a conceptual sense, on both of the levels described. One of the primarily empirical reasons for the widespread predominance of connectivity as a desirable principle stems from the notion that it facilitates the maintenance of social relationships. Conceptualisations of connectivity tend to rest on assumptions of progressive globalisation and multiculturalism, as much as relying upon the rhetoric of innovation (particularly as a technology) to reproduce these conceptualisations in the public sphere.

Burns and Thompson (2013) take a more critical approach to the notion of recognition theory at the level of the global. They suggest that, 'From the perspective of cosmopolitan political theory', most thinkers in the field of recognition theory, with a few notable exceptions noted by the authors, 'have ignored the fact of globalization and have therefore failed to take on board its normative implications'. This is highly problematic because, '[. . .] in a world in which the fates of all human beings are bound tightly together, it is impossible to deny that the values by which we should seek to live together should be universal in their scope' (2013: 2). In a world where a state of semi-permanent connectivity via SNS applications and dense mobile communications infrastructure has transformed and accelerated the media ecosystem at a global level, there is a discernible underdevelopment of theory in the field. It would seem to me sensible that any overview of social interaction and recognition practice in social media connectivity would necessarily need to be cosmopolitan in outlook, and seek to address questions concerning the distribution of resources and the divisions of labour underpinning the social media economy on a global scale. The point of a cosmopolitanist approach is to add something new and distinctive to accounts of global justice through a focus on recognition as a concept, and this can be extrapolated to general arrangements concerning the ethical life of contemporary communications practices and a global level of connectivity.

I briefly return to the rhetoric of innovation later in this chapter in relation to such globalised practices, but first I shall outline the traditional arenas of recognition theory and scholarship from a number of key disciplines of humanist inquiry to argue its relevance as an empirical and conceptual entity in contemporary online communications and Web 2.0 practices. In this way, I hope to illustrate recognition, and its politics, as a theme at the heart of the understanding of connectivity, and as essential to the construction of a connectivity ethics.

A note on recognition theory

In his *IEP* entry on 'Social and Political Recognition', Paddy McQueen argues that, for recognition theorists, 'recognition can help form, or even determine, our sense of who we are and the value accorded to us as individuals'. Recognition theory often focuses on the role recognition plays in individual identity formation as well as the normative, and in some cases emancipatory, foundation this can provide to theories of justice (McQueen n.d.). In the context of online interpersonal communications, and social media use in particular, this baseline is extremely useful in establishing the role of recognition in the way users establish and mobilise identity, within what is often described as anonymous or lo-fidelity communications contexts. It is also useful in thinking through the ways that users sometimes act within intra- and inter-group communications and community contexts specific to a subculture or neo-tribe. In recent and contemporary debates, recognition theory tends to be influenced primarily by the political and moral philosophy of Nancy Fraser and Charles Taylor, and the philosophical anthropology of Axel Honneth.

In what follows, I will outline Honneth's recognition theory in particular. In common with Nicholas Smith, I believe that Honneth's work, more than other recognition theorists, has as its root an emancipatory ambition shared with predecessors in the Frankfurt School, '[. . .] providing insight into the sources of social conflict, social suffering and social pathology characteristic of the times, insight that might also reveal sources of social emancipation' (Smith 2012: 2). There are common elements with this emancipatory project found in the communitarian ethics and convivialist politics featured in this book so far, and the emancipatory elements of the Frankfurt School tradition are useful in any attempt to prevent critiques of connectivity from running into an unnecessarily negative corner. For, as Danielle Petherbridge has noted, Honneth's '[. . .] concept of recognition is intended to provide a framework for analysing social conditions of individual self-realisation and the development of social relations and institutions' (2011: 13), providing a thick description of this development into a number of fields including rights, justice and equality, in an affirmative mode of critique.

The political philosopher Aivishai Margalit suggests that his own normative politics differs from Honneth's because it is arrived at by thinking through injustice, inequality and despotism, whereas Honneth emphasises justice, equality and freedom (2001: 127). In short, it is often much clearer what counts as humiliation, and less clear what counts as respect. His examples where humans are treated as non-humans, 'e.g. as animals, as instruments, as mere statistics, as sub-humans', have obvious twentieth-century political and ideological precedents in context of dehumanising the other, and so on. One can therefore see that there are productive ways in which Margalit's negative politics could be used as a vehicle to critique notions of connectivity, particularly in relation to clearly toxic practices such as trolling and doxing – highly visible and readily identifiable negative aspects of everyday social media interaction. More generally, we can see this in the way that accelerated media often operate with more immediate feedback in a negative, rather than positive, loop precisely because the negatives are that much easier to identify and call out.

But through engaging Honneth's positive politics in the round, an emancipatory potential is possible. In fact, in dealing with this bipartisan comparison in the recognition theory of political philosophy, one can see a clear correspondence to notions of online recognition politics specifically. There, the main issues form two parallel (and often in popular and academic discourses, opposed) positions in relation to participatory media. First, a positive position for participation based upon creativity, equality and freedom of information (e.g., Jenkins, Ford and Green 2013; Jenkins, Ito and boyd 2015; Gauntlett 2011). Second, a negative position which attempts to tackle modes of alienation from different perspectives (Lanier 2010, Singh 2014a, 2017; Kowalski, Limber and Agatston 2012; Fuchs 2014; Fuchs and Sandoval eds 2014; Curran, Fenton and Freedman 2012). One could argue that the urgency to which Margalit refers here is particularly apt in the context of, for example, forms of cyberbullying which have insidious and subtle influence on self-performance choices (both online and in real life). These practices find their most obvious cues in trolling, public shaming and doxing (themes I will tackle in Chapter 7 and revisit in the Conclusion).

As discussed in previous chapters, connectivity, whilst on the surface a utopian project, also carries within it the materials of conflict, suffering and pathology ingrained from the particular social and cultural condition of the times: neoliberal late capital. To my mind, this provides the justification for centring a construction of recognition theory for social media connectivity on Honneth's particular perspective: a *struggle* for recognition. Attention to Honneth's work in the field of media and cultural studies is underdeveloped, and in what follows I aim to lay some groundwork for others to consider the productiveness of his emancipatory recognition theory in gaining further insights into social (media) relations.

I will chart how this work has been influenced by continental philosophy and Hegel's early-career work on intersubjectivity – and, also, how in this regard Honneth has profoundly influenced my perspective on the role of recognition in the context of accelerated media ecosystems. I have already discussed Taylor's work in the context of communitarian approaches to connectivity in Part I of this book. Here, I foreground aspects of self-realisation in Taylor's ethics, in comparison with Honneth, to anticipate the discussion on authenticity of self in the final three chapters. For the moment, I consider the implications of Honneth's emancipatory project of recognition for the politics of connectivity within always-on contexts. I do this with a view to exploring his applications of developmental psychology in his discussions of self-realisation, and the general grounding of a mature sense of both self and identity in social relations. These self-realisation dimensions of his work are, for me, the most important in terms of thinking through the psychosocial aspects of social media use most relevant to practice in the contemporary accelerated media ecosystem. I intervene in this aspect of his work by drawing upon object-relations as Honneth had himself drawn. However, I take this appropriation much further, through an exploration of Kohut's self-psychology, Jung's depth notion of persona and a development of Benjamin's theory of mutuality in the direction of connectivity ethics. Through this intervention, my aim is to strengthen the psychological aspects of Honneth's theory of recognition, and fortify the role it will play in my arguments about online pathologies, and in my development of a theory of social media as a 'false-self system' in Chapter 7.

Recognition, emancipation and self-realisation

In his book *The Struggle for Recognition* (1995), Honneth's motivation for reconstructing Hegel's theory of recognition was primarily to rethink the concept of justice, but also to give a better account of the relationship between socialisation and individuation as well as between social reproduction and individual identity formation. Through this reconstruction process, as set out in his book, he came to reconsider earlier positions on Hegel's intersubjectivism, to develop an interpretation of Hegel that sought to consider social reality as a set of layered relations of recognition (Honneth 2012: vii–viii). Essentially, Honneth's project eventually extended from the young Hegel's Jena lectures right through to Hegel's mature writing, as featured in *The Philosophy of Right*. To me, this work encapsulates an idiosyncratic Hegelian narrative of recognition theory, which embodies the constitution of identity in intersubjectivism, to the development of moral agency, esteem and dignity. In short, to know another is to know oneself; to recognise oneself requires a recognition of the other, in the fullest of measures.

For recognition theorists who follow *The Philosophy of Right*, these layers of recognition encompass a strong ethics dimension. For example, according to Margalit in what is to my mind a brilliantly concise summary of Hegelian-influenced recognition theory (2001: 129 [my emphasis]),

[. . .] recognition in the sense of endorsement and respect (recognizing the status of the other) has deep moral and political implications. Thus what turns out to be constitutive to self-knowledge (self-consciousness) is vitally important to ethics. *Both self-knowledge and ethics require the point of view of the other.* This point of view is the meeting-point between ethics and epistemology.

There is, thus, a specific need to acknowledge that recognition, communication (in social relations), ethics (in terms of recognition-as-fairness, at the very least, if not justice) and self-knowledge are fundamentally intertwined. Furthermore, the complexity of this intertwining of intersubjective relations is superimposed upon online communications, where the recognition of status (in its most empirical sense) is often the only thing one has to go on in terms of meaningful communication and social intercourse with another. This suggests that recognition has a more full and foundational role in online communications practices than previously thought in critical social media studies.

When we closely consider the etymology of the term 'recognition', we discover that we use the term at an everyday level perhaps more often than we realise, but that also the term has several distinct meanings. First, as an act of intellectual apprehension – as in, when we 'recognise' mistakes made by ourselves or others, or perhaps we 'recognise' the traditional informal relationship and mutual influence of institutions such as church and state, or media and government. Second, recognition can be understood as a form of identification, such as when 'recognising' a friend in the street. Third, recognition might refer to the act of acknowledging or respecting someone, as in recognising someone's status, achievements or rights (McQueen n.d.; Inwood 1992: 245–7; Margalit, 2001: 128–9). It is more likely that in the philosophical treatment of the term, particularly in traditions drawing from the young Hegel's work, the last kind of recognition tends to be foregrounded, as it tends to be more overtly political and social in character; and is also generally understood to play a role in self-understanding too. The key here is that we ought to acknowledge the interplay between these different levels of recognition, as not mutually exclusive, but as *mutually inclusive.* This is because, in the treatment of recognition from the viewpoint of interpersonal interaction, it is difficult to conceptualise recognition in the context of online communications without that *mutual interplay of apprehension, identification and status.* In this sense, one could concede that connectivity as a conceptual framework for the exchange of online identity has an interior logic of mutuality, pregnant with the potential for human social elements such as apprehension, identification and status. However, these human elements are contained, and superseded, by competing logics of the neoliberal kind discussed at length in Part I. Therefore, such potential of connectivity is foreclosed.

Michael Inwood, in *A Hegel Dictionary*, notes that the verb *to recognise* has five broad meanings or senses. These are: to identify; to realise; to admit; to endorse; and to take notice. It is, therefore, not simply a case of intellectual identification of a person or thing, but the assignment to it of a positive value and the explicit expression of this assignment. An individual becomes a person, a recognised and recognising subject, in this exchange of value. Hegel can thus be read as dealing with the problem of how one becomes a fully fledged person by securing the acknowledgement of others (1992: 245). Note the crucial dimension of *evaluation*, in the assignment of values, the importance of which will become clear later in this chapter. It is enough at this juncture to point out that recognition theorists of various persuasions hold in common the notion of evaluation as a dimension of recognition. I refer the reader to Margalit's point about recognition-as-endorsement above, for which evaluative judgements need to be made and from which social relations take on a value relative to the parties within that relation. For Honneth (2012: 3–4), in the *Phenomenology of Spirit*, Hegel sought to

> [. . .] demonstrate that a subject can only arrive at a 'consciousness' of its own 'self' if it enters into a relationship of 'recognition' with another subject. [. . .] elucidating not an historical event or instance of conflict, but a transcendental fact that should prove to be a prerequisite of all human sociality.

In Honneth's reading of Hegel's subjectivity, one can trace a distinct transcultural and, to an extent, trans-historical element in this generalisable prerequisite. Lysaker and Jakobsen note that for Honneth, although there is an acknowledgement of individual and cultural differences, '*all* human beings seek to realise themselves in three basic ways: as bodily-emotional beings, as rationally and morally responsible persons, and as individuals with particular traits and abilities' (2015: 3 [emphasis in original]). This is based upon the three forms or patterns of recognition drawn from Hegel's *Philosophy of Right*: love (private spheres of care, personal relations, family); respect (institutional spheres of state and legal rights); and esteem (achievements in work, markets, civil society). Human self-realisation is therefore understood in Honneth's thought as both an ontogenetic process of the individual's life history, and a phylogenetic socio-historical and institutional process. The three basic forms of recognition are laid over these two senses of historical process in intersubjective self-realisation and so, in this model, one can discern the importance of recognition for individuals, groups and communities on the registers of both the personal and the political (see Table 4.1). For Lysaker and Jakobsen, 'Honneth claims that it is only through processes of socialisation and internalisation of norms that we can learn to articulate and pursue our own interests as simultaneously *recognising* and *recognised* in the public sphere' (2015: 4 [emphasis in original]). Hence, for Honneth, the foundation of recognition as a personal and a political process is essentially intersubjective. It requires, to refer back to the parlance of British Telecom and Bob Hoskins, 'reciprocated confidences'.

The fundamentally ethical character of mutual intersubjective recognition stems from this tangential purpose of self-realisation. That is, without recognition as experienced in social relations of self-realisation (love, respect, esteem), we cannot possibly develop self-understanding and the traits, abilities and competences necessary to become engaged citizens (Lysaker and Jakobsen 2015: 4), or what Hegel had formulated in his model of an ethical life. Self-realisation and ethical personality, therefore, are articulated, one in the other. The psycho-political emancipatory project that Honneth constructs is therefore a powerful and attractive one that, at its heart, has the normative notion of a common good. This articulation is akin to what Danielle Petherbridge has termed Honneth's framework for analysing both '[. . .] social conditions of individual self-realisation and the development of social relations and institutions', the normative function of which is grounded in his philosophical anthropology and '[. . .] conceptualised as an originary notion of undamaged intersubjectivity which is understood to provide the fundamental preconditions for successful subject-formation and the development of ethical life' (2011: 13). This formulation of self-realisation, so close to phenomenological descriptions of the intersubjective encounter – the 'wild communication' of pre-linguistic and pre-theoretic knowledge in and of the world, to paraphrase Vivian Sobchack (1992) – provides the material from which Honneth draws the justification for his emancipatory project, and for the ethical provision of intersubjective recognition. It also acknowledges the dialectical movement fundamental to Hegelian intersubjectivity between the material world of the contingent (immanence) and the transformational promise of potential for change (transcendence).

The 'originary' element here is Honneth's attempt to safeguard a normative construction of the subject as authentic lifeworld subject. Although probably one of the most problematic assumptions in his *oeuvre*, he nonetheless attempts to consolidate this by pointing out that, '[. . .] one of the main problems confronting contemporary critical social theorists today, is determining which instances or experiences can be pre-theoretically located within social reality that also contain "system-bursting" potential to compel change within a given social order' (Petherbridge 2011: 1–2). Honneth is therefore optimistic in his view that conditions for social change can be located in social interaction. This is part of his emancipatory project, and 'an attempt to redirect Habermas' original idea regarding damaged relations of recognition in the lifeworld' (Petherbridge 2011: 5).

The continuity and progression between Habermas and Honneth can be further elaborated in three instances (see Table 4.1 for a broad overview). In the first instance, Honneth accepts the shift from a Marxist paradigm of relations of production to Habermas' relations of communicative action, so there is at the heart of recognition theory a baseline acceptance that any emancipatory project for social progress rests upon social interaction rather than social labour. For our immediate concern, which is that of connectivity ethics, this provides us with a problem: the implications for SNS interactions which are fundamentally based on data automation. Data automation is essentially fuelled through human-machine interaction (and the labour-materiality of interactions between humans and machines). As many political economists (such as Scholz ed. 2013; Lovink 2008, 2011, 2016; Fuchs 2013, 2014; Allmer 2015) have pointed out, social media tends to have a reductive or eliding effect between social interaction and social labour. Here both bear an equivalency in terms of signifying connectivity with other users, rather than ostensible interaction or labour used to generate the materials for social media consumption (news feeds, likes, shares etc.). There is, then, a cultural turn at work where the data generated through social technologies remains fundamentally social (and is the product of the relation between social interaction and social labour). However, the culture driving the data automation turn is computational in character, and therefore an embodiment of material labour processes; it does not necessarily *also* incorporate social interaction itself, and therefore it is difficult to imagine a communicative action solution to the problem of data automation.

As Honneth's approach suggests, however, the dynamics of social change ought to be understood in the moral struggles between social groups. That is to say, emancipatory forces and manoeuvres take place in the moral architecture of social interactions. To my mind, this is essentially a recovery of class struggle as a formal social dynamic which has the potential to drive social transformation. This is crucial to understanding Honneth's notion of struggle for recognition as both intersubjective and political on a wider scale, and has implications for the political power held in stasis which could be leveraged by users and social organisations themselves. This also brings back into focus a concern with digital labour materiality which sits alongside this social dynamic as an ongoing issue of uneven exploitation, at least from a broad political economy perspective.

In the second instance, Honneth's theory of recognition articulates 'the normative intersubjective conditions necessary for autonomy understood in terms of successful individual self-realisation' (Petherbridge 2011: 6). This shares a common grounding with Habermas' intersubjective rationality that makes argumentation and thus communication possible (Habermas 1984, 1987). It seems fundamental to me that the political recognition of the other should have as a precondition a reciprocal political recognition of oneself; in other words, a self-realisation. Last, Honneth develops an institutional order of recognition relations: 'whereby all spheres of life can be organised recognitively, including the organisation of social labour' (Petherbridge 2011: 7). This constitutes a move away from Habermas' modes of integration ('Lifeworld' and 'System') in mediated *sociation*, and towards social life seen in terms of three forms or patterns of social relations of recognition: love, law and achievement. Honneth's main task is therefore to bring together a notion of social struggle and conflict with a normative theory of social action.

TABLE 4.1 Corresponding forms of recognition and mutuality

Intersubjective recognition	Self-relation	Institutional context
Love	Self-confidence	Personal relationships – first selfobjects, family
Law	Self-respect	Moral responsibility and autonomy within the context of legal and institutional relations
Achievement	Self-esteem	Self-worth, integrated into shared value-community Principle of mutuality

According to Petherbridge (2011: 14), he does this through a reading of Hegel's Jena lectures on recognition.

> The three spheres of love, law and achievement, which recall Hegel's divisions between family, state and civil society, are central to the development of three corresponding forms of self-relation. The formal concept of ethical life is to be understood as a normative ideal in which specific patterns of recognition enable individuals to acquire the self-confidence, self-respect, and self-esteem necessary for full realisation.

We might summarise these three spheres of intersubjective relations of mutual recognition as aspects of love, rights and solidarity which interact in everyday practices of social and interpersonal communication in any number of contexts. When taken in detail, these aspects address the following.

1. Familial relations – where love is the basic sense of familiarity, trust or self-confidence to enable the individuals concerned to flourish.
2. Rights and law – where social and political institutions endow individuals, groups and subjects with social self-esteem.
3. Work and social interaction – which facilitate the individual's worth and value to the community, contributing to the sense of social solidarity.

As Sinnerbrink comments, '[. . .] failures within any of these three spheres of recognition – misrecognition as social disrespect in the spheres of familial relations, legal rights and social contribution – constitute a form of *moral injury* motivating various kinds of social struggle' (2007: 119 [emphasis in original]). The question I wish to pose here is: what happens to these self-relations in SNS communications and, hence what, therefore, happens to self-realisation in processes of misrecognition in online interactions? Further, what forms of misrecognition occur via SNS contexts, and what forms do moral injuries take in response to such kinds of misrecognition?

Misrecognition as social disrespect

There are a number of scenarios which, to my mind, provide tentative answers to this set of questions around misrecognition as social disrespect. One of the clearest examples may be found in the trend towards the so-called Quantified Self. Elsewhere, I have written about this phenomenon by applying the associated concepts to celebrity YouTubers, and the performance of self in online lifestyle and reality programming on social media and video streaming platforms (Singh 2017). Here I will note briefly that the most readily familiar aspect of the Quantified Self in popular culture would be the everyday practices of self-tracking performed at a personal level via tracking applications of various descriptions. FitBit, for example, or any number of applications associated with measurements of body-mass indexing, jogging-route mapping, *stepometers*, and other wearable technologies or mobile phone applications all form familiar aspects of everyday media engagement and are examples of the Quantified Self. Indeed, Deborah Lupton's critical sociology study, *The Quantified Self* (2016), discusses the Quantified Self movement in some detail – an extremely popular social and consumer movement, both online and offline, through which people devote time, resources and spending power, to achieve gamified goals and targeted personal rewards. The way that individual users build up the data necessary to enable the function of self-quantification is through building content via a combination of methods. For example, front-end social media profiling, field-form content and browser or click-through patterns; through mid-points of consumer profiling via tracking software; to back-end data production which feeds into datasets to produce visualisation for the user to view and share. As I state (2017: 211) elsewhere,

> In this way, contemporary media interaction has taken on (to borrow from classic Marxian terminology) the *appearance-form* of consumer-as-agent which sublates a deeper, atomised version of consumer-as-commodity, and tends to reduce the character of customer satisfaction to the choice of trade-off: access to Web 2.0 services for a surrender of data.

As stated a moment ago, users devote considerable amounts of their time and resources to these activities, but a question remains regarding the status of an individual self that is 'quantified' in this way, and in what ways quantification at these multiple levels constitutes a misrecognition. In terms of misrecognition in the self-regarding individual, on the surface at least, it could be argued that this set of practices constitutes very little real harm. Certainly, the conventional wisdom here is that in the Quantified Self movement gamified targets are an efficient way to get consumers to 'buy in' to healthier lifestyles and closer communicative practices via always-on connectivity. This is an empirical statement of fact, and the way in which it lends itself, not only to a specific *consumer* lifestyle of 'self-improvement' but also more generally, to the authentic idea of a more productive and healthier existence is difficult to bring an argument against. However, on an ethical level, this argument merely follows a logic that eternalises the notion that gamification exists merely to satisfy the system. So, a goal-oriented, individualist trajectory, particularly with financial or services-in-kind rewards as incentives to remain online and data-active, exists because this is how people are incentivised. Whilst it may be empirically true that this kind of incentivisation logic predominates in neoliberal philosophy, the argument remains circular and constitutes a logical misrecognition as social disrespect for other kinds of incentive to action. It forecloses on an emancipatory sense of recognition, and one can apply a failure at the level of social contribution to this example, as a social disrespect – even as the empirical argument would declare that the social contribution of the Quantified Self movement is proven via the data generated through quantification, and shared through connectivity.

Therefore, one might say that, even at the level of functionality and facility, the general use of gamified apps is misrecognised; they are sold to customers (and to industry opportunists alike) as the latest trend in transformation and lifestyle must-have. I would go further, stating that the operationalisation of this 'untrue' arrangement is precisely the surface playing ground overlaying the automated culture of Quantified Self apps. The kind of 'false self' to which I have occasionally referred, and the subject of discussion towards the end of this book, might be therefore more fully described as an 'untrue-to-the-case' self, rather than an out-and-out falsification or denial of truth.

I argue that there are further questions to be addressed regarding how intrapsychic processes are transformed in routines of a Quantified Self. In what ways does this kind of reification between individuals and the social-facing personae of such individuals appease the needs of the social media system, fail the individuals who build the data (the community of users) and frustrate self-realisation in its classic forms (love, law, achievement)? These aspects of intrapsychic process where there is a real danger, by proxy, in over investment or identification in the quantified self persona as 'the whole thing' are addressed in Chapter 7 in some detail and relate to another matter to which I referred some moments ago: that of the transformation of self into a commodity-form.

Where the quantified individual is transformed into a commodity-form, the individual experiences alienation from the world of the social – the false or untrue self is recognised over and above the true self. This is the case on the level of data profiling, where the quantified version of self is explicitly addressed through routines of automation, such as targeted advertising, suggested links, recommendations, rewards or reputation systems and so on. In this sense, one may argue that data profiling, as a practice and a process, actively encourages what post-Jungian perspectives might consider the pathology of persona identification. It is, in some ways, closely tied to what I have described elsewhere (Singh 2014a) as a version of the self that resembles an automaton rather than a person; where automata simulate personhood through the phenomenon of selfies. This may seem a stretch to assume: that a phenomenon as ubiquitous and harmless as the selfie can be regarded as a remove from personhood and towards a simulation of personhood. However, to hold such a radical position on this is to acknowledge the binary thought embedded in contemporary culture that opposes self and society, and disregards or disavows commonality as a measure of authenticity.

Here I take my cue from Charles Taylor's ethics of authenticity, and the emancipatory thread running through his body of work on the subject. Taylor argues that the contemporary culture of authenticity 'encourages a purely personal understanding of self-fulfilment, thus making the various associations and communities in which the person enters purely instrumental in their significance. At the broader social level, this is antithetical to any strong commitment to a community' (1991: 43). There is, thus, an increasing privatisation of experience, a reactionary anthropocentrism, where empirical distinctions in the choice of one thing over another (in the general sense, the cultural value of individual over and above community) become privileged at the expense of commonality. Commonality in this sense recognises that an autonomy *worth having* is one in which some issues (a sense of community and, hence, recognition in the sense of esteem) are more significant than others (egoistic self-fulfilment at the expense of others). In a passage (1991: 40–1 [emphasis in original]) that curiously seems to predict the contemporary culture of always-on, and my radical reading of the phenomenon of the automaton-as-selfie, Taylor provides the grounds to develop a philosophical basis for a critique of so-called digital narcissism, writing that

> That is what is self-defeating in modes of contemporary culture that con-centrate on self-fulfilment in *opposition* to the demands of society, or nature, which *shut out* history and the bonds of solidarity. These self-centred 'narcis-sistic' forms are indeed shallow and trivialized [. . .]. To shut out demands emanating beyond the self is precisely to suppress the conditions of signifi-cance, and hence court trivialization. [. . .] Otherwise put, I can define my identity only against the background of things that matter. But to bracket out history, nature, society, the demands of solidarity, everything but what I find in myself, would be to eliminate all candidates for what matters. [. . .] Authenticity is not the enemy of demands that emanate from beyond the self; it supposes such demands.

Whereas I have touched upon misrecognition as a kind of social disrespect, here we find the materials for developing a theory of social respect based upon the rec-ognition that a full ('authentic' in Taylor's description of the fulfilment beyond the demands of self) sense of self and personhood necessarily emanates from a mean-ingful engagement with our own horizons of significance. These are constituted, rather inevitably, within social communications and interactions. Furthermore, this commonality emanating from sources beyond the self seems to bear resemblance to a proper notion of 'reciprocated confidences' in the sense of leading an ethical life within the social sphere, where recognition plays a key role in the unfolding of intersubjective social being. This happens at a number of levels, from the intrapsy-chic, through the intimate, to the fully social (Taylor 1991: 49).

> On an intimate level, we can see how much an original identity needs and is vulnerable to the recognition given or withheld by others. It is not surpris-ing that in the culture of authenticity, relationships are seen as the key loci of self-discovery and self-confirmation. Love relationships are not important just because of the general emphasis in modern culture on the fulfilments of ordinary life. They are also crucial because they are the crucibles of inwardly generated identity.

This dialogical relation of intersubjective recognition is a continuity between the communitarianism of Taylor and the critical theory of Honneth. In thinking about a crucible of generated identity, such dialogical thinking offers an affirma-tive and emancipatory ethical potential of interaction at the level of individual agency. The culture of narcissism (and, one might suppose, digital narcissism) is empirically self-fulfilling; that is to say, it fulfils the functions that we suppose it does (and might conventionally expect it to do) and therefore is generally viewed as causing trivial harms, if any. This view does not take ethics and the ethical life into proper consideration.

The love-respect-esteem model of ethical self-realisation

In order to properly consider relationships as crucibles of inwardly generated identity, we must make the connection between emancipatory interest in recognition and feelings of disrespect – what Honneth has described in his work as 'moral grammar of social conflict', arguably the concept central to his theory of recognition. In other words, the emancipatory movement in Honneth's work argues for an ethical self-realisation, or 'ethical personality', that is able to accommodate such feelings of disrespect. This 'ethical personality' is also able to recognise in the other the interest or capacity of respect and disrespect in order to avert social interaction descending into misrecognition as social disrespect. For Petherbridge, this is indeed the case: 'The three intersubjective patterns of recognition constitute Honneth's version of a good or ethical life in the sense that they provide the conditions for successful identity-formation or the development of an "ethical personality"' (2013: 167). In social interactions, this is accomplished in a number of ways. Love tends to be realised through ethics of care, respect is realised as moral or legal rights and esteem works within the cultural sphere, within the 'framework of a horizon of shared values' (Burns and Thompson 2013: 7).

As an interesting caveat to this model, Nancy Fraser (the main rival for Honneth in some circles of recognition theory) argues a case that does not regard self-realisation as a significant aspect of recognition at all. Rather, participation and parity frame any consideration of justice, and therefore of recognition (See Honneth and Fraser 2002). For individuals to be able to enjoy the parity of participation, they need to possess status, resources and a voice, which is one of the main reasons that Fraser places more emphasis on redistribution over recognition in any emancipation project. In other words, in social interaction, aspects of redistribution and representation play key roles that are at least as, if not more important than, recognition. I argue that Fraser's approach thus has the discernible character of an underlying political economy of recognition, thanks to its closeness to the notion of social capital as human resource, in her model crucial to any emancipatory project. The struggle for recognition in Fraser's approach is based largely on her critique of an 'inadequacy' in Taylor's account of group identity. Indeed, Fraser seems to abandon identity politics as too ambiguous to be useful, and regards self-realisation as a project of recognition theory as being too psychological, and inadequately sociological, to account for the role that distribution has to play in shaping social justice. Her argument emphasises parity of participation as adequate to the question of justice, whilst making 'no reference to the idea of self-realization' (Burns and Thompson 2013: 7). This critique of identity politics is important, as Nicholas Smith (2012: 2) has pointed out.

> Not only was culture just one aspect of identity [. . .] but identity too was only one aspect of politics: struggles over the distribution of resources were just as important from a moral, political and social point of view, as struggles over the recognition of identity.

However, for the context of online platform culture, where questions of identity persist in the foreground of debates, it is worth noting that both Fraser and Honneth argue for the social character of *difference* in identity politics. They both move towards a broader conceptualisation of identity politics where relationships of difference between individuals and groups make a contribution to an individual's identity. It seems a sensible move to consider this within contexts of social media interactions and how these have shaped identity politics during the past decade and, given the online interaction between individuals and groups, of the kind discussed in Chapter 3. In terms of populist models of self-realisation, this seems to embed itself in a psychology of individual personality. However, Fraser's often-cited criticism of Honneth as 'too psychological' can be read as a criticism that his approach is inadequately grounded more generally, as it downplays the material, historical and class dimensions of politics. Whether this criticism is fair is open to question. For instance, Lysaker and Jakobsen (2015) read in Honneth's later work attempts to address Fraser's critique of excessive psychology, giving the example that denial of equal rights is wrong, even if the misrecognised are not psychologically damaged. This seems of vital importance; just because some people are able to 'get over' inequalities, injustice or social negligence, it does not excuse these abuses.

This is relevant in the culture of online trolling where victims are seen as fair game. Publicly visible phrases used to undermine others and channel public displays of disrespect such as 'Tits or GTFO' ('Tits or Get the Fuck Out') are prevalent in online gaming, for example, where casual misogyny is accepted as an everyday occurrence (if not universally accepted as a social practice). This kind of interaction is indicative of a more overt and cultural prevalence which assumes that such behaviour causes relatively trivial harms. Contra to Fraser's criticisms, Lysaker and Jakobsen state that 'a reduction of issues, such as freedom, justice and democracy to issues of psychological injury is not at stake. [. . .] Psychological harm becomes an injustice only if the ethical status of a person is disrespected' (2015: 8). Therefore, Honneth might be read in the context that whereas justice and psychological wellbeing are related, they are distinct registers of social experience. However, I would say that scenarios such as the one just outlined show a carving-out of cultural space which accepts disrespect in the moral sense of ignoring the interests of others, and, indeed for some commentators, makes a virtue of it (see Penny 2013). Additionally, a growing body of social psychology scholarship seems to support this. This work associates online disrespect (in the moral and ethical senses) with challenges to psychological integrity and social standing, and to the general presentation of symptomatological decline in wellbeing (e.g., Kowalski, Limber and Agatston 2008; Navarro, Yubero and Larranaga eds 2016; Betts 2016; Sorbring, Skoog and Bohlin 2014; Giota, and Kleftaras 2013; Lapidot-Lefler and

Barak 2015; Brooks and Longstreet 2015). To my mind, it would seem unwise to attempt a disassociation of the two phenomena of moral and psychological harms. This is a psychosocial problem, and relative harms relating to psychology and connectivity ought to be treated in terms of the three forms of recognition identified by Honneth (love, respect, esteem) in order to acknowledge that respect and disrespect have a psychological dimension.

Additionally in this regard, for the purposes of this current study, my view is that being 'too psychological' is not something that we should accuse of Honneth's work. Indeed, as I shall develop in the final chapters, a more pertinent question (especially in terms of self-realisation) ought to consider if Honneth's work is psychological *enough*. The turn to Kohut and thence Jung to lend a depth dimension to the object-relations approach used by Honneth (via his reading of Winnicott) will produce a more rounded psychology of recognition in this context. The aim of this synthesis is to enable a rethink on the possibility of an emancipatory social project such as Honneth's critical social theory ultimately aims to establish. At the same time, one might establish an equivalent emancipatory psychological project – through a model of recognition that allows for both existential self-realisation, which is predicated upon wellbeing and self-confidence, and for social realisation through fair redistribution and moral respect.

What this self-realisation model of recognition seems to hinge upon is that the relationship between not recognising others as human beings with interests (that is to say, as persons) and the horror of oneself not being recognised as a person by others is part of the crucial process of mutual demarcation in self-realisation. I would argue that this process allows intersubjective relations to map pathways to dignity, as well as providing some kind of assurance against feelings of shame, tied into the emotional luggage of disrespect. As Honneth himself noted, social struggle tends to be motivated when people's notions of justice are violated: 'It is for this reason that when deep-seated normative expectations of intersubjective recognition are not met, people react with negative feelings of "shame, anger, or indignation"' (Petherbridge 2011: 18). These are deep-seated emotive and affective dimensions for which depth and relational psychology have the conceptual tools adequate to the task of robust analysis.

This process is also the mechanism through which individuals and groups face off reification in social interaction. In relation to Honneth's model, Bob Cannon writes that '[. . .] it is not possible to reground critical theory within the struggles of participants to realize the normative promise of modernity without challenging the system's diremption of "ethical life"' (2001: 136). This systematic diremption, or forceful splitting, is experienced by individuals as an intuitive injustice and indignation at the prospect of being treated as a thing rather than as a person. By the same token, one can surmise that the striving for dignity for oneself as well as for others is the basis in Honneth's model for achievement of self-realisation as well as the achievement of social community. This, we might say, is the basis of civil society in the first place, and gives form to the struggle for justice and basic rights in intersubjective relations. A brief return to Margalit on this aspect of self-realisation, and his reading of Hegel, reveals continuities between his own work and that of Honneth. On this question, Margalit notes that '[. . .] what turns out to be constitutive to self-knowledge (self-consciousness) is vitally important to ethics. Both self-knowledge and ethics require the point of view of the other. This point of view is the meeting-point between ethics and epistemology' (2001: 129).

This self-knowledge aspect of self-realisation, that is to say, knowing oneself and recognising in oneself the capacity for acknowledging the interests of others, is especially useful in understanding why such a simple rhetorical device as 'recip-rocated confidences' can make such a lasting impact. The identification of others, of events and of objects; detecting flaws in others, and the admission of one's own mistakes; the acknowledgement of others' traits and abilities; and the capacity to publicly endorse the status of others – these are all distinct aspects of recognition and have been intimated so far in this chapter as powerful psychosocial enterprises. What they hold in common is the importance with which we accord such aspects in our social interactions and communications practices. In a world discernibly characterised by semi-permanent, persistent conditions of connectivity, these prac-tices of intersubjective recognition become immediate, amplified, publicly visible and therefore fraught with risk. The stakes are high in social media declarations of recognition precisely because of these reasons. But I would argue that, superficially at least, the rewards too are immediate, amplified and publicly visible. This public self-realisation is a powerful, emotive motivation that engages our time, effort and energies. But what exactly is going on when we engage with such interaction practices, and is this level of self-realisation the same kind of realisation alluded to by recognition theory?

Self-realisation, always-on culture and the principle of mutuality

I argue that asking such a question immediately suggests that always-on aspects of everyday life have impinged, in some ways, upon self-realisation as a process in both psychosocial and moral senses. To address this social risk and reward balancing act, we need to be mindful of the always-on contexts within which Web 2.0 arose in the first place, and through which social media interaction became the preva-lent mass form of communications practice. Always-on is an interesting concept precisely because it describes the way that we seem to be constantly networked, constantly connected; in a state of semi-permanent connectivity, as I have alluded to so far. I have also written about this at length elsewhere (Singh 2014a) and in slightly different contexts, so a very brief outline of that argument here will suf-fice to engage how I see self-realisation within social media interaction practices as fundamentally tied-in to the always-on condition. Howard Rheingold (2002a) describes collective behaviours of individuals who use mobile media and techno-logical networks to organise collective action. This typifies Rheingold's utopian, and in my opinion somewhat nebulous, approach to technologies and the way people tend to use them. It is a problematic position because it seems to reproduce positivist rhetoric of innovation and connectivity uncritically. However, more recently, he has developed a more direct political stance, outlining the challenges of demands on people's time and attention and the repercussions of such challenges upon our ability to respond in an informed way (2012: 50), asking his readers to

> Consider the possible danger of alienation from ourselves as well as others. What might be called 'the Thoreau objection' to the siren call of digital distraction is worth examining, since the always-on availability of information to inform or amuse along with perpetual possibilities for social interaction may be depriving us of something humans have always drawn on: solitude.

Rheingold's reference to Thoreau evokes a sense of challenge upon one's free will to engage with others, and the question of whether this engagement is compelled in some way – a sense of duty to participate in social media connectivity. This is a powerful psychological image with which we respond in patterns of self-disclosure, play and impression management, in social media interactions. It also brings up the important question of solitude, which is simultaneously both culturally valued because of its scarcity *and* devalued because it appears anathema to connectivity. This is an important cultural distinction precisely because of the appearance-form which masks the philosophical error inherent in this dichotomy; solitude in the sense employed by Rheingold – something akin to self-reflection or self-awareness – does not equate easily with feelings of loneliness or with social ineptitude. However, because it is often misrecognised as such, solitude tends to carry with it a mythic collective image of antisocial 'self-ish-ness': that is to say, in the myth of connectivity, in quite literal senses, 'sharing is caring', whereas solitary behaviour is viewed in the somewhat opposite terms of selfishness or anti-social behaviour. The problems with this stem from the way that always-on connectivity demands of us a kind of attention that takes us away from solitary behaviours, and from the reflective spaces that solitude can bring. In his book *You Are Not a Gadget*, Jaron Lanier (2010: 4) remarks that

> Anonymous blog comments, vapid video pranks, and lightweight mash-ups may seem trivial and harmless, but as a whole, this widespread practice of fragmentary, impersonal communication has demeaned interpersonal interaction. Communication is now often experienced as a superhuman phenomenon that towers above individuals. A new generation has come of age with a reduced expectation of what a person can be, and of who each person might become.

The impetus to manage oneself on social networking platforms, the impression that one makes and the profile that one builds (and is built through data automation) is charged with this expectation of superhuman proportions, of the demands for immediacy that far exceed anything pre-existing the Web 2.0 era. But Lanier is quite correct in his phrasing about what happens to the status of personhood (and indeed, by implication, what happens to individual persons) in this collective image of superhuman, and precisely *machine-like*, expectation. The expectations we have of ourselves and of each other, whilst highly demanding in terms of quantity of engagement with process, is impoverished in terms of quality. This relative image of self is of an entirely different order to the fragmentary nature of online communications practices that Lanier describes. This is close to Sherry Turkle's view (2011) that the excessive demands of the media surround tend to exacerbate tensions where persistent connectivity leads to loneliness. This position is even clearer in her more recent work, *Reclaiming Conversation: The Power of Talk in a Digital Age* (2015), where she claims, persuasively, that solitude is a key socialisation process for the development of empathy – essential for a meaningful social life where mutual recognition allows for multiple interests to engage. Giving the example of children having to learn to socialise through such persistent connectivity, including the capacity for engaging the real-world consequences of anti-social behaviours such as cyberbullying, Turkle writes (2015: 61) that

> It's the capacity for solitude that allows you to reach out to others and see them as separate and independent. You don't need them to be anything other than they are. This means that you can listen to them and hear what they have to say. This makes the capacity for solitude essential to the development of empathy. And this is why solitude marks the beginning of conversation's virtuous circle. [. . .] Without empathy [. . .] we don't understand the impact we have when we bully others because we don't see them as people like ourselves.

In other words, the consequences of behaviours can be lost because social media tends to make the experience of others (and of ourselves) a fragmentary one, where the interests of others go unrecognised or easily dismissed, and opportunities for self-reflection and growth of empathy are missed. The relational psychologist Heinz Kohut (2011) provides an avenue of insight into how this fragmentary state is not only qualitatively and morally impoverished, but also psychologically problematic. His self-psychology approach, to which I give extensive treatment in Chapters 5 and 6, points to the value of reflection and self-introspection, and their role in facilitating both recognition in interpersonal relationships and in securing a resilient, mature personality. The constant pressure in always-on contexts to *perform* connectivity mirrors the psychological struggle to stabilise personality, to safeguard against its fragmentation. Over-mechanised identification with our connected selves has the potential of fragmenting a coherent self in spatial terms. A growing body of scholarship in the field of social psychology attests to issues associated with self-esteem, body-image and de-individuation in social media interactions (e.g., Coleman et al. 1999; Lewallen and Behm-Morawitz 2016; Ho, Lee and Liao 2016; Carah and Dobson 2016). Indeed, Kohut might describe this, in the psychological sense, as related to a loss of bodily cohesiveness, elaborated as a form of hypochondriasis[1] (2011). It would also be expressed as a fragmentary experience of time, again expressed in social psychology studies as issues associated with compulsive behaviour and so-called Internet addiction (e.g., Giota and Kleftaras 2013; Brooks and Longstreet 2015; Sorbring, Skoog and Bohlin 2014; Widyanto and Griffiths 2007; Baumer et al. 2015).

For Kohut, the self-psychology in these kinds of scenarios is expressed as the subject experiencing a loss of feeling her/himself continuously, elaborated as worries about being unreal and lacking uncertainty about the future. I expand on this in the next chapter as I argue this is tied-in to both existential and embodied notions of personhood – crucial to a depth psychology of recognition. For now, I think it relevant to establish the importance of this fragmentation in space and time as a discernible move, in cultural as well as psychological terms, away from reflection and introspection. The former is important for Honneth in relation to the self-realisation aspect of recognition, and the latter is important for Kohut, which he saw as crucial to the stable development of the self and its constituents.

For Kohut, experience of the self through introspection is vital in three respects. First, in the '[. . .] sense of being the same person throughout life – despite changes in our body and mind, in our personality makeup, in the surroundings in which we live.' Second, that self-perception encompasses '[. . .] our sense of abiding sameness within a framework of reality that imposes on us the limits of time, change, and ultimate transience.' And, third, an awareness of what Kohut describes as a 'tension gradient' between various constituents of self (ambitions, ideals, skills and talents) that enables the individual to establish a sense of continuity of self through time (2011: 453). I would argue, therefore, that solitude is an important condition which facilitates the necessary reflection of, and thus self-realisation and experience of, self in the sense of recognising one's own self-confidence, self-respect and self-esteem. Whereas self-realisation is possible only through meaningful social interaction in Honneth's model, it is often through solitude that we realise the value of those relationships of recognition through searching one's own feelings. This seems to be substantiated through Kohut's self-psychology. So, we might refine the problem here as one in which we are always connected (networked) but that this is often misrecognised, on a cultural (and political) level, as a *meaningful* connection. At the same time, we are alone, but in a state that could be described as *disconnect*, rather than solitude. This is being alone, but not in the sense of 'quality', reflective time to ourselves – indeed, all of that time is taken up with social media platform engagement, where it is difficult to see any reflection occurring in the sense that Kohut describes it.

This state of disconnect is picked up by Sherry Turkle, a key thinker in this area. Her approach, which I have touched upon here and in previous chapters, echoes the more politically engaged side of both Rheingold and Lanier, where she states that, 'Networked, we are together, but so lessened are our expectations of each other that we can feel utterly alone. And there is the risk that we come to see others as objects to be accessed – and only for the parts we find useful, comforting or amusing' (2011: 228). She describes this atomisation of whole personhood or self as being 'tethered' to the technologies we use at an everyday level. For Turkle, this extends through the language we use to describe the relationship (e.g., 'I'll be on my mobile') through to behaviour (e.g., in terms of how practices of communication problematise the boundaries between public and private). Additionally, in a McLuhanesque turn of thought, this extends even to our own sense of embodiment (e.g., the physical intention we mobilise towards communication, such as closing off real-world spaces through gesture, as when one uses a finger in the open ear whilst having a telephone conversation in a public space).

danah boyd has also written extensively on this subject (2012), and her approach continues this thinking, to an extent, although perhaps occupying a more positive space. She observes that boundaries between reality and virtuality appear to have become blurred, somehow artificial; or at least that these distinctions no longer seem to matter as much as perhaps they once did. This is largely down to the condition of always-on, where connectivity is assumed and ubiquitous. But also, most importantly perhaps, that when we refer to 'network', we are not necessarily referring to the technology itself, but to social interactions. In other words, technological networks really imply social networks, real relationships and real-time lives. boyd then poses questions concerning what counts as online, considering that, at least as far as cultures with developed communications infrastructures are concerned, there is no consensus on where this distinction might be, how clear it is nor where the 'real' ends and the 'virtual' begins. It is at this juncture in her argument that we can read a critical strand of thinking towards fragmentary experiences of online interaction. She argues that the distinction between on- and off-line is actually so untenable (it can no longer be maintained in any straightforward way) that we need to consciously declare 'off time'. Indeed, since boyd's work in this area, a whole literature has emerged in recent years regarding the phenomenon of abstention from social media use. This is when users consciously declare 'off time', and there is a tacit cultural acknowledgement that we are somehow spending 'too much' time engaging social media (Allen 2012; Portwood-Stacer 2012; Kaun and Stiernstedt 2014; Light and Cassidy 2014; Baumer et al. 2015). This acknowledgement recognises that engagement as something other than engaging with recognising-others. In other words, the principle of mutuality upon which the cultural predominance of social media is based (i.e., the maintenance of relationships, staying connected, reciprocating confidences and so on) is not necessarily being serviced in a meaningful way by our social media interactions. Perhaps we are engaged with the platform itself, and less so with others (as persons) as a result.

One of the problems that has characterised this account of always-on so far is that it tends to reproduce a rather binary way of thinking in popular discourses on the impacts of communications technology. Grant Bollmer has noted that 'Assumptions about the political effects of network technology reduces politics and experience to these properties of networks: the conjoined beliefs that *connection is freedom* and *connection is resistance* are held as axioms in spite of any counterevidence' (2012: 1 [emphasis in original]). But equally, as Bollmer points out, claims in both popular and academic discourse tend to be polarised to take on directly oppositional positions in relation to connectivity: 'Either the Internet enables the direct action of individuals linked together as never before or political disaffection permanently wanes away through online participation' (2012: 1). The truth of the matter is rather more untidy than popular and academic discourse would appear to allow, and yet there are ways in which social media interactions tend to move towards the mechanistic as a matter of course, according to the affordances of the platforms themselves.

For example, Geert Lovink recognises that social media users are 'No longer encouraged to act out a role, we are forced to be "ourselves" (in a form that is no less theatrical or artificial) [. . .] There is no alternative reality' (2011: 13). The 'selves' that Lovink refers to here are the versions that express and are expressed through data profiling on social media platforms. Such relatively bleak perspectives on social media identity, and the descriptions of how that identity cannot serve as a crucible for self-realisation (largely due to the artificial nature of such interaction), are becoming more common in academia, and stand in sharp contrast to more positivist approaches. What ought to be recognised in Lovink's position is the level at which such 'roles' are performed. For example, in relation to blogging and opinion expression, Lovink writes that 'The freedom to speak the "true" self while remaining hidden is replaced with the belief that liberation comes from the "complete" revelation of self, fully connecting to the totality of the network, defined by the limits of social technologies' (2012: 2). This transparency in online social interactions paradoxically means that performative play of identity is *de facto* denied; data automation and connectivity fixes identity as a surface value because the regimes of profiling are ultimately predicated upon the processing of activity through platform algorithms. In turn, these shape how that identity is expressed through the SNS profile. This betrays a discrepancy at the heart of social media interaction and identity for which questions regarding the status of utopian approaches might be reconsidered and usefully engaged as countermeasures.

For example, Siebers and Fell (2014) produced an executive report for the Connected Communities project in the UK, which reviewed literature on the relation between community and future as concepts. Drawing from the philosophy of Ernst Bloch, Siebers and Fell remarked (2014: 5) the need to

> [. . .] take seriously idea that at the bottom of our temporal communal existence lays [sic] an openness towards the future, and the idea that only in (political, social, cultural, existential) praxis which strives towards human dignity lies the adequate response to that openness.

Therefore, utopianism is not just about impossible no-places, but is a 'concretely anchored response to a foundational openness of existence [. . .] the central contents of our experience are characterised by being unfinished.' This is essentially a philosophy of hope, predicated upon a trust that openness can work to establish and strengthen communities and improve the lot of the individuals within them. It is interesting the Siebers and Fell emphasise the role of dignity here; as I have discussed previously, this is as a key element in the development of moral self-respect in Honneth's model of ethical personality. Honneth viewed this kind of utopian project in terms of a primacy of affective recognition in human relations with social structures, emphasising lived human relationships as the building blocks of communities and ultimately civil society. In this sense he is a communitarian, in that his emphasis on human associations as a source of identity formation is key to thinking how social interactions nurture communities as they come into being, and sustain them as crucibles of trust, dignity and mutuality.

As I shall explore in more depth in the next chapter, Kohut noted that a mature self has 'accepted the independent motivations and responses of others, and has grasped the notion of mutuality' (1971: 50). Even in the sense where relationships can be recognised as based on social asymmetry, there is, at a more ontological level, a basis of symmetry, where each person has a point of view and that point of view is recognised as an autonomous interest. This is, of course, a deeper understanding of point of view than, say, acknowledging an opinion posted online and leaving a comment on the post. In a sense, even though such an exchange might be deemed a welcome development in the freeing up of movement of information in a functioning democracy, I argue that this does not constitute a struggle for recognition on the same levels that Honneth, Margalit and Kohut are discussing. It would be an impossible stretch, surely, to argue for this, and one can imagine that even utopians would balk at such a position; it is not necessarily the case that every person is capable of supplying an equal point of view. This is a qualitative question, of a particular order more properly relating to social capital. However, this assertion might pertain to an ethical imperative to seek equitable expression – not merely to press the rights of individuals to express their opinion, but that deliberative mechanisms such as free movement of opinions ought to provide some grounds for mutuality, where responsibilities of trust are also fully acknowledged as dimensions of rights to free speech. So often, as we have seen through various examples (in relation to toxic online practices such as trolling) this trust breaks down, and perhaps this is due in part to the notion that social media interactions cannot, as apparatus of recognition, properly form the grounds for self-realisation.

There is an instrumentality at work in social media interaction that, whilst by no means universal, might be generalisable through acknowledgement of data automation and governance. The temptation here might well be to say that, insofar as I need the other only enough to recognise me, to achieve recognition and hence self-knowledge, the other is in some way a mere object or tool. Margalit, for example, in his reading of Hegel's master/slave dialectic, correctly engages this instrumental solution as a Kantian objection. It is framed in such a way that such recognition is not fully autonomous (it is contingent and not, perhaps, freely given as a recognising consciousness) and therefore cannot satisfy the conditions for moral respect. It might therefore be accurate to suggest that without such satisfaction, recognition cannot be truly valued as such. Margalit's treatment of Hegel acknowledges a further step, beyond instrumentality, where two individuals in an asymmetric relation are capable of recognising the other as a person, beyond the status of mere instrument. They also recognise one as master and one as slave, crucial to 'their social understanding as based on asymmetry in their respective status. But this social super-structure is grafted onto an ontological base that is based upon symmetry: each person has a point of view' (2001: 133).

It is troubling, therefore, to attempt an application of this notion to one's point of view in social media interactions. Precisely because of the fragmentary aspects of social media interactions as I noted by Lanier and by boyd a moment ago, our own point of view seems to be at least one remove from others' due to the algorithmic nature of news feeds on Facebook (to give one example). Fragmentary, and driven by automation, they are never wholly autonomous and therefore susceptible to an instrumentalism that appears to not even permit a master/slave recognition (even as real-world asymmetry has long persisted in online contexts – see Crawford 2002). Once again, such a situation raises the principle of mutuality as a psychological precondition to authentic self-development. Without mutuality, the individual cannot get beyond an instrumental, narcissistic order of self and others. It is towards these questions that I now wish to turn.

Note

1 Hypochondriasis, in this sense, denotes a shift of norms towards actual ill-health or a vulnerable state of wellbeing.

5

TOWARDS A DEEP PSYCHOLOGY OF RECOGNITION AND MUTUALITY IN ALWAYS-ON CONTEXTS

In Chapter 4, I put forward some tentative arguments towards a recognition theory for social media interaction. The discussion was necessarily wide-ranging and captured the essence of Axel Honneth's approach to establish a bottom-line recognition process that could account for misrecognition as a kind of social disrespect. It also outlined the potential for both moral and psychosocial self-realisation within the context of a world characterised by an always-on condition of semi-permanent, persistent connectivity. In this chapter, I will significantly extend that discussion, particularly in the direction of Honneth's application of object-relations theory, which he drew from the developmental and relational psychology of D. W. Winnicott. Honneth's philosophical anthropology was also influenced largely by Hegel's Jena lectures (as well as Hegel's mature work, including the *Philosophy of Right*), and the social psychology of the self, primarily taken from George Herbert Mead. To this background, he applied Winnicott's ideas to give a more detailed account of the role of familial relations in the shaping of personality in personal and social interactions, as well as to more fully develop and account for the role of the human psyche in self-realisation and mutual recognition. What I aim to achieve is an extension and strengthening of the psychological dimension of his framework by synthesising this with Kohut's psychological theory of the selfobject (1971, 1977, 2011), a wholly original intervention in the theory of social technologies, which I present both here and in Chapter 6.

Honneth has claimed that '[. . .] social relations of recognition can only develop under the precondition of corresponding structural developments within the human psyche, such as have been investigated in exemplary fashion by object relations theory' (2012: ix–x). In making this bold claim within the field of social research, he has identified the need to draw connections between external social recognition and structural psychological formation (2012: x). As noted in Chapter 4, Nancy Fraser has been critical of Honneth's use of psychoanalytic concepts, claiming that his work is too psychological, and does not give a strong enough account of the need for redistribution within an historical materialist framework. It may be true that a full acknowledgement of material conditions (such as class) playing a role in the exaggeration of asymmetric recognition would be necessary to give a rounded political economic argument. However, I argue that an extension of the psychology of self and identity is also necessary. This would aid the construction of a more complete account of the structuring presence of social media interactions and always-on connectivity in relation to psyche, as well as explore in more detail the notion of an 'ethical personality' in this context. Additionally, it would constitute, in some regards, an extension of Honneth's later work which, according to Petherbridge (2013: 146), turned to object-relations psychoanalysis

> [. . .] to undertake an empirical reconstruction of the primary forms of intersubjectivity and self-formation. This orientation towards object-relations theory constitutes a major reformulation of the theory of recognition that has become central to Honneth's project and the fundament upon which his later work is based.

I leave the work of political economy to others to fully explore, although note here some excellent contributions to the contextual analysis of such questions. I acknowledge the role that this field has in influencing my position on these matters, specifically in the field of digital and social media studies (e.g., Allmer 2015; Fuchs 2013, 2014; Fuchs and Sandoval eds 2014; Scholz ed. 2013; Dyer-Witheford 1999, 2010; Webster J. G. 2014; Webster F. 2002; Sandoval 2013). Where I intend to make my original contribution is through developing a synthesis of ethical personality and self-psychology, with a view to extending towards a depth psychology approach. I will apply this synthesis to interaction in contemporary always-on connectivity. With regards to this in particular, I would like to focus on issues of social justice in online communications practices – specifically, in relation to toxic and benign practices of disclosure and disinhibition. In doing so, this chapter and Chapter 6 will prepare the ground for a discussion of social media as a false-self system in Chapter 7.

We might begin extending Honneth's account of personal identity by borrowing the following question: how do persons develop and maintain their identity, their sense of themselves as practical, moral beings with unique characteristics and distinctive places in the social world? (Zurn 2015: 6). This is a question that, so far, I have addressed at the periphery, and that speaks to aspects of social justice that are underdeveloped in digital and social media studies. Of course, in a general context of social relations, Honneth proposes an answer: '[. . .] individuals become who they are in and through relations of mutual recognition with others' (2015: 6). However, we might amend Zurn's question slightly in order to apply more directly to our context, which takes into consideration the persistent connectivity of the always-on world. In this context, we need to take account of the complexities of the symbolic and practical distinctions existing between online and real-world identity, and how identities are mobilised in imagined and lived spaces in cultural practice.

Therefore, the questions I would like to address in the current chapter are these: how do persons develop and maintain their identity, their sense of themselves as practical, moral beings with unique characteristics (and acting in distinctive moral spaces) in the social media world? In addition, as a development of the argument in Chapter 4, to what extent is it necessary to develop the psychological aspects of Honneth's model of self-realisation to more fully account for fragmentary notions of personhood found in the always-on? And furthermore, within this ethical personality framework for semi-permanent connectivity, how might we start to engage a depth approach to account for the structuring presence and mythic content of connectivity in order to begin the work of developing an affirmative and workable mutuality in online contexts? As with the approach espoused in Part I of this book, these questions are intended to be framed in fundamentally ethical, rather than empirical, ways. In this context, would Honneth's proposal, that individuals become who they are in and through relations of mutual recognition with others, remain valid?

Self, identity and reflection in Kohut's self-psychology

To prepare a response to these questions we must first reconsider the approach Honneth takes in asserting his claims about ethics and personality. In particular, how does his model give us an opportunity to begin to rethink what is meant by the development of *self* as distinct to the development of *identity* in social interaction? As previously noted, Honneth's main focus tends to be in the field of social justice, where he identifies the place of mutuality and recognition as a starting point for meaningful discussion. He states that 'social justice is to be defined in terms of the requirement of mutual recognition, and that we must take our point of departure in historically developed and already institutionalized relations of recognition' (2012: viii). Ultimately, this approach to social justice underpins mutual recognition because it mobilises freedom as a good within modern democracies. Importantly, the approach demands of individuals, as part of wider institutional groups (families, communities, organisations), an awareness of the interests of others and of the group in order to give proper meaningful social value to that freedom. It provides for a practice of restricting the interests of the self (through reflection as much as deliberation) where those self-interests are fundamentally at odds with other interests and may lead to relative harms.

This is an idea influenced by Hegel's *Philosophy of Right*. As Honneth points out, 'For the mature Hegel, recognition refers to an act of moral self-restriction, which we must be able to perform on ourselves in the face of others if we are to arrive at a consciousness of our self'. He points to an internal connection between recognition and freedom, because for Hegel, 'it is only by taking part in institutionalized practices of self-restriction that we can experience our own will as being completely free' (2012: viii).

It is important to note here that in applying Hegel one needs to remember that he is most often interpreted as attempting to account for recognition as constitutive of all social reality. According to Honneth (2012: 3–4), in the *Phenomenology of Spirit*, Hegel sought to

> [. . .] demonstrate that a subject can only arrive at a 'consciousness' of its own 'self' if it enters into a relationship of 'recognition' with another subject. [. . .] elucidating not an historical event or instance of conflict, but a transcendental fact that should prove to be a prerequisite of all human sociality.

As Honneth suggests, we need to ensure that if this recognitive mechanism is applied to social processes, then the influence of prevailing norms, principles and practices need to remain central: 'Claims and demands, obligations and beliefs are just as much a part of reality as supposedly purely "objective" matters' (2012: ix). It is within this frame, then, that Honneth is able to suggest that *self-realisation*, as a process, is experienced by all human beings. This is in full acknowledgement that individual and cultural differences persist in everyday experience, and that institutions such as family and community play a crucial local role in the kinds of demands and obligations faced by individuals in negotiating moral self-restriction and civic action. Self-realisation constitutes and underscores our experience of social reality in three basic, intersubjective forms of recognition. On a bodily, emotional level, self-realisation is experienced as a development of self-confidence, through private spheres of care, in personal relations, within close institutions such as family. This is a *love* recognition. On a level of responsibility, self-realisation is experienced as a development of moral self-respect, through institutional spheres of state and legal rights. This is a recognition of *law* and *respect*. Finally, self-realisation is experienced as a development of social self-esteem, at a level emphasised through a public-facing, socialised identity with social traits and abilities. This is a recognition of achievements in work, markets, civil society – the recognitive basis of *esteem* (see Table 5.1).

In all of these aspects of recognition, what is immediately discernible is that they are founded upon a principle of mutuality – that is to say, that recognition proper does not occur without a recognising other. This is a fundamentally Hegelian conceptualisation of self-realisation in human beings, which is contingent upon *trust*. Perhaps in our first love relations (centred conventionally as a child-mother relation within the family, or less conventionally as a significant figure within a family-like structure), this trust takes on the character of dependence, at first, before developing into fully independent choices. However, in later life, such vulnerability (not to mention the amount of good faith and resilience required to undertake such a risky enterprise) centres on the tensions inherent between self-regarding and other-regarding at the heart of our social interactions where dependence takes on far less significance. It may be true that such mutual trust is a leap of faith that some may be reticent to make. However, in psychosocial as well as ethical terms, it is a risk that we might regard as having an exponential pay-off in recognition terms.

The kinds of bonds made in early life, which help shape rudimentary identity, remain influential in the kinds of bonds we strive to make in later life to express and explore that identity in social interaction. As touched upon in the previous chapter, Charles Taylor (1991: 49) put it this way: 'Love relationships are [. . .] crucial because they are the crucibles of inwardly generated identity' (1991: 49). Indeed, the opportunities for the self-reflection that Turkle (2015) has argued as essential to the building of empathy are frittered away through persistent connectivity. As I have also noted, the absence of solitude that comes with this persistent, semi-permanent connectivity means that the space for self-reflection, an essential grounding component for the 'virtuous circle' of conversation, meaningful engagement, introspection and empathy, is missing. At the very least, it exists in an impoverished form. The same self-reflection that we find wanting in always-on connectivity turns out to be a requirement for consistency of identity to build relationships in everyday life. Love relationships provide a conceptual and experiential bridge between the political and the psychological aspects of personal identity, particularly in early life, where opportunities for reflecting upon one's behaviour are tried and tested through the approval and disapproval of others. At the same time, reflection provides the grounds for mutuality because, as Taylor implies above, it involves the developmental understanding of the importance of human interaction as well as the foundation for identity as an autonomous human agent capable of freely making decisions that take into account the interests of others in social interactions.

Honneth recognised this, turning to Winnicott's developmental approach. He saw that mutuality in social relations rests upon the ability to recognise and accept the independent motivations of another, thereby providing the opportunity to reflect upon one's own motivations and the potential consequences of one's actions. This has a number of implications on the distinct levels of freedom, moral respect and psychology of relationships, associated with Honneth's model of ethical personality. In most developmental approaches, Winnicott's and Kohut's included, there is a stage in which the infant, incapable of self-reflection in the mature sense, misrecognises herself as omnipotent, and all-encompassing. This omnipotent stage in development is overcome, according to Winnicott, through interaction with another – usually the mother or a significant attachment figure. That figure reacts to the destructive behaviour of the child, behaviour driven through the misconception that she is omnipotent, through approval or disapproval. Through this socialisation process of trial and error the child usually begins to accept the fact of intentionality outside of her own. For Honneth, once again in an echo of Sandel's notion of 'reciprocally constitutive' relations, 'Individuals achieve self-determination by learning, within relations of reciprocal recognition, to view their needs, beliefs and abilities as worthy of articulation and pursuit in the public sphere' (2012: 46). In Kohut's self-psychology, this is an acceptance of the independent motivations of others, and a grasping apprehension of the notion of mutuality, from early life into maturity (1971). It forms the key to understanding how mutuality plays a role in the development and functioning of self and identity.

TABLE 5.1 Development of 'ethical personality'

Honneth Intersubjective forms or patterns of recognition	*Relational PSA* (e.g., Winnicott)	*Hegel*	*Kohut* Constituents of self	
Love (ethics of **care**)	Basic self-confidence (bodily–emotional)	**Family**	Ambitions; basic layers of personality: strivings for power and success; first selfobjects (family)	Depth psychology concept of **personality**
Law/respect (**rights**)	Moral self-respect (responsibilities)	**State**	Ideals; central idealised goals (including, perhaps, idealised persons, images of figures whose competence is idealised)	
Achievement/esteem (**solidarity**)	Social self-esteem (traits and abilities)	**Civil society**; social community	Skills and talents; (related to social competence and social capital)	**Identity** (parasocial interface)

Self-realisation | The principle of mutuality | Recognition
Ethical personality

In his essay, 'Four Basic Concepts in Self Psychology' (2011 [1979]), Kohut makes a clear distinction between the concepts of self and identity. To begin with, 'The self is a depth-psychological concept and refers to the core of the personality made up of various constituents in the interplay with the child's earliest selfobjects' (2011: 451). He goes on to distinguish identity as 'the point of convergence between the developed self (as it is constituted in late adolescence and early adulthood) and the sociocultural position of the individual' (2011: 451). So, Kohut conceives of identity as a kind of psychological or psychosocial interface. Whereas his concept of self is a deeper structuring presence that incorporates the basic layers of personality (the strivings for power and success that Kohut describes as 'ambitions'), as well as 'ideals' – central, idealised goals (including, perhaps, idealised persons, psychological images of figures whose competence is idealised as more fully rounded and 'complete' individuals in the mind of the beholder). Together these layers of personality and identity form what Kohut calls the *constituents of self*. This has implications for the ways in which parasocial attachments and imagined relations with unknown others in social media contexts (relations that are commonplace in popular culture, particularly regarding celebrity and lifestyle cultures) might be regarded according to their relative authenticity. It also has far-reaching implications in terms of the cultural importance accorded to such remote relationships in contemporary popular culture.

At the same time, it might be true to suggest that online contexts further complicate the inner and outer aspects of individuality so important to analytical psychology, making it necessary to rethink how inner lives are reflected through social interactions and social media interactions – and, by that same process, how the outer worlds of such very different forms of interaction are reflected upon in one's own counsel, in self-reflection. In the teleological sense of individuation (the concept which describes the process through which individuals are living towards end goals including self-realisation) Jung introduced a complexity of meaning and uniqueness to the deeper understanding of the process of achieving selfhood. It is difficult to say to what extent, if any, a life lived partly through fragmented and often illusory online interactions achieves this sense of meaning and uniqueness at an unconscious level. After all, Jung was working at a time when, although certainly the space-time compression effects of communications technologies and practices were felt (through, for example, cross-Atlantic telecommunications), the current era of persistent connectivity was still some way off. It is difficult to imagine that he would have been able to anticipate the scale and character of the fragmentary effects of connectivity described so far in this book, or the extent to which connectivity might disrupt or impoverish self-realisation.

Kohut went some way to bridging the gap between Hegelian self-realisation and Jungian depth psychology. Identity in Kohut's model is distinct as a socio-cultural phenomenon – a psychological or psychosocial interface enabling the individual to develop a distinct personality made up of both deep structuring self-presence and an outward social status. Jungian models sometimes tend to overemphasise the individuation process as an inner process of self, whilst de-emphasising the role of the social interface overlaid upon the core personality. The inner core, in some ways, motivates the outer layer, and the whole model tends to over-emphasise duality. It may be true to say that this interpretation can be seen to work in real-world situations and in face-to-face communications as an empirical, conscious phenomenon (i.e., most people tend to not risk *full* self-disclosure, even in the most self-serving branding exercises characterising professionalised social media marketing practices today). However, the problem with this interpretation is that it tends to break down in social media contexts, where frequent-but-impoverished interaction amplifies personal detachment rather than reducing it.

This idea of impoverished interaction is the 'alone-together' effect so eloquently described by Turkle (2011). It also sits at the heart of the main ethics argument laid out in Part I of this book, where I foreground the distinction between the empirical and the ethical in social interaction. What I wish to add to that ethical dimension here is that although the Jungian notion of individuation is problematic, its usefulness can be found in Jung's take on formation and mobilisation of personality, where self and identity are quite distinct psychological entities that necessitate specific approaches. It is important that Kohut describes *self* as a depth-psychological concept though, because, as one might best understand it, it is from depth psychology that we can take insights regarding the structuring presence of psyche, the archetypal presence of self and its role in online interactions. These are, after all, interactions driven through a corresponding structuring presence of persistent connectivity – connectivity between humans and other humans, and between humans and the machines that govern information flows. This always-on structuring presence of connectivity may be considered an allegorical parallel with the similarly all-encompassing presence of psyche, which finds conscious, cultural expression in our notions of identity.

I will develop intersections between Kohut's approach, other relational approaches and a depth perspective on these contradictory impressions momentarily. To get to that point in the argument, it is useful to extend the distinctions made between self and identity as an underpinning of social (media) interactions. The basis of thought in this area stems largely from observations made by practitioners in the psychotherapy room. For instance, Kohut describes a belief that many psychoanalysts develop a strong core self which protects against fragmentation in dealing with the process of therapy – a situation that understandably places a lot of strain on the analyst, where the interaction of personalities is a key component of the analytical journey. This is coupled with a relatively diffuse identity which allows for empathy with many different types of people. By contrast, some people are characterised by a relatively weak self, but a strong identity – perhaps aligned with an intensely experienced social role, and a strong identification with that role necessary to achieve everyday success, or even survival. Such people are prone to psychological disintegration when their social order is disrupted or destroyed. Examples of this might be found in displacement due to war or famine. There are others still for whom a strong, rigid identity rests on a strong, established self (2011: 451–2). This is expressed as a fully realised personality coupled with a consistent social identity.

It is possible for individuals to possess neither strong sense of self nor strong identity. Such cases are highly problematic in that both fragile personality and weak social identity would make for difficult socialisation and maintenance of cohesive relationships in the first place. Indeed, when Kohut gives detailed descriptions of the fragmentation of self in the context of weak self and weak identity, this is largely expressed in terms of the fragmentary experience of space and time, whose cohesiveness is vital to a cohesive sense of continuity of self. As a fragmentation of space, this is experienced as a loss of bodily cohesiveness, often elaborated as a form of hypochondriasis. As a fragmentation of time, this is experienced as a loss of subjective continuity, elaborated as worries about being unreal or perhaps, in less extreme cases, lacking certainty about the future. It occurs to me that in such situations, individuals might be caught in a spiral of searching for role models with idealised competences. We see this so often in popular culture where the parasocial engagements, emotional investments and publicly shared intimacy of fans with their celebrities are amplified in intensity and in frequency of opportunity through Web 2.0 connectivity – for example, in the way that celebrity YouTubers such as Zoella, PewDiePie, shaycarl and others have garnered mass appeal through their affability as public personas, and the kinds of aspirational values they seem to embody provide a neat fit for para-social alignment in the way audiences (whether in possession of relatively weak or stable identities) engage with their content. The comments sections that trace a narrative of such interactions with online celebrities suggest both high levels of emotional investment and attachment are a recipe for emotionally charged fan interaction, and a palpable sense of emotional fulfilment (when celebrity action is met with approval) and betrayal (when fans feel let down by the actions or words of their celebrity). Where this fits in with Kohut's model, in cases where parasocial alignment is an eventuality of fragmentation of self for such individuals with fragile personalities, their own psychological paths might lead to various, and serial, partial *ambitions*. These are momentary fixations on specific details that, in the ordinary run of things, would be far less important for healthy development of self and identity. However, in social media interactions, such details are loaded with an entirely different magnitude of cultural value.

A particularly well-known example of this within online celebrity culture can be found in (vlogger and YouTube celebrity) Chris Crocker's 'Leave Britney Alone' YouTube post (September 2007). In this vlog post, Crocker, in a direct-to-camera monologue, appears to have an emotional meltdown in response to Britney Spears' much-publicised troubled personal life. In particular, he details the negative (sometimes threatening) responses from public commentary (on social media feeds as well as in entertainment news and on broadcast networks) towards Spears, expressing his concerns that this will tip her over the edge. He even threatens to 'throw himself off the nearest bridge' if people don't stop harassing her. The video went viral, becoming one of YouTube's most rapidly viewed and most commented video posts to date and led to a complex, protracted public reaction towards Crocker himself.

The complexity with which the performative aspects of vlogging culture mean that we can never be totally sure to what extent Crocker is consciously performing or merely self-disclosing, and the very public space through which Crocker shares this moment means that comments made from viewers on the platform itself were loaded with observations about the post at face value. Crocker's effeminate appearance and emotional outbursts were the target of ridicule precisely because these were the details picked up on by the viewers themselves. The evaluation of the video overall was profoundly negative, but largely because these attributes were the aspects subject to evaluation rather than the subject matter itself. Evaluation was predominantly based on prevailing social and cultural norms surrounding how young men should look and behave in public (rather than Crocker's underlying message, which implied concerns that public trolling might lead to an extreme response from Spears, such as suicide). Such instances are extremely common in contemporary vlogging culture today, but were relatively new in 2007 when the technology was emerging, which is the reason Crocker's video garnered the attention that it did. But one aspect of this, which is perhaps the most important lesson to be learned here, is specifically related to this commonality. Public self-disclosure, emotional breakdown and subsequent harassment via social media feeds occurs all the time, on all platforms, in relation to all sorts of cultural content. It is largely afforded through a combination of free speech discourse, deregulated media environment and hyperconnected Web 2.0 platform culture.

Beyond face-value, one might be tempted to rethink Crocker's video post as an attempt to outline the way celebrity (in this case, embodied in a specific person, Britney Spears) emphasises the idealised competence of a celebrity other. The expectations collectively placed upon such figures are high, and the impossibly superhuman task of maintaining such competence in the public eye generates the perfect conditions for failure. It is in this aspect where Kohut's model of self psychology is illustrated in practice. Admittedly, there is a danger in the Crocker case that one would fall into a trap where stereotypes (and their public evaluation) of normative masculinity, femininity, sexuality and even ethnicity elide with certain kinds of (approved) behaviour online. Crocker's visible and public expression of sexual orientation and performative gender ambiguity came under both scrutiny and rabid public assaults in comments relating to his videos. It is also true that there is a temptation to read a certain cerebral 'whiteness' into the concerns of the interactions at work here. The reason that I bring this particular example up here is that the doubling of celebrity (Britney as pop star, Crocker as YouTube superfan) led to some extreme emotional responses from commentators (mostly homophobic, but others just plain cruel). One must also be mindful that this is not isolated to instances of homophobic response to a specific expression of popular culture. Here, one could easily argue that celebrity culture in general, and the aspirational values embedded in the parasocial relationships between celebrities and their fans, is merely an amplification of real-world, everyday investment. This 'searching for role models with idealised competences', as a description for the combination of weak self and weak identity in Kohut's model, becomes important for an additional reason – it is symptomatic of popular culture, and happens so commonly that it barely registers as being of observable value. The various, serial and partial ambitions and the momentary and fragmentary character, of social media interaction, lead to fixation on specific details that become the 'whole thing' – an argument that I have developed in detail elsewhere (2017) in response to other relational approaches to social media (especially Balick 2014b).

This *to-be-looked-at-ness* of role models in celebrity and fan cultures is perhaps nothing new, but the intensity and amplification of the scopic and optic attitude towards others in social media contexts is a recent development coinciding precisely with the Web 2.0 era. What has become clear in this short period of time is that the fragmentary experience of self is driven through two forces, contradictory in definition but complementary in their aggregated effects in a dialectical exchange. These forces might be described as experience of self and others through introspection (and subsequent self-disclosure) and experience of self and others through narcissistic investment (and subsequent oversharing). In fact, for Kohut, as with many relational approaches, all psychological experience of self is in some way beholden to these forces. They are somewhat essential to the development of self and identity. The difference here is that, in the contexts of persistent connectivity, these forces exacerbate the fragmentation aspects of that experience and are, in some ways, discernible features of social interaction, commented upon and observed through what is commonly described (both with broad accuracy, and in vulgar misappropriation in popular culture) as 'digital narcissism'.

In terms of the experience of self via introspection, Kohut breaks this down into three aspects (2011: 453). The first of these focuses on a 'sense of being the same person throughout life' which remains consistent through time. This is consistency despite changes in appearance, the effects of aging upon mind, memory and functionality, changes over time in our personality makeup and also changes in personal circumstance. The second aspect draws from a perception of self as a 'sense of abiding sameness within a framework of reality that imposes on us the limits of time, change, and ultimate transience' (2011: 453), and therefore speaks to our sense of finite existence, and mortality, through the experience of time, aging, illness and so on. Finally, the experience of self via introspection draws upon aspects of Kohut's constituents of self – our ambitions, which are built from the most basic layers of personality, our ideals, which are formed of idealised goals drawn from relative self-respect and the respect for others, and our skills and talents, which make up the materials of our social interactions. It is not the *content* of these constituents that defines the self, but the 'tension gradient' between them. This 'tension gradient' enables the individual to establish a sense of continuity of self through time. It is also key to understanding the distinctions and relationships between the psychoanalytic definition of narcissism and the popular or folk understanding of the term.

"Selfobjects", self-disclosure and digital narcissism

Kohut, to an extent, redefined the psychoanalytic method through his emphasis on what can be observed with introspection in ourselves and with empathy (a sort of vicarious introspection) in others. This approach is loosely built upon the introspection-empathy models originally developed by Breuer and Freud in the 1890s, but in Kohut's thought has evolved in terms of considering methods such as free association and resistance analysis as auxiliary instruments 'employed in the service of the introspective and empathic mode of observation' (Kohut, cited in Ornstein 2011: 29). Considering a further definition of self, formulated by Kohut, we can see the importance with which he accords this mutuality: the self is 'an independent center of initiative, an independent recipient of impressions' (2011: 454). Implied in Kohut's 'centre-recipient' model here is the acceptance of the independent motivations of others, and a grasping apprehension of the notion of mutuality. This is achieved through what Kohut termed 'selfobjects': narcissistically invested psychological objects; or, objects either used in the service of the self or which are themselves experience as part of the self. Typically, in early life, the first selfobjects experienced are focused on family figures, and the attributes associated with them. In his book *The Analysis of the Self* (1971), Kohut explores this experience as a sort of psychological testing ground where the self (as a conception and experience of subjectivity), and identity (as a social interface), are first developed. He writes (1971: 26) that

> The small child [. . .] invests other people with narcissistic cathexes [psychological energies, engagement] and then experiences them narcissistically, i.e. as selfobjects. The expected control over such (selfobject) others is then closer to the concept of the control which a grown-up expects to have over his own body and mind than to the concept of the control which he expects to have over others.

The selfobject, to be clear, is not another person, but the psychological image or idealised experience of a significant other, invested with associations the child attributes to it. Additionally, Kohut (2011: 457) recognises the need to differentiate the notion of selfobjects (objects that are experienced as part of the self) from true objects (independent centres of initiative and motivation, or autonomous beings, experienced as such).

> There are two kinds of selfobjects: those who respond to and confirm the child's innate sense of vigor and perfection; and those whom the child can look up to and with whom he can merge as an image of calmness, infallibility, and omnipotence. The first type is referred to as the mirroring selfobject, the second as the idealized parent imago.

The first kind of selfobject mirrors an archaic striving for power and success, and is the beginning of the development of self-confidence. The second kind embodies the central idealised goals of a developing personality, providing figures whose competence is both idealised and imagined as fully realised. The anticipation of control over selfobjects, experienced narcissistically, is an anticipation of self-control. It is interesting to compare this aspect of narcissistic experience with the folk definition of narcissism as understood in the popular imagination: self-love, control over others. One might begin by saying that this folk definition is incomplete at best, particularly as it has been recognised in the scholarship on blogging and other online communications practices that narcissism in such contexts describes a process that amounts to an incredibly complex social performance of autonomy. Indeed, as Zizi Papacharissi puts it in her book *A Private Sphere* (2010), the human element of social networking embodies a complicated balance of ego-centred networks that engage age-old traditions of tension between public and private spheres, as well as the tensions between individuals and their social engagements. She writes that, 'The values of *autonomy, control,* and *expression,* prioritized in developed democracies, are generously afforded via SNSs. The technology invites expression, affords autonomy, and enables control of the self and its multiple performances' (2010: 143 [emphasis in original]).

So, here again we see echoes of self-control as key to understanding the psychology of narcissism. Papacharissi's take on narcissism in social media interactions resembles Kohut's selfobject mechanism quite closely. Control over selfobject others is closer to the concept of a mature self-control or self-composure than to the control one might expect over others in the folk definition of narcissism. Social media, and the kinds of interactions afforded through such platforms, therefore amplify this apparent control of self – little wonder social media is such a massively popular and compelling pastime. As a desideratum, one might start to think of this in the context of a collective, mythic image of connectivity as the embodiment of values promised and (to some extent, perhaps) realised around the notions of democracy, free expression and so forth. These aspects were, of course, the subjects of lengthy coverage in Chapter 1. For Papacharissi (2010: 144),

> Autonomy, control, and expression, as realized via the social networks of the private sphere, present ego-centered needs and reflect practices structured around the self. This would suggest liberating practices for the user, but not necessarily democratizing practices for the greater society.

So, where one might be tempted to describe such technologies as embodying democratic values, they ought not to be framed as *democratising* technologies as such. However, there is a realisation aspect to these processes which suggests that the value of autonomy, as an expression of democracy, is also a specific end-goal condition springing from mutuality and recognition. As Christine Kieffer (2013: 124 [emphasis in original]) has pointed out, in the developmental life-stage

> The selfobject is an outside other who is needed by the child whose experience is broadened through participation in the other's capacities as if they were the child's own. This includes developing a capacity for empathy with oneself *through* selfobject experiencing of the parent's empathy.

In other words, the participation in the selfobject other's capacities as one's own capacities is essential to the potential growth of empathy, which develops in the experience of self and others through the reciprocity of narcissistic investment and introspection. It leads to mutual recognition and, ultimately, to autonomy in its authentic sense.

As others have commented, the broad understanding of a narcissistic person in popular or folk psychology is someone who is vain and enamoured with themselves. For Jacoby, 'Those usually characterized as narcissistic then, are people who admire only themselves. The people around them serve but one purpose, to echo that self-admiration' (2006: 1). However, narcissism in Kohut's approach is closer to the idea of self-control and self-value than the control of others and particularly the control of how others see us. Indeed, as Jacoby points out, psychoanalysis in general tends to take a view of narcissism as an idealised form of self-control, projected onto the expectation one has of others in their response. And this is very different from popular definitions. It is important to note that the term narcissism is widely recognised in the psychoanalytic community as both amongst the most important in the field, as well as one of the most confusing (Pulver, cited in Jacoby 2006: 4). In fact, psychoanalytic descriptions of narcissistic disorders often seem precisely the opposite to popular descriptions, 'involving more or less serious disturbances in self-valuation and an overwhelming self-hatred' (2006: 3) rather than intensified self-admiration. This complexity, and the contradiction between the popular and specific conceptions of narcissism, is a source of the term's strength if anything, because it points to complex everyday psychological experiences and social phenomena that require complex description.

Jacoby notes some interesting convergences between Kohut and Jung in the approach to the psychology of self, particularly around the notion of narcissism, which begin to unpick this complexity. In particular, he considers Kohut's work on the lines of maturation in narcissism to have strong convergences with Jung's work on the individuation process, although he is careful to point out that the term 'narcissism' itself is rarely used in Jungian circles. He also considers there to be clear convergence with Winnicott (2006: 6). What he considers as a common factor in these relational and depth approaches is that 'It is not narcissism itself that constitutes a personality disorder, but rather the failure of narcissism because of the unrealistic demands of the "grandiose self"' (2006: 4), this is, the part of the personality that emphasises idealised, exceptional expectations of oneself. Additionally, according to Kieffer, 'For Kohut, the archaic selfobject experience gradually evolves into mature selfobject experience. This process involves recognising the other's subjectivity through mutual empathy and introspection' (2013: 124).

So in a sense, one might think of narcissism as an everyday, normal pathology, in much the same way that persona is sometimes considered an everyday pathology of interpersonal exchange in classic Jungian thought. There are many ways in which distinctions between healthy and pathological narcissism are distinguished and manifested, but these are difficult to sustain without a mindful consideration of the term's clarification and revision. Narcissism is 'like a well-worn coin, almost without clearly defined contours yet still of considerable value' (Jacoby 2006: 4). In Kohut, there is a sense of attempting to consider narcissism in the round with a neutral value attributed to it, which contributes to a process of empathy acquisition through mutuality, recognition and introspection. It is in this sense that I consider and apply the term, although with certain caveats involving its negotiation and manifestation in social media interaction. In the following chapter, I outline my approach.

6

SELFOBJECTS AND INTERSUBJECTIVE MUTUALITY IN THE CONTEMPORARY MEDIA ECOSYSTEM

Following on from the last chapter, Papacharissi (2010) discusses the term narcissism in the context of what is popularly described as 'digital narcissism'. In many ways, her approach is as careful as Kohut's more psychologically based approach in dealing with the clarity of defining narcissism as a concept and as a phenomenon: 'employed to understand the introspection and self-absorption that takes place in blogs and similar spaces, and to place these tendencies in historical context' (2010: 145). In this approach, whereas narcissism is often associated with preoccupation with the self that is self-directed, this is not necessarily motivated through selfish reasons. It is a more neutral and less unilateral characteristic of blogging, vlogging and other popular social media practices (2010: 145). This is echoed in an aspect of Christine Kieffer's intersubjective model of recognition through mutuality and empathy. She writes (2013: xxii) that:

> Mutual recognition develops as two people meet and engage with one another – within a context of bi-directional influence. However, mutual recognition, in which there is an awareness and acceptance of the other's autonomy, is, in my opinion, often a developmental achievement. Thus, therapeutic action is aimed at helping the patient to develop a cohesive state that permits a sense of one's subjectivity while recognising the subjectivity of the other.

This technique of disclosure acts to facilitate empathy, to build and maintain trust within therapeutic contexts, but it also helps to shed light upon general processes of self-disclosure, confession and over-sharing in everyday online communications contexts. This is because it is difficult to maintain an argument where a network of social media interactions is a true example of bi-directional influence. Joinson and Paine (2012) point out that self-disclosure is 'the telling of the previously unknown so that it becomes shared knowledge.' This exists in everyday face-to-face encounters, occurring in a variety of contexts which determine its purposes. Taking the example of one-to-one relationships, 'Since self-disclosure is often reciprocated, within a dyad disclosure, it often serves to strengthen the ties that bind people in romantic or friendship-based relationships' (2012). Joinson and Paine also point towards the act of writing, particularly about traumatic or highly personal accounts, to be in some ways cathartic.

However, in the context of contemporary online communications, and the short-form micro-blogging contexts of social media in particular, the effects of online disclosure are both amplified and attributed specific, problematic social values. For a start, the public nature of disclosure between oneself and one's network amplifies the connection that would be made at a one-to-one level. It may be an act of personal communication, but at the same time is a strangely impersonal act – confessing something deeply personal to one person is very different to confessing that same detail to a multitude. In addition, the asynchronous nature of a large percentage of online communications practice reduces the context within which one is able to reciprocate and, of course, that reciprocation is not as immediate as in face-to-face communication. Disclosure in a multitude context of communications is certainly more in tune with a broadcast mode of communication, and less related to a mutual sharing of introspection to establish trust.

This happens at industrialised levels, as much as everyday uses, thanks in part, to the economic apparatus of contemporary creative industries. For instance, Jill Walker Rettberg (2014) has noted that the most successful blogs in Norway are run by young women, and have a higher daily readership than many of the top-selling Norwegian newspapers. The fact that young women have found platforms through which to speak to large audiences without censorship is something that ought to be both acknowledged and supported. However, despite this success (or indeed, because of it, perhaps) the bloggers themselves come up against incredible responses. These responses range from public commenters directly posting on their articles, to professional criticism from the established press. This criticism, most often negative, is partly attributable to a perception of narcissistic practice that stems from exhibitionism (and here, blogging and vlogging is seen as an exhibitionist practice), and the norms and values associated with expected behaviours for women in society. Walker Rettberg writes that 'blogging and selfies are not phenomena that are exclusive to women – far from it – but the accusation of blogging or selfies as being narcissistic or exhibitionistic is particularly common when women engage in these practices' (2014: 18). Therefore, there is evidence to suggest that the folk definitions of narcissism are conflated, in cultural practice, with the politics of gender norms – with the tendency to be directed negatively towards female practitioners.

The relevant aspect of this phenomenon, aside from the worrying gender politics of regulation, discipline and foreclosure against female blogging activity, is the appropriation and extension of folk definitions of narcissism into the digital realm. This aspect of 'digital narcissism', with its focus on self-admiration and the instrumental seeking of affirmations from others in order to sustain that self-image, has very little to do with Kohut's recognitive self psychology. And yet, this version of narcissism permeates the assumptions that we tend to have about heavy social media presence, and the crossed-purposes to which disclosure is put under such circumstances. Indeed, if one is to take a cynical view, then the disclosure of details to establish trust could be read as a key strategy for professional or semi-professional bloggers who wish to project a sense of authenticity and familiarity to their audience, in order to establish and maintain parasocial investment, and a 'following'. Where numbers flow, the money tends to follow. Walker Rettberg makes some interesting observations about well-known (not necessarily professional) bloggers, who resolutely maintain the attitude that they are having a conversation when they use social media to 'connect'. Indeed, she cites evidence where this bears out in a number of contexts, particularly on micro-blogging platforms such as Twitter. But it is perhaps the impersonal form and structure of the micro-blogging medium that leads us to rethink it as one of a number of mechanisms that amplifies narcissistic failure, as Kohut would put it.

Things become exponentially more complicated when the boundaries of professional and amateur are challenged in everyday micro-blogging, however. This is certainly in the way that broadcast modes of communication have become widespread, and subvert notions of celebrity that pre-existed Web 2.0. For dana boyd, everyday users of micro-blogging platforms, particularly teenagers whose heavy use has necessitated a strict level of attention to the maintenance of their social media feeds, have ended up becoming 'objectified in ways that parallel what celebrities face' (2014: 151). She goes on to write that

> This is a process that media scholar Terri Senft calls 'microcelebrity.' Teens who are famous among niche crowds get to face both the costs and the benefits of being on the receiving end of tremendous attention, but without the structural support that celebrities have—including the handlers, managers, and financial resources to cope with the onslaught of attention. This can create a heady situation, with teens simultaneously relishing that positive feedback and being deeply affected by the cruelty and pressure that often comes with it.

To my mind, this has similarities to the phenomenon of 'FOMO', or 'fear of missing out'. What is curious here is the possibility that people would tend to self-disclose more in order to increase their perceived chance of being 'let in' to a conversation (no matter how unidirectional) to participate in the social discourse of a given in-group. Such a claim may seem a little strong. However, it would perhaps help to shed light on toxic practices such as trolling which seek to draw out disinhibited acts of disclosure and cathexis. The reasons trolls do this, essentially, is in order to capture material to hold the disclosed party to ransom, both emotionally and socially. Ultimately, to expose people, for whatever reasons. Cyberbullies and trolls prey on this broadcast mode of authenticity, which is an extension of the social values of inclusion and participation.

'Contrived perfection made to get attention'

Less obviously toxic, but perhaps equally pernicious, practices in online communications and social media interactions also seek to draw out acts of disclosure and cathexis, in order to capture attention. The architecture of monetised platforms such as YouTube, for example, affords this process, and the success of very famous examples in the YouTubing community (PewDiePie, Zoella, shaycarl, Miranda Sings) evidences the way that the use of these arrangements to leverage user engagement into monetised outcomes is phenomenally effective. In fact, this architecture, and the practices afforded through the technical and cultural apparatus of YouTube, gives us insight into what happens to selfobjects and the relations afforded selfobject interaction within the context of an accelerated media ecosystem. In essence, the instrumental nature of disclosure mechanisms (not to mention the sheer amount of data generated and the automated governance of that data within the technology itself) on a platform such as YouTube feeds back into the predominant conventional forms of social interaction in contemporary societies. Kieffer (2013: 123) offers an insight, through deconstructing Kohut's original selfobjects approach in the maturing personality.

> Kohut's theory emphasised the function of the selfobject, that is, other people providing selfobject functions for the individual. Kohut emphasised this aspect of relating since he was trying to explain how infantile vitality and exuberant self-regard, as well as archaic idealism, got derailed into pathological narcissism. He was also stressing an alternate view of optimal psychological health as rooted in continuous connectedness to others – rather than an illusory autonomy.

We may take this deconstruction, and break it down even further in order to explore the implications for social media interactions, within the contexts just mentioned. In claiming that people provide selfobject functions for the developing individual, what Kohut is suggesting is that the recognition of a significant other upon which the phantasy of idealised competences may be projected is a process that provides the basic ingredients for healthy, functional interpersonal connectedness. Following on from that insight, true autonomy can only exist through that connectedness, in mutual recognition. Kohut describes a typical scenario in which a significant other such as a close family member (usually the mother) would provide the archaic vehicle through which the psychological construction of the selfobject could occur. The aforementioned projection of self-control plays a central part in the developing personality and its coming to an accommodation with the realities of dealing with external autonomous beings – and, in turn, oneself becoming a truly autonomous being. However, the problem here might be identified as a semantic one, as much as a matter of pathology.

The kinds of *connectedness* that Kieffer describes, and to which Kohut devoted his attention, relate to this mutuality and a proximal, interpersonal connection. It is clear that the mediation brought to bear through persistent *connectivity* might afford certain kinds of connection, but that mediation itself changes the *quality* of that contact. Without implying an evaluation of that quality, we may say that there is a qualitative distinction in the kinds of connectedness that are shaped through dimensions of medium-specificity. However, it is difficult to separate that level of distinction from an evaluation of those qualities. Indeed, as mentioned elsewhere, an entire literature in social psychology of communications has sprung up around this question in relation to the notion of fidelity and how the quality of communications can be judged according to the relative fidelity to face-to-face interactions (Sproull and Kiesler 1986; Joinson 2003, 2007; Joinson and Paine 2012; Joinson et al. 2012). These arguments provide evidence suggesting that fewer social context cues and non-verbal communicative forms (all of which remain more or less present in face-to-face interactions) present themselves as the level of fidelity to face-to-face interaction diminishes. The lower the fidelity, the poorer the quality of the communication. It follows that such fidelity, and the relative qualities of interaction associated with medium-specificity and connectivity, provide conditions through which the selfobject process is disrupted.

However, even in proximal, face-to-face interaction, the selfobject process has immediate derailing potential, where the exertion of self-control becomes a struggle to overcome shortcomings and a descent into self-loathing and inadequacy. In social media interactions, this struggle is lived through time and time again, where idealised images contribute to defining the cultural worth of the profile (and the person) they represent. This struggle is, additionally, amplified and accelerated through an intensification of real-time media surrounds. As Charlie Gere remarked (and, it should be noted, some time ago), this real-time ecosystem has evolved a '[. . .] general trend toward *instantaneity* in contemporary culture, involving increasing demand for instant feedback and response, one result of which is that technologies themselves are beginning to evolve ever faster' (2006: 1 [my emphasis]). When one adds to this the rapid-response of selfie culture and its accoutrements of commentary and criticism, associated in part with notions of image, beauty, perfection and self-esteem, one ends up with a potent cultural topography of value and esteem, the shared meaning of which is established and traversed, through social interaction.

The well-publicised example of Essena O'Neill is a case in point here. O'Neill, a teenaged fashion model from Australia, who had captured modelling contracts ostensibly thanks to her massively popular Instagram and Vimeo following, described the practices involved in finding the perfect selfie as 'contrived perfection made to get attention' (Hunt 2015). By her own admission, O'Neill's saturated presence on social media 'served no real purpose other than self-promotion' and left her deeply unhappy, unfulfilled, disconnected from people and the everyday world and disillusioned with the cultural weight placed upon appearance and conventions of beauty. In an interview with *Teen Vogue* (Ceron 2015), O'Neill gave a candid, reflective account of her experiences:

'When I started wearing makeup at school, I guess I started to become popular. Boys started liking me. When I started posting photos like this, it received so much attention. So I guess for me, it was like, oh, I'm better like this. Or actually, I'm not enough without this,' she says. [. . .] 'I wore makeup to feel better about myself, which is ridiculous because I actually wasn't feeling better, per se.' She added that, 'This perfect girl in this picture that got 23,000 likes, this girl looked in the mirror most days and hated her appearance.'

The instrumental nature of social media interaction and, in this case, the specific focus on image production on Instagram, amplifies these cathecting processes and increases the rapidity of feedback in an accelerated mode of engagement. This is necessary for two reasons. First, in a purely economic sense, the monetising function of Instagram lends itself to a potential (and in many ways, realistic) career aspiration where the very successful are able to achieve substantial earnings. According to Hunt (2015) O'Neill was able to make at least 2000 AUD income for each post, from marketing and endorsements, to her 612,000 followers. This creates a potent incentive for the social media celebrities themselves, not to mention incentive for the formation of considerable industrial apparatus surrounding and facilitating professional social media careers. But there is a second, intertwined reason. For a user fanbase, this establishes a powerful parasocial investment in a selfobject whose existence seems to attest to or 'prove' idealised competence. Her fanbase, fully aware of the constructed nature of O'Neill's image, nonetheless abided it because it fulfilled the phantasy of idealised competence. Perhaps this emotive fulfilment, writ large through social media interactions on the various feeds and platforms across O'Neill's online presence, provided the platform for fans to seek approval and esteem (from themselves and each other). This reveals the need to entertain the more phenomenological dimensions of self and, in particular, regarding the concept of self as subjectivity (rather than self as self-sustaining, as an isolated or unitary ideal). For Kieffer, this acknowledgement highlights 'the essential and una-voidable contextual embeddedness for ourselves in relation to others – whether in the dyad, the small group of the family, or in the larger community' (2013: 173). We may add to this the context of relationships that are forged and maintained through semi-permanent connectivity.

Essena O'Neill was successful, influential and, conventionally speaking, seemed to possess an awe-inspiring beauty. At the same time, the lessons learned from O'Neill's case suggest that such fixation on ideals can stall the process of full self-realisation on both sides. It diminishes the concept of self as subjectivity, and instead engages self as a unitary idealised form. She was not happy, and her fans were even less happy to see her lift the veil, withdraw from social media and pub-licly expose its constructed nature. Her behaviour in withdrawing from her social media career provoked what seems to be disproportional negative commentary from users. But I think that, although undoubtedly unfortunate and certainly unfair towards O'Neill, this kind of reaction is understandable. With so much parasocial, emotional investment in this narrative world of the 'Essena O'Neill' brand, fans had much to lose. O'Neill provided the idealised competence necessary to face the image (the imagined, psychological construct) that the fans had of themselves when they looked in the mirror, and evaluate according to the criteria consented to in the process of social and brand interaction.

What is at stake here, aside from the worrying dimensions of body-image fixation, is that in the accelerated world of social media interaction, this focus on unitary, idealised competence, amplified and endlessly reflexive, ultimately pushes away mutuality as a possibility. As Kieffer states, 'While people need selfobjects throughout their lives, the development of insight about other people's rights and feelings, along with the capacity to "shore up the self" of the other, is also essential to self-development' (2013: 126). The continuation of this relational capacity towards imagined ideals is important and necessary, as it facilitates empathy. However, in cases like O'Neill's, it is difficult to see in either direction (towards celebrity or fan) the facility to maintain a 'shoring up of the self of the other.' This has implications for recognition theory, where mutuality is essential as a developmental achievement. Where the journey towards an ethical personality ends at the stage of idealised competence, criticism rather than recognition becomes the measure of success. Projected self-control is effectively returned to sender.

It is interesting that, in writing about the psychological functionality of this in a psychoanalytic context, Kieffer questions this self-regard aspect of an imagined critical ideal. She asks: 'Can an empathic stance truly be broadened to include the occasional, well-timed criticism – can the mirror reveal the patient to himself viewed as others may see him or must it only mirror him as he wishes to be seen?' (2013: 125). If this question is broadened to focus on social media interaction, how does the accelerated surround of reflexive, image-driven communication amplify these views? There seems to be another 'tension gradient' at work here, this time not only between the constituents of the self, but between the constituents of self- and other-regarding. Reflexive and image-driven communication lends itself to, and ultimately affords, an amplification of self-disclosure – of making oneself vulnerable to idealised and real criticism – in order to maintain a semblance of connectedness to others.

There may well be a temptation here to elide the notion of continuous *connectedness* with the kinds of persistent *connectivity* that I have been describing throughout the book so far. However, this is more a case of a need to connect and feel recognised, as being in tension with the compulsion to enact connectivity through social networks. The former requires the social, the latter, although arising from and pertaining to the social perhaps, does not require it. Connectivity, as explored in Chapter 3, merely needs its mythic content to sustain itself. This distinction and tension gradient between connectedness and connectivity is based upon the principle of continuity of being, in the relational sense, rather than any appeal to psychological ill-health through semi-permanent connectivity. The mythic content and formal elements of connectivity that Jacoby has written about, and the desire for connectivity in everyday discourse, is brought together in tension through the practice of self-disclosure, which can be seen in the context of social media interactions, to have a disinhibition effect.

Here, my perspective on disinhibited acts of self-disclosure is informed by John Suler's highly influential essay, 'The Online Disinhibition Effect' (2004). Suler's social psychology approach is perhaps most useful for our context in relation to his notion of 'Solipsistic Introjection', a dimension of online disinhibition that describes a projection of imagined otherness in the communications practices between users where aspects of anonymity necessarily justify self-disclosure in order to finesse a semblance of trust between users. Where online communications most often operate within reduced-social-cue contexts (lacking facial expression and non-verbal cues especially), Suler suggests that people's self-boundaries can become significantly altered to account for this. Suler suggests (2004: 323) that

> People may sense that their mind has merged with the mind of the online companion. Reading another person's message might be experienced as a voice within one's head, as if that person's psychological presence has been internalized or introjected into one's psyche. One may not know what the other person's voice actually sounds like, so in one's mind, often unconsciously, a voice is assigned to that person.

To take a dramaturgical metaphor for interaction performance, there is therefore a certain sense in which the online other becomes a player in one's intrapsychic world. This is a player whose character is based partly on the other's self-presentation, and based partly on the representations formed through one's wishes and needs, as well as through images of relationships experienced and imagined. For Suler, this is developed to the point that 'Online text communication can evolve into an introjected psychological tapestry in which a person's mind weaves these fantasy role plays, usually unconsciously and with considerable disinhibition' (Suler 2004: 323). Therefore, one might suggest that the mediation of interpersonal communication disrupts what might be described as a motivation towards intersubjective connectedness. After all, in always-on, real-time contexts where demands for interaction are multiple and couched in values associated with immediacy of response, full-disclosure and psychologically projected self-control to a multitude audience, the user's responsiveness fuels connectivity, adding to its mythic content as a desirable social lubricant.

However, the pressure to self-disclose within such contexts leaves little room for nuance or other-regarding, and this may have an adverse cumulative effect on one's own self esteem. Kieffer sees self-disclosure as a critical function in interpersonal communications, and 'Judicious self-disclosure is fine if well-timed and should occur within the context of a dependable self-selfobject' (2013: 135). What Kieffer refers to here is Kohut's notion of self-selfobject: a self-ideal, which needs to be attainable in order to provide the affirmative materials necessary for a beneficial result, and lead to a progressive measure of self-esteem and mutual respect. This mirrors the anthropological practices that Honneth identified in the *Struggle for*

Recognition, when he writes that the reproduction of social life is '[. . .] governed by the imperative of mutual recognition, because one can develop a practical relationship-to-self only when one has learned to view oneself, from the normative perspective of one's partner in interaction, as their social addressee' (1995: 92).

However, in social media interactions, I argue that the psychological dimensions of this acquisition of self-affirmation through the practical relation-to-self is amplified by several magnitudes out of proportion. The superhuman feats which we have to undertake in order to manage all of these online tasks and respond to demands in real time, *in addition to* the always-already need to fulfil self-affirmation, feed into the mythology of connectivity as a standard where all users are (necessarily) idealistically competent. The mythic content is further underpinned through the systematic rewarding of interaction quantity between the levels of technological system, user-base and the nexus of cultural-economic value; interaction generates the data, which draws in the money, which further incentivises the generation of encouragement for increased interaction. And so it goes, in a self-fulfilling circle involving human and non-human interactions, mirroring Jaron Lanier's observation that 'Communication is now often experienced as a superhuman phenomenon that towers above individuals' capacity to keep up, or indeed, even to be able to observe with any great accuracy or awareness, of those interactions and real-time pressures. This is a context in which 'A new generation has come of age with a reduced expectation of what a person can be, and of who each person might become' (2010: 4).

What is crucial here is to remain mindful that intersubjective mutuality is still a possibility, where it emerges through *striving* for connectedness (as much as connectivity) in social interactions, and that this connectedness can happen regardless of the medium (and, sometimes, despite it). The circular mediation process outlined above certainly provides a distraction from this striving for mutuality, but its derailment is far from inevitable. This brings us back to the notion of mutual recognition as an embodiment of this human capacity to strive for connectedness, and is a cornerstone of the influential work of psychoanalyst Jessica Benjamin. Marie Hoffman has suggested that 'Benjamin depicts mutual recognition as the capacity to see others as equal subjects with needs, desires, and perspectives that can differ from one's own, and the reciprocating experience of the other's acknowledgement of oneself' (2011: 12). This is fundamental to the notion of interdependent mutuality and self-affirmation alluded to some moments ago.

In her essay 'Beyond Doer and Done to: An Intersubjective View of Thirdness', Benjamin defines intersubjectivity '[. . .] in terms of a relationship of mutual recognition—a relation in which each person experiences the other as a "like subject," another mind who can be "felt with," yet has a distinct, separate center of feeling and perception' (2004: 5). Clearly this position on the intersubjective has notable antecedents, which Benjamin duly acknowledges. The thoughts of Hegel (1994 [1807]), Kojève (1969) and Winnicott (1956) all make influential contributions to the notion of intersubjectivity as a fundamental aspect of human consciousness and mutual recognition, and all, if in quite different ways,

'[. . .] try to specify the process by which we become able to grasp the other as having a separate yet similar mind' (2004: 5). However, Benjamin's perspective emphasises 'both developmentally and clinically, how we actually come to the felt experience of the other as a separate yet connected being with whom we are acting reciprocally' (2004: 5).

It is this capacity for mutual recognition in the development of a felt experience of connectedness that forms the basis for Benjamin's intersubjectivity theory. In her synthesis of Hegel's struggle for recognition and Winnicott's formative experience of the other as differentiated subject, Benjamin 'views recognition of separate objectivity as both the necessary predisposition for ethical behaviour and "love, in the sense of discovering the other [. . .]"' (2011: 13). Love is here used in the same sense as the first form of intersubjective recognition in Honneth's thought. What is novel in Benjamin's extension of this, however, is the idea that love as an expressive form is a *discovery of the other*. So, whereas for Hegel a common interpretation might be to see the struggle for recognition to be a struggle that ends in domination (and this is certainly an interpretation that colours Hoffman's perspective on Benjamin's Hegelian recognition), 'For Benjamin, struggle ends in mutuality, an achievement of holding the tensions of difference rather than reaching a zero-tension equilibrium' (Hoffman 2011: 13). It is an ongoing process that remains an *opera aperta*. It is unfinished, unresolved, yet it is essential to the connectedness and empathic capacities afforded through mutual recognition. For Benjamin, recognition is, essentially, 'a paradox that is never fully resolved but rather continues as a "state of constant tension between recognizing the other and asserting the self"' (Kieffer 2013: 127). It is worth quoting Benjamin in full here, because in her notion of intersubjective recognition Benjamin develops mutuality as a depth concept of developmental achievement, profoundly influenced by Winnicott and, by association, Kohut. For Benjamin, recognition arises through the development and process of mirroring by an idealised other. She writes (2004: 6) that

> In highlighting this phenomenological experience of other minds, I [. . .] emphasize the reciprocal, mutually influencing quality of interaction between subjects, the confusing traffic of two-way streets. But this theoretical recognition of intersubjective influence should not blind us to the power of actual psychic experience, which all too often is that of the one-way street—in which we feel as if one person is the doer, the other done to. One person is subject, the other object—as our theory of object relations all too readily portrays.

Such aspects of object-relations theory tend to emphasis a dualism and dyadic relation between agents in social interactions, and there is a certain reduction in this scenario, of people to things. It is entirely likely that, in the light of what I have been discussing so far in this chapter, this reification process is intensified in conditions of persistent connectivity. However, Benjamin does give pause for thought on this, and offers a potentially liberating, third direction – a space which she actually terms as the *third*, and which is experienced subjectively and intersubjectively as *thirdness*. She writes that 'I think in terms of thirdness as a quality or experience of intersubjective relatedness that has as its correlate a certain kind of internal mental space; it is closely related to Winnicott's idea of potential or transitional space' (2004: 6). In enacting this third space in our interactions, and in mobilising an awareness of how thirdness connects us in fundamental ways in a mutual recognition of subjectivity, one in the other, there is a sense here that Benjamin holds on to the notion that self-disclosure forms a mutual ground. This is the grounding through which the other's point of view or reality can be taken into account and empathically acknowledged. To do this, a certain surrendering of self (a surrendering of 'ego' in the folk sense of the term) is necessary. It is this aspect of mutuality that Benjamin claims is recognitive. Surrender implies 'recognition—being able to sustain connectedness to the other's mind while accepting his separateness and difference. Surrender implies freedom from any intent to control or coerce' (2004: 7). Thus, the development of autonomy can be understood, recognised in oneself and in the other and applied accordingly in social interactions.

In the previous chapter, I asked a question along the following lines, suggesting that some of the issues discussed in Chapter 4 could be usefully extended: to what extent is it necessary to develop the psychological aspects of Honneth's model of self-realisation to fully account for fragmentary notions of personhood found in the always-on? During the course of this current section, I have attempted to extend this aspect of connectivity to take into account some of disinhibited effects that emerge through the challenging environments presented to us in contemporary accelerated media ecosystems. Benjamin's notion of mutual recognition through intersubjective experience and the possibility of a third space may provide an elegant solution to these challenges. However, one must fully acknowledge the difficulties in building up the trust and skill required to maintain such a space in real-world social interactions, let alone the altogether 'superhuman' zone of reduced expectation that Lanier has suggested exists in today's social media world. Whether the possibilities for building and maintaining a third space are disrupted or diminished though persistent, always-on connectivity is a matter for further empirical study beyond the scope of this book.

However, one might begin to consider from a communitarian and convivialist perspective, a theoretical assertion that the process towards the development of an ethical personality, in Honneth's terms, is compromised in the always-on condition. A potential disruption of this compromise may be found through the possibilities of thirdness. It is certainly a challenge to be met in future thinking on connectivity ethics. In particular, I would argue that this might form the basis of an approach to inform the design of processes and interfaces whose purposes are ostensibly to afford connectedness between people as autonomous subjects (rather than people as governed elements of a system, or between machines). Such design needs to take the role that mutual recognition plays within connectivity ethics seriously. In this sense, we may reconnect a line of inquiry from Chapter 2, namely, R. D. Laing's notion of a 'creative relationship with the other', in which there is a mutual enrichment of the self and of the other. For Laing (1965) such mutual creativity can be thought of as a 'benign circle': a good in itself that promotes well-being and accommodates difference, without resorting to a sterile relation between anonymous and equal entities. The co-creative space that Benjamin describes has much in common with Laing's benign circle, because in both concepts we find a reciprocally constitutive and convivial way of being which at the very least recognises the possibility of other-regarding, and mutual self-development.

Another question I had asked earlier in this chapter referred to the development and maintenance of identity: how do persons develop and maintain their identity, their sense of themselves as practical, moral beings with unique characteristics and distinctive places in the social media world? As intimated, I think that the common practice of self-disclosure plays a key role in this process, and has both benign and toxic aspects. As discussed earlier, people tend to self-disclose for any number of personal reasons. In face-to-face communications, the trust that develops through shared disclosure is a social mechanism helps to furnish such interactions with a sense of recognition that there exists autonomous interests in each party. In online contexts, people tend to self-disclose in order to build and maintain trust in a real-time, accelerated context, in which feedback is immediate, instantaneity and availability are expected and criticism is standard (in particular, with regards to image-driven judgement). Therefore, the space and time in which to develop trust through self-disclosure in this depth sense is missing and, as suggested earlier, is replaced with value-judgement as a substitute. My feeling is that, once again, further empirical research is necessary to establish the extent of this substitution and the extent of awareness that such processes occur. Such work would seek to assess the impact of this pressure upon practical everyday strategies. Additionally, the key to understanding these processes revolves around a systematic mapping of digital and data awareness in a range of contexts, and across a wide range of demographics to assert educational and cultural need at the point of practice. At the time of completing this book, I have just begun work with colleagues on a project to assess these issues at a regional level (specifically, Scotland), with a view to extending this work nationally, and replicating the studies and exercises developed on an international level (Singh and Borges Rey, forthcoming).

Within these contexts, I think it is a fairly safe claim that, following Honneth, individuals become who they are in and through relations of mutual recognition with others, and that this remains a valid argument. However, a further development of this in relation to aspects of self as online entities (which paradoxically are associated with real-world entities – i.e., people) is required to extend this argument to its logical conclusion. To what extent might we agree with Lanier when he suggests that the [. . .] 'widespread practice of fragmentary, impersonal communication has *demeaned* interpersonal interaction' (2010: 4 [my emphasis])?

This appears to be a moral argument, with practical, ethical implications for everyday interactions. However, there are additional complications. As Jill Walker Rettberg (2014: 63–4) has commented:

> Although people have been tracking their personal data for centuries, the combination of data generated through wearable devices and online services that can automatically log personal data with our increasing ability to store and process large quantities of data has led to a surge of interest in personal tracking and data analysis. The interest isn't solely driven by technology. Society in general is increasingly invested in quantitative measures that we hope will allow us to improve our performance.

Walker Rettberg's take on this may well go some way towards addressing the more open-ended questions I have deliberately left remaining in this chapter, particularly regarding the possibility that mutual recognition is disrupted or degraded at best when considering social interactions within the accelerated media ecosystem. For Walker Rettberg, society seems to be invested in moving away from qualitative differences, and towards quantitative systems, which are traditionally associated with cultures of productivity and efficiency. She mentions the terms 'performance', which is common enough in persona studies, and in the study of identity politics. However, there seems to be a secondary implication – performance *of* what, exactly? Performance *for* what? Locally, and empirically, we could suggest that this kind of 'quantified self' practice fulfils a perceived need to engage in (and disclose one's engagement in a publicly viewable arena) with the process of self-actualisation. The transformative discourses around such processes have established a commonly understood ground for mythologising the practice of 'becoming who you really are'. I discussed this paradoxical aspect of popular culture elsewhere (Singh 2015), which finds expression in many different areas of consumer culture: celebrity culture, the cosmetics industry, the beauty myth, public relations and, of course, reality television programming. There seems to be, common to all of these threads of popular culture, a performative aspect of personhood – a 'versioning' process of the self, which escapes recognition in the depth sense because it is perfectly satisfied to settle for a recognition based upon relatively superficial acknowledgement of socio-economic success or cultural achievement. In this scenario, there is again little incentive to allow for a thirdness to develop, and in fact, there could be a strong claim to the very opposite – that, essentially, thirdness would disrupt the quantification process, because it seeks to recognise autonomous claims and qualitative differences between people that are in some way expressions of authenticity.

In the next and final chapter, I triangulate a number of perspectives to bring together an argument around some of the questions I have left open here. This includes the notion that, for Walker Rettberg at least, there is a sense of self that is not only quantifiable but is also, through common cultural practice, quantified, and that this is regarded by many to be a desirable, positive, liberating phenomenon. We might describe this as a 'self-commodification' process, where individuals act as agents to populate data profiles that 'perform' their representation in connected systems. And, although related to the idea of the 'commodification of self', ostensibly a political economic concept that addresses monetisation, the division of labour and the distribution of wealth flows in online business models (amongst other things) is a quite different approach. Self-commodification as a cultural practice seeks to justify its own processes through psychosocial mechanisms of versioning and establishes authenticity through identity-performance in what I call the 'false-self system' of the social media world.

7

SOCIAL MEDIA AS A FALSE-SELF SYSTEM

In the Charlie Brooker-helmed television drama *Black Mirror* (Ch4/Netflix 2011–present), there is a moment in the episode 'The Entire History of You' when the two main characters Liam and Ffion (played by Toby Kebbell and Jodie Whittaker) are having sex in their marital bed. We are witness to their lovemaking as a discernibly passionate encounter full of physical satisfaction, signified through energetic heavy-breathing, moaning and sweat. We see the couple enthusiastically snatch at each other's bodies, apprehending each other in a grasp of mutual body-recognition – one in the other, each as one whole part of a greater union. It is, in other words, a representation of an idealised sexual encounter between two people who would seem very much in love. The scene is abruptly intercut with another in which the same couple, in the same bed, are still having sex – but something altogether disturbing is revealed in this alternating effect. The premise behind 'The Entire History of You' is based around speculative prosthetic memory technologies, where nearly all of the characters in the episode have had a small device implanted in their head called 'grains'. These implants record everything they see, and from these recordings they are able to re-watch (and thus, to an extent, relive) moments from the past, either privately, or in company through television monitoring. This documentation lifestyle is very much an extrapolation of the ways in which people have adopted social media technologies to share abundant images of their lives. From holiday snaps to breakfast to ultrasound images, photo albums and social media galleries and 'stories' act as evidence to satisfy the lifestyle clarion call of 'pics or it never happened'. It is also reflective of the normalisation of this evidential behaviour – characters who have not had 'grains' fitted are considered curiosities, anomalies; much like those who have not adopted Facebook and other massively popular Web 2.0 technologies in real life, they are outliers.

Throughout the episode, various characters use the playback function to re-examine aspects of their lives. Most instances are fun and rather trivial, involving selfies and the production of other recordings that can be watched in company on a television screen. In the scene described above, it is revealed to us through intercutting that Liam and Ffion use the memory technology to watch playback from recordings of their lovemaking past, in order to augment the sex of the present, each viewing their own perspective privately. The revelation for us as viewers, sutured into a complicity with the characters thanks to the extensive use of point-of-view shots in the episode, is the disturbing realisation that both of the characters are entirely focused on their own playback image, rather than the person they are actually having sex with. This masturbatory mode of technologically enhanced sexual activity is made all the more alienating to watch because of the blank expressions on Liam and Ffion's faces – exacerbated by the way the technology makes their eyes turn pure white when viewing private playback. The sex is consensual, there is little doubt on that count – and a conciliatory kiss is shared by the couple once the sex is finished. However, one is left with the feeling that both characters are deeply into a privatised experience of sexuality – transactional, almost. The kiss signifies care, but there is a discernible distinction made between that and the sexual act during the course of this particular scene.

The main problem, somewhat ironically (given that many popular cultural representations of autosexual activity focuses on the relative dysfunctionality of masturbation), relates to the fact that neither character is alone – they are actually in the physical presence of another, and so, to borrow from Sherry Turkle's phrase once more, they are 'alone together' (2011). In some ways the facilitation of solitary fantasy might be more understandable given that the other would *not* be present. In fact, one of the other characters relays such a use during a dinner party scene. Furthermore, one might imagine this technology in a more positive light where, say, a partner is away working and physical intimacy is simply impossible; or perhaps where a disability might hamper physical mobility, and such technology is used as an augmentation. In such cases, one might speculate that technology can facilitate a relationship. But the scene described in *Black Mirror* is a case of an altogether different kind – it looks routine, perfunctory, joyless. On the one hand, the characters have literally objectified one another's bodies, for the sake of reliving a past sexual encounter, and then adding a real-time sexual component to it; on the other, they have both literalised the objectification of the other as an image, rather than as a whole person. Indeed, the impression we are given is that the other body in this situation could be anyone's. However, because they happen to be married to the person they are watching, and to the person they are having intercourse with (although the two experiences are on distinct experiential registers), no adultery is being committed. The evidence from this scene may be summed up in that, to an extent, both parties in the marriage are on fairly safe moral ground, but ethically speaking there are issues around the disruption of mutuality in a fully matured relationship that are troublesome. In addition, the moral status of Ffion's actions come under scrutiny later in the episode, as do the ethics of Liam's actions in the use of the technology and the consequences he sets in motion as a result.

Of course, such disturbing imagery is easy enough to condemn, but the realities of married life, with children in the mix, are challenging, and a technology that could conveniently augment one's marital expectations might be viewed as a straight-forwardly transactional solution. Indeed, these are issues that form a favourite subject of discussion in both popular culture and on the psychotherapist's couch. In *The Divided Self* (1965: 86), R. D. Laing describes a case in which one of his patients, who otherwise conducted his life along normal lines,

> [. . .] could never have intercourse with his wife but only with his own image of her. That is, his body had physical relations with her body, but his mental self, while this was going on, could only look on what his body was doing and/or imagine himself having intercourse with his wife as an object of his imagination.

This account describes, in quite stark terms, the fullest expression of false-self as a normal pathology in Laing's thought, and reflects, psychologically, what is literalised in 'The Entire History of You'. Not necessarily an aspect of contemporary culture that is unfamiliar – we do, after all, live in image-driven times – nonetheless, Laing drives home the objectification apparent in everyday life which has the power to disrupt congress, impoverish what we are told should be a moment of absolute intimacy with someone we love the most, through an existential pattern of objec-tification and alienation. The relative pleasures which one may experience as a sexual and sexualised being are here offset by a psychic deadness, and a disconnect between the inner world of one's emotions and the outer world of social being. It is problematic enough, one suspects, to even countenance the discretion with which inner and outer are treated here – as a binary, as if the two are somehow separate aspects of consciousness. But given that Laing's work is often mobilised through dialectical- rather than picture-thinking, once suspects that this is not his empha-sis. Rather, the binary is a symptom of the disconnect, and this disconnect forms through the breakdown of mutuality as a principle in our most valued relationships.

So far in Part II of this book, I have discussed similar descriptions of rec-ognition (and its disruption) from a number of fields relevant to the study of interpersonal communications in Web 2.0 contexts. Having outlined Honneth's rich description of recognition in light of the notion of 'reciprocated confidences' and the 'reciprocally constitutive', I offered a strategy whereby Honneth's application of object-relations theory to the concept of recognition could be reinforced through the self-psychology of Heinz Kohut, and in par-ticular Kohut's pathology of narcissistic success and failure. This psychosocial mechanism of narcissism in self-psychology is the same mechanism that affords the development of mutuality through confidence, respect and esteem in social interaction and ultimately provides the foundation to enable human actors to develop empathy. I progressed this approach by describing Kohut's transhistoric narrative of self-realisation, as a narrative that embodies an interpersonal princi-ple of mutuality that encapsulates recognition as a bodily-emotional, moral and social phenomenon; and it is this aspect of self-realisation that allowed me to tentatively outline a depth and relational approach towards ethical personality (in Honneth's parlance) in social (media) relations.

In this final chapter, I wish to elaborate the depth dimension of this approach, by expanding on my discussion of self-realisation as a psychosocial phenomenon that hinges upon the recognitive principle of mutuality. I shall do this through discussion of classical and post-Jungian thinking on persona, as well as drawing from other psychological schools. I then engage a specific derivation of the term 'complex' from Jungian depth psychology to explore the intricacies of authenticity as a recognitive notion in social media interactions. The complex in this sense brings together the building blocks of the psyche, often experienced as partial personalities in the Jungian terminology, but in addition raises the question of 'cultural complexes' as constellations of psychic and social space interacting and mutually impacting. This is, specifically, a psychosocial development of the original term in post-Jungian thought and psychotherapy (Singer 2000; Singer and Kimbles 2004; Singer 2004; Kimbles 2000). In what follows in this current chapter, I hope to make an original contribution to the understanding of the psychology of online interaction, within a framework that might describe social media as *a false-self system*. I begin my discussion by developing my application of Laing and his existential approach to psychology. In considering his contribution to our understanding of separateness and relatedness as an existential equilibrium, we might begin to further understand this as underpinning broader social interaction in the relationship between self and other, and how Web 2.0 technologies amplify this equilibrium.

Personae, separateness and relatedness

The existential-phenomenological work of the psychiatrist and psychotherapist R. D. Laing has been influential in my thinking on the development of personality, social interaction and, in particular, familial relationships and their role in the development of an 'authentic' sense of self. I fully acknowledge that Laing's approach, and some of his practices, were not without controversy. However, his overview of the existential equilibrium of separateness and relatedness in everyday pathology, as developed in his influential book *The Divided Self* (1965), ought to be of particular interest to students of social media. The somewhat under-acknowledged observations he made on the notion of authenticity in one's attitude to the self, and the parasocial interface of identity, have immediate relevance for the ways in which contemporary connectivity shapes how we see ourselves, in relation to others. It underpins a sense of self-recognition (through aspects of what might be framed in popular discourse as self-esteem) and also the recognition of others (especially in the sense of other-regarding and empathy). When read retrospectively, in some ways to my mind at least, Laing's work also pertains to a distinctive Jungian tone. This is especially discernible in the implications of his acknowledgement of the role of the *imago*, the psychological *image*, so to speak, in the relationship between self and other. His approach draws explicitly from the Jungian notion of *persona* as a structuring archetype. For example, he writes (1965: 95) that

'A man without a mask' is indeed very rare. One even doubts the possibility of such a man. Everyone in some measure wears a mask, and there are many things we do not put ourselves into fully. In 'ordinary' life it seems hardly possible for it to be otherwise.

This concept of social masks, worn to suit the occasion, is a familiar one; as is its application to social media interactions, and to Web entrepreneurship, where microcelebrity depends largely upon reaching audience segments in ways that tap into popular typology. This is a conscious strategy, to build alignments of identification or sympathy and, ultimately, audience engagement (and emotional, parasocial investment).

The etymology here is instrumental. As I have often discussed with students when examining the performative aspects of Instagramming, or Facebook status updates for example, the etymology of persona works as a reminder of what we might already intuitively know about persona as a psychosocial mechanism. The persona in ancient Greek theatre referred to the mask a performer wore, symbolising a character's traits and representing something of the character's inner nature or essence. It signified the true role of the character in the drama, for the audience to evaluate and engage with. The performance, through use of the persona, invited the audience to infer qualities inherent in the wearer, encouraging a belief in the verisimilitude of performance, where the masquerade is fully acknowledged as a representation. The performative or dramaturgical aspects of this have not gone unnoticed social media scholarship, where aspects of performativity lend themselves to the notion of masquerade, and aspects of dramaturgy lend themselves to notions of staging, iconography and *mise-en-scène*. These kinds of approaches are noted particularly in social interactionist approaches where the application of Goffman's notion of performance of self in everyday life drew heavily from the accoutrements of theatre, staging and performance as an analogy for self-presentation (Athique 2013; Goffman 1997; Papacharissi 2010; Walker Rettberg 2008, 2014).

One may take this analogy further, by considering the allegorical and psychic aspects of self-presentation in social interactions; Jung used the notion of persona to describe the phenomenon of social role-playing as a structuring psychic phenomena (or *archetype*), complementary to the social mechanism employed in interpersonal communications. To put it another way, persona in the Jungian sense is the psychic structuring presence refracted through the social face an individual presents to the world. It is a psychological figure that speaks to both inner and outer dimensions of one's consciousness, and is essential to self-expression in social situations, to the relative stability of personality and to the establishment and maintenance of mature relationships. In his *Two Essays on Analytical Psychology* (1953), Jung described the archetypal notion of persona as '[. . .] a kind of mask, designed on the one hand to make a definite impression upon others, and on the other to conceal the true nature of the individual' (1953: 190). So, for Jung (pre-empting Laing), persona performs this dual masking function of revelation and concealment to protect the sense one has of a coherent self. This facilitates the interpersonal aspects of social life by enabling individuals to enter into the risky business of social relationships, through both opening 'oneself' to others and through protecting those aspects of the personality that lie in a more fragile state, akin to ego. This is similar in many ways to the 'tension gradient' between the various constituents of self, found in Kohut's self-psychology as discussed in Chapter 5, where the materials of our social interactions are defined and realised through the distinctions and continuities of self- and other-regarding. This is done, ultimately, in a trust-themed everyday drama where both conscious choices and unconscious notions of what we ultimately share of ourselves with others define the relationships we find ourselves in.

In his own approach to this relationship structure, Jung tried to account for the depth and complexity of the human personality, in its dialogical nature. This dual function of revelation and concealment is similar in many ways to subsequent theorisation of the psychological notion of 'false-self': a social face of personality and that aspect of oneself that presents in interpersonal interaction. We have already seen similar notions in the example of Laing, but this notion additionally appears in several different traditions in psychology. In another well-known example, Donald Winnicott wrote that the false-self is a defensive mechanism, designed to facilitate personal relationships through 'compliance' with what others might expect of us (1965). As with Laing's approach, and to an extent with Kohut, there is a sense in Winnicott's version of false-self, especially in more extreme pathological cases, that the presentation of self is a show, masking a feeling of inner deadness or a creeping sense of inauthenticity.

In this version, the false-self works in social contexts by deflecting from others' suspicion of one's detachment from relationships and the world. It also reflects Jung's version in which there is an everyday normal pathology of feeling fake or phoney in some way that leads the individual ego to build a deception or persona as a defence mechanism against emotional distress. In Winnicott's approach, this is built up in infancy, and is subsequently reinforced through life, as relationships develop or fall away, and as our social networks are established. Through unconscious processes of introjection, internalisation of the experience of others and, in more extreme cases, through the imitation and internalisation of other people's behaviour, this false-self comes to be (mis)recognised by others and even by oneself as the whole thing, the 'real me'. This has real-world implications for which accelerated forms of misrecognition have developed in social media interactions. I have written about the specifics of these implications elsewhere (2017), and this was the topic of discussion in Chapter 4, referring to misrecognition as social disrespect.

Although the same individual could 'put on' different personas (or personae) in order to deal with the various relationships in his/her life (e.g., wife, mother, sister, daughter, employee, carer, party animal), these are not just conscious decisions and personal choices made to suit the social occasion. For Jung, in the proper sense, the persona is part of an intrapsychic apparatus, an ego operation interfacing between one's internal experiences and one's social being. Where there are obvious, conscious choices to be made in social interactions, the psyche uses the less-conscious operations of persona to cope with the demands of maintaining sophisticated social relationships by mediating between the internal world and the external world. Notions of acceptance and acceptable behaviour, awareness of context, collaboration and competition – these interactions all demand a complex social interface such as persona, because they impact upon the integrity of one's personality and one's status as a person with distinct, autonomous interests. To put it another way, social compliance places a number of demands upon the individual to curb unfettered self-ish-ness, and a functioning persona copes with these demands, helping to facilitate a coherent and continuous sense of self. Although rarely referring explicitly to theories from classical Jung (a notable exception being Balick 2014b), and even more rarely relating to disclosure practices that amount to much beyond conscious strategies for finessing social management, these aspects of social interface are fully acknowledged in some approaches to the critical study of social media. For example, Mendelson and Papacharissi (2011: 252) note that

> In everyday life, people consciously and unconsciously work to define the way they are perceived, hoping to engender positive impressions of themselves. This effort entails emphasizing certain characteristics, through dress, hairstyle, behavior and/or speech, while hiding or diminishing other characteristics perceived as flawed, depending on the context.

This is literalised in everyday practices of 'impression management' in social media and other online interactions. In fact, it is commonplace to use different social media applications to facilitate different kinds of social interactions, expectations and levels of relationship intimacy. A number of studies, including social research of practices in interactions between teenagers (e.g., Vandebosch et al. 2013) show that it is common practice to manage multiple FB and SNS profiles for different audiences, expressing different public faces or personae for different situations. For example, so-called *Rinsta* and *Finsta* profiles – respectively, a 'real Instagram' profile to interact with one's peers, and a 'fake Instagram' profile to work as a decoy to assuage parental anxiety around 'stranger danger', grooming and other perceived threats to children. The Finsta account is the one that (typically) a teenager will allow a parent full access to, using it as a front of sorts to distract from activity disclosed on the real account that might be deemed by an authority figure as inappropriate, shameful or prohibited.

It ought to be noted that although this is ostensibly deceptive behaviour that most parents would hesitate to endorse, it is one mechanism among many through which teenagers are able to explore and develop their sense of identity independent of an authority whose psychic image comes to symbolise restriction and curtailment upon the development of a dignified self with autonomous interests. In Jungian terms, this commonplace adolescent response may be read as the 'trick' to counter the parental *trickster*, whose operations materialise through surveillance technologies and practices of supervision (as discussed by Samuels, 1993). Such are the psycho-political tensions pulling at the heart of the separateness-relatedness dialogue in contemporary adolescent life.

On these questions one might return to Laing for a moment. We may also think of his model of existential equilibrium at the heart of separateness-relatedness as a departure from the kinds of self-certifying subjectivity found within many classical strands of psychoanalysis. This is thanks in part to his acknowledgement of the phenomenological aspects of interconnectedness between mind, body and world. This is an influence from French existentialism and, in particular, the work of Maurice Merleau-Ponty. Merleau-Ponty openly saw mass media forms of the twentieth century, the cinema especially, as materially representative of this interconnectedness (1964). Perhaps most of all, aside from his development of the existential approach to imaginative misrecognition of an authentic self in relation (especially to others – the focus of discussion in previous chapters, and a topic I shall reprise in the next section on data identity) we find in Laing a significant departure from the kinds of recognition and authenticated difference found in, for example, the Lacanian infant. It is enough, for Laing (and echoing my comments regarding the Jungian 'trick' some moments ago), that we are able to acknowledge the capacity to experience oneself as autonomous: 'that one has really come to realize that one is a separate person from everyone else. No matter how deeply committed in joy or suffering to someone else, he is not me, and I am not him' (1965: 52).

This has perhaps obvious applications in the way that we might think of the role of social media interactions in the development of adolescent identity more generally, and in the social and cultural practices of adolescents whose lives so often embrace the accelerated convenience of social media applications. Additionally, in this realisation one might also acknowledge the important fact here that late capital societies in general have committed to the status of autonomous subject a role as some sort of barometer of free will. That is to say, *individuation-as-separateness* is prized to the degree that, on a psychosocial level and within a psychic economy, there appears to have been a fall in the currency of the 'relatedness' vector in the existential equilibrium.

Separateness seems to be considered more valuable, politically and economically speaking. Aside from institutional commitments such as to one's family (as an institution especially), to community (in the institutional arrangements of such, like taxation, charity donations, volunteering and so on) and democracy (a commitment to the procedures of the state, as well as to consumerism) relatedness disappears from view. This general shift is noticeable in the kinds of loneliness and lack of solitude as discussed in Chapter 5 (see also Turkle 2015), typical of social interactions in contemporary accelerated media ecosystems characterised by always-on, persistent connectivity. It is also reminiscent of the way that the experience of capital has been narrativised in the historiography of Western democracies more generally, as outlined by Frederic Jameson (1981, 1988) and Max Weber before him (2001). This kind of existential disequilibrium therefore sits within the logic of late capital, as the privatisation of experience intensifies, and one can imagine the gradual dissipation of mutuality accelerate in pace through the myth of connectivity.

The lack of reflective and recognitive space necessary to foster empathy, as I have already outlined in previous chapters in relation to Sherry Turkle's work in particular, may be indicative of this problem. However, Laing goes further than this in relation to the feeling of autonomy. If we are compelled in this upwards movement towards individuation (in the late capital, rather than the Jungian, sense of the term), then we are robbed of the fullest experience of autonomy such that, for Laing, one 'can experience neither his separateness from, nor his relatedness to, the other in the usual way' (1965: 52). The existential equilibrium between a sense of separateness and a sense of relatedness is crucial, for Laing, to enable individuals to cope with the reality of existential disquiet as social beings. This existential disquiet is the lived knowledge that, expressed in Sartre's terms, one cannot love for someone else, nor can they do the same for me (2001); or in Heidegger's thought that we cannot die another's death, only our own, towards which we are thrown (2000).

The benign and vicious circles of data materialisation

The added complication of living the disequilibrium, through which we hurtle towards a mythic point of self-actualization or individuation, is that a condition of persistent, semi-permanent connectivity requires that we give something up willingly in order to participate in this journey. It is worth quoting Laing in full here (1965: 52–3), to illustrate the 'something' we give up:

> A lack of sense of autonomy implies that one feels one's being to be bound up in the other, or that the other is bound up in oneself, in a sense that transgresses the actual possibilities within the structure of human relatedness. It means that a feeling that one is in a position of ontological dependency on the other (i.e. dependent on the other for one's very being), is substituted for a sense of relatedness and attachment to him based on genuine mutuality. [. . .] Therefore, the polarity is between complete isolation or complete merging of identity rather than between separateness and relatedness. The individual oscillates perpetually between the two extremes, each equally unfeasible.

This oscillation is compounded in the contemporary media landscape by the fact that the entire ecosystem is underpinned by (and is reliant upon) networks of data. Several recent studies that engage with aspects of political economic critique of data generation, management and monetisation (e.g., Allmer 2015; Fuchs 2012, 2013, 2014; McChesney 2013; Srnicek 2017; Terranova 2004) tend to highlight the enormity and sheer amount of data, and the valuation of that data as a commodity in driving global digital economies. There are fewer studies that explicitly engage the affective and psychological position of the individual subject in relation to either the identification of self with data presence, or to self-identification with one's data profile, especially in relation to psychic processes (notable exemptions include Balick 2014b; Krüger & Johanssen 2014; Singh 2017).

Accessibility to convergent media content, in its various formats, using various platforms and hardware and from an array of access points, is becoming open to increasingly individual, personalised choices. This condition lies at the very heart of what might be described as a Web 2.0 ethic of connectivity: the notion that media forms are inclusive, participatory, writable from the perspective of an end-user, immediate and, ultimately, democratised through practices of access, sharing and gift economies. At the front end of these services, it would seem that the extent of that freedom of choice, of paramount importance in a deregulated media ecosystem, signifies an individuated agency that is at once participatory and empowering. However, this position has increasingly become prone to criticism from a number of disciplinary approaches where, even at this front end of service provision, choice has an illusory dimension (see, for example, Zelenkauskaite 2016). I refer here to the algorithms associated with, for example, massively popular streaming services – specifically, Amazon Prime, Netflix or YouTube serve as key examples. These services operate within economies of attention and affect to present the consumer with front-end suggestions according to not only personal preferences based upon prior consumer choices (a narrowcast-based, 'pull' tendency), but also complexities associated with third-party arrangements for profile and data monetisation, and content provision (a more ostensibly broadcast-based 'push' tendency, partially based on long-tail economic models).

Another case in point here: various algorithms have been developed to increase market potential for YouTube producers – note the use of that term, 'producers', which is a professionalised recuperation of the more interactive, participatory and amateur-ish 'produsage' model often referred to in Web 2.0 scholarship (e.g., Bruns 2008). As if to illustrate the extent of this recuperative turn, for example, DigitasLBi and Outrigger Media developed OpenSlate – a social media analytics platform partnered with YouTube and designed to anticipate stars of the future before they break. The results of analysis guide investment choices for corporate players to develop new online talent and decrease risks of such investments whilst simultaneously increasing the chances of return on investment. Essentially, according to Learmonth (2013), OpenSlate produces predictive, qualitative data of a kind not available from YouTube's own analytics systems. Webster (2014) stated that, at his time of writing, OpenSlate tracked over 50,000 channels, and 25 million individual videos on YouTube, giving scores based upon specific qualitative criteria: audience engagement, frequency of new content added, influence and reach.[1] For Webster, 'It's possible the talent identified in this way would hit it big without intervention. But using metrics to identify winners can create winners. Unlike the weather, social predictions can change outcomes'; and, unlike in the physical world, predictive 'algorithms powered by big data have the potential to create "self-fulfilling prophecies" in the social world' (2014: 93).

Although writing about a slightly different aspect of the data studies field, one of the more radically infused book-length critiques of this logic can be found in the aforementioned work of Deborah Lupton – *The Quantified Self* (2016). To reiterate, Lupton's study explores the forms and practices of self-tracking via various lifestyle applications powered by Web 2.0 connectivity, from a critical sociological perspective. Once again, the mass popularity of these technologies should not be underestimated – this is at the very popular end of popular culture. Such self-tracking practices – the phenomenon of FitBit, for example, or any number of applications associated with measurements of body-mass indexing, jogging-route mapping, stepometers and other wearable technologies or mobile phone applications – all form familiar aspects of everyday media engagement, as well as, one could argue, impression management. The implications of Lupton's work also necessitate that one considers ways in which such practices partake of a broader culture associated with self-improvement, modification and technologies of wellbeing or work productivity within relations of power. I have discussed some of the intimate correlations and dialogues between self-image, lifestyle and cultures of self-improvement elsewhere (Singh 2015) so I do not wish to repeat too much of that here, but it is noteworthy that such questions have begun to be addressed from a post-Jungian critique.[2]

Although social media platforms and other Web 2.0 technologies may be identified with affirmative possibilities for expressive freedom, lifestyle and politics (transgression, action or subversion), they equally have tendencies to exacerbate what Laing described as the otherwise 'normal' pathological split between an 'inner' self and a generalised deadness of the embodied 'false-self'. Elsewhere, I have argued that in contemporary media ecosystems interactions can quickly disaggregate into moral positions of diminished recognition of others as whole persons with unique interests. This false-self attitude is characterised by an objectification of others, an amplification of unreal perceptions, unreal expectations and futile actions, the kinds of which are encountered in and mobilise online filter bubbles (Singh 2018: n.p.).

This is perhaps best expressed in Laing's vicious circle of falsity – that: 'Love is precluded and dread takes its place', where 'The self by its detachment is precluded from a full experience of realness and aliveness' (1965: 82). Nowhere is this demonstrated to its most complete degree than in the false ideal of body image found in image-driven social media platforms, where people are both quick to judge bodies and quick to call out body-shaming. On the one hand, if we enter into this point of debate, there is a sense of reification of self and other; we are fundamentally disembodied from ourselves in the sense of over-identifying with persona(e) in a false-self system, thus foreclosing on lived, warm relationships based on mutuality. On the other, the body itself becomes a sublime reified object, coded as an idealised unit of exchange, where selfies are currency for the mobilisation of identity in social exchange. Furthermore, such identity is bound up with a notion of data, such that it is reduced to a set of preferences and, ultimately, a quantification of choice (a system of presets and 'preferences'), out of which contained choices present themselves. In the image-driven emphasis of optic-privileged culture, the evidential value of the selfie (Walker Rettberg 2014; Sturken and Cartwright 2000) as expression of lifestyle should not be underestimated, both in the sense of its representational face-value aspect, and in its monetised data-value aspect. If nothing else, the phenomenon of the selfie demonstrates that we are, in the false-self system of social media, quite literally what we consume; or, we are nothing.

The aspect of Lupton's work that I would like to emphasise in relation to these issues through dialogue with some of the post-Jungian ideas around psychologies of the self I outlined a moment ago is her emphasis on the ways in which practices of self-tracking are 'spreading from the private realm into diverse social domains, and the implications of the self-tracking phenomenon for the politics of personal data, data practices and data materialisations' (2016: 1). In other words, the intensification of private experience is being drawn into the social. Indeed, we saw a speculative dramatisation of this in the chapter's opening example from 'The Entire History of You', where intensely private aspects of the personality (perspective, memory) are being disclosed openly, and relational aspects (sexual congress) are subject to atomised privacy. Additionally, according to some research, this tracking includes intensification of privatised places of work, institutions and other transactional spaces, where the labouring body is objectified, and the imperative to *perform*, has become internalised (Moore and Robinson 2015). The vehicle through which this intensification is moving is in the materialisation of data identity.

This is where the idea of a false-self *system* starts to make more sense. The quantification (at least, the *attempted* quantification) of selfhood through standardised systems of profile building, data-mining and so on in everyday online transactions, is a totalised and totalising system of sorts. Underpinned by data identity, social media interactions of various descriptions systematically push towards traffic increase. The most obvious way to achieve this is through pushing what is already conventional and popular, risk-averse and culturally immediate. This totalising, recuperative movement is found in the diversity of cases I have discussed so far in this book. For instance, the impact of multichannel networks often owned by major media multinationals such as Maker Studios (Disney) and machinima.com (owned by Time Warner), and the music-oriented content of Vevo (Universal Music Group, Sony Music Entertainment and Warner Music Group). Additionally, the role of microcelebrities, characters and influencers to draw traffic through personality attraction and endorsement (such as Shay Carl Butler, Colleen Ballinger and many others), Instagram and other platform stardom (and in the case of Essena O'Neill, an extreme example of totalising image convention). These visible cases overlay an invisible foundation level of data appropriation, mining, analytics and manipulation operating at the back end of Web 2.0 technologies, driving smart tech interaction and providing frictionless consumer profiling.

Although on an everyday level as consumers, we may not be aware of, nor necessarily concerned with, the transactional character of these aspects of data-driven identity, these are questions in need of address. As discussed at length in Chapter 5, the experiential, existential human self is not expressive of, nor can it be expressed in, data. Identities of various descriptions might be materialised through data, and this is an interesting notion, but it is misleading to attempt an elision of identity with expressions of selfhood here. An authentic sense of self cannot be sustained through data transactions, nor a sense of self be managed by and through data, for similar reasons. Individuality may be identifiable as and through data-driven systems of *identity*, but in this kind of 'self system', the notion of self is reduced to the status of ident, brand presence and lifestyle choice. To refer to previous discussions, in this sense, the 'falsity' of this false-self refers not to fakery or imagined selves, but to a sense of the untrue, and the inauthentic, as in: 'untrue to itself'.

Presets and preference settings, vicariously shared through social media updates and ostentatiously pushed through practices such as 'Like-farming', Snapchat 'streaks' and other methods used by ordinary users to acquire some aspect of recognitive contact, are in danger of being misrecognised (by systems as well as by users themselves) as expressions of the whole person. As we have seen in the various discussions on recognition offered over the course of this book, this is a fundamental ethical and existential error.

If further support for this argument is needed, we might appeal to Hegelian intersubjectivity and Hegel's well-known account of the struggle for recognition in *Phenomenology of Spirit* (1994 [1807]) to tease out what is necessarily 'false' about this particular kind of 'self system'. This argument is relevant as an influential precursor to relational psychology's intersubjective interaction between more than one psyche as meaningful interaction. Following Aristotle's notion that one's relationship to others always runs parallel to one's relationship with oneself, Hegel's idea of self-consciousness is as a self-consciousness existing only as something recognised. The need for others outweighs every other need or desire, and this is a crucial precondition in any society that pertains to conviviality as a 'living together' or 'living well' ethical value. Hegel writes that 'Self-Consciousness must orient itself toward superseding the other independent being, in order to become certain of *itself* thereby, as the being that it is; it must concomitantly be oriented toward superseding *itself* (since this "other" is itself)' (1994: 51, §180 [emphasis in original]). In other words, self-consciousness must negotiate with an other (self-) consciousness, recognising itself in the other in order to become certain of itself so that, eventually, 'The consciousnesses recognize themselves as *mutually recognizing each other*' (1994: 53, §184 [emphasis in original]). However, false-self systems seek, through this process, to define self-consciousness as individuated, and this mutuality is subject to various intermediaries of the kinds just described. This intermediation is a problem for a consciousness that desires to be recognised as itself, above all else. As (Hegel translator) Kainz notes (1994: 50, note 5) in his annotated edition of *Phenomenology of Spirit*:

> [. . .] a human being's existence as a self-consciousness is in a very real sense dependent on recognition by alter egos; so that if [. . .] someone were to exist without any recognition at all (not even of a negative sort), this person would not exist as a self-consciousness.

An argument could be made here that, in a media ecosystem defined through social interactions that are mediated through data materialisation, the moment and sustaining of recognition in order to maintain a sense of life and security overrides other principles (and this could include moral ones). Such an argument also recognises that freedom (to act, speak, assemble – in general, but also specifically, in social media interactions and Web 2.0 activities) is a commodity in the exchange of recognition. It permits, in a synoptic sense, the licence to say and act in ways that surpass moral value and social obligation. This is because, in a recognition economy driven through data materialisation, one's only obligation would be to recognise another as another would recognise you – however negative or alienated.

In human interactions, healthy personas are characterised by both robustness and strong differentiation. However, social media communications have an in-built tendency for communication shorthand, and this tendency systematically favours the personally convenient, and the immediacy of identification with per-sona as a quick-response, 'easy version' of the self. On this basis, assumed versions of oneself and others have a tendency to become estranged, and relations become objectified. Self, in this sense, is systemic and simulated, rather than expressed in any strong sense by the user; the routines that characterise the practices of 'quanti-fied self' movement (Lupton 2016) are the governing principle at the data level in all social media platforms (Singh 2017).

To take trolling as an example of this sort of objectification that lies upon a more visible level to the user (i.e., comments threads), although an act ostensibly subject to popular criticism, trolling also becomes, controversially, something of an exonerated act. This is because it ostensibly fulfils the logic underpinning obliga-tions of recognition in the most superficial, non-mutual sense: I recognise you, albeit negatively, because I either respond to something you have posted online, or, I deliberately provoke you into a false debate on a controversial subject. It also expresses a vulgar definition of freedoms of speech (advocates of which have been popularly described in online contexts as 'speechers') without fully acknowledging the responsibilities that necessarily associate themselves with those freedom rights: you recognise me because, albeit negatively, I have expressed a right to freedom of speech. In such unfortunate, somewhat solipsistic circumstances, in the practice of trolling *the consciousnesses do not recognise themselves as mutually recognising others* with independent and unique interests.

The problem here rests on the notion that recognition is not only affirmative in the positive sense of life affirmation but is also subject to, and circumscribed by, conditions through which that recognition takes place (a commodified and com-modifying environment). In this case, a data materialisation is built within various instances of capital (economic, social, cultural and – perhaps most immediate and potent given the mediated environment of social interactions in Web 2.0 contexts – symbolic). Additionally, the limits of recognition are also shaped through the pre-dominant value system: a value system that takes freedom of speech to its limits and beyond, whilst ignoring the parameters of responsibility and justice associated with those rights in moral and legal frameworks is a value system that, however misplaced, exonerates trolling and other forms of cyberbullying. Essentially, what we are dealing with, therefore, is a variation on Hegel's 'unhappy consciousness', described by Robert Sinnerbrink as an *alienated* form of subjectivity: 'As Hegel contends, however, alienation can be overcome only through the rational com-prehension of our historical condition and through *the social achievement of mutual recognition*' (2007: 55 [my emphasis]). So, whereas it may first appear that dialectical movement of recognition is corrupted through the conditions of commodity-identity and data materialisation prevalent in social media interaction, effectively fueling corrosive practices such as trolling, the principle of mutuality once more provides a solution. This time, mutuality augments the self-psychology of Kohut and Benjamin, and the philosophical anthropology of Honneth, with an appeal to Hegelian phenomenology and to his philosophy of right.

This leads us to another aspect of Laing's work that fully appreciates the necessity to engage productive and positive aspects of interpersonal interaction. In addition to the vicious circle of the false-self, Laing describes mutual recognition between persons as a benign circle, a 'mutual enrichment of self and other'. He writes that 'The reality of the world and of the self are mutually potentiated by the direct relationship between self and other' (1965: 82). For Laing, this mutuality forms the intersubjective basis of an existential equilibrium. He furthers this observation by emphasising the fundamental expression of mind, body and world as a creative expression of consciousness, in a relationship with other consciousnesses. However, without a principle of mutuality guiding the full recognition of others as whole persons with autonomous interests, this expression is impossible. He states (1965: 84) that without such mutuality,

> What one might call *a creative relationship* with the other, in which there is a mutual enrichment of the self and the other (benign circle) is impossible, and an *interaction* is substituted which may seem to operate efficiently and smoothly for a while but which has no 'life' in it (sterile relationship). There is a quasi-it-it interaction instead of an I-thou relationship. This interaction is a dead process. (1965: 82 [emphasis in original]).

To avoid dead, 'quasi', inauthentic interactions, and to reinvigorate the I-thou status of fully recognitive being, Laing's creative relationship necessitates a leap of faith to retain a warm, lived sense of mutuality. I argue that it involves risk in revealing enough of oneself to another to facilitate the openness that trust requires to establish mature relationships. It also requires a full recognition that the contemporary communications media ecosystem does not necessarily have the capacity to facilitate such openness, because of the representational regime and data materialisation of online identity as if it were the whole thing (a self). To borrow once more from Aaron Balick, 'Pathology develops only when the individual identifies with their persona at the expense of other attributes of their personality: when they believe the persona to be "the whole thing"' (2014b: 16). The 'pathology' at work here is the inauthentic false-self.

Social media and the complex of authenticity

Following Joseph Henderson's pioneering typology of social, aesthetic, philosophical and spiritual dynamics, the psychiatrist and Jungian analyst Thomas Singer (2000, 2004), along with his colleague Samuel L. Kimbles (2000), developed the concept of the 'cultural complex'. This is a term which derives specifically from the notion of 'complex' found in the analytical psychology of Jung and post-Jungian thought. In this school, complexes operate at the personal level, and are made up of the building blocks of the psyche, often experienced as partial personalities or distinct psychological entities. Ultimately, these experiences derive from the tensions and interplay between archetypal, unconscious materials in the psyche, and the necessity to deal with the outside world. The term 'complex' is often used in depth traditions to describe the constellation of affects, images, emotionally charged associations and collective psychic material.

The 'cultural complex' is a development of the original term in post-Jungian thought and psychotherapy. It came about through a necessity to acknowledge the role of interaction between intrapsychic processes of individuals and those of others, and also between the psychic world and the world of the social in general. The cultural complex describes powerful moods and behaviours characterised by repetition, lived out at a cultural level as part of a *zeitgeist* of attitudes, behaviours and worldviews. In time, these tend to become internalised by individuals through various identification processes, and accepted as certain ways of thinking about and doing things (although, crucially, remaining not necessarily the *best* way to think and do). Singer writes that, 'For Jungians, Henderson's work opened the door to the vast realm of human experience that inhabits the psychical space between our most personal and our most archetypal level of being in the world' (2004: 19). He goes on to suggest that, 'like personal complexes, cultural complexes provide a simplistic certainty about the group's place in the world in the face of otherwise conflicting and ambiguous uncertainties' (2004: 21). It is a process whereby one's own sense of self mingles with larger notions of identity in a collective sense, and then further: when one's own cultural complexes mingle with other cultural complexes in reciprocal amplification. As Singer (2004: 32) writes:

> We hold up strange mirrors to ourselves and to one another when we start to explore cultural complexes as part of our personal and historical development. Our cultural complexes get all mixed up not only with our personal history and complexes but with other cultural complexes as well.

There is, arguably, a more materialist outlook to the notion of cultural complex when compared to the classical Jungian notion of personal complex; it tends to emphasise the social, and may be regarded as fundamentally historical in its character, as it reflects diachronic shifts in modes of worldview, shaping norms and values over time. However, this is a sense of personal or shared history that is present, that is unfolding as one interacts with others and with the world. It is almost as if an aesthetic of being operates through this experience and gives one a sense of being present and alive in the moment. It is therefore a powerfully seductive aspect of authenticity and carries with it a sense of both identity and recognition.

I would argue that the notion of authenticity, although certainly mythic in character (certainly in the kinds of aesthetic experiences just described), and problematic in its relationship with essentialist truth claims and so on, relates closely to the notion of cultural complex. This is particularly the case when the struggle for authenticity, for a feeling that is true to oneself, is amplified through social media interactions. Indeed, one might tentatively argue that authenticity is *itself* an instance of complex. I have noted elsewhere, for example, that persona tends to amplify the individual and, likewise, the interaction of cultural complexes will amplify and extend conventions of worldview and of social interaction. So, persona on an interpersonal level (the psychological operations that reveal and conceal to keep the personality intact) and cultural complexes of authenticity at a wider level (that address the social necessity to express and remain 'true' to oneself, in the individualist sense) together distort the view of the true self for others. However, as I have mentioned elsewhere (Singh 2017) it is never *fully* a false-self that is presented. The term 'false' is not intended to signify 'inauthentic'. As already noted in a number of contexts during the course of this book, inauthenticity as a concept ought to be reserved for cases where individuals and others identify with the false-self as if that is all there were. This appears to be a characteristic of *zeitgeist*, and reflects the complexity (and arguably, the complex) of the struggle for authenticity.

In order to complete this argument, I turn once again to the thought of Charles Taylor. His work on the intensification of privatised experiences, and the inflated cultural value of what he terms 'self-realisation' (closely related to the concepts and practices of individualism, self-actualisation and 'lifestyle' individuation), is of particular interest here. He writes that the contemporary culture of authenticity, which characterises modern life, 'encourages a purely personal understanding of self-fulfilment, thus making the various associations and communities in which the person enters purely instrumental in their significance. At the broader social level, this is antithetical to any strong commitment to a community' (1991: 43). This increasingly intensified, private experience intimately fosters a transactional approach to relationships, where one's relationships are viewed as being subservient to personal fulfilment. For Taylor, as it stands, the predominant and impoverished principle of individualism does not offer a view on how individuals should live with others. It is a curious echo of the convivialist ethos, coupled with echoes of Hegel's struggle for recognition, as well as the psychosocial principle of mutuality that I have mapped out in this book. Taylor's acknowledgement of the problem speaks to an unfolding and unfoldedness of inter-subjective (social) being that seems to be all but absent in the transactional and data-driven versions of selfhood promoted through social media interactions. He writes (1991: 47–8) that

> My discovering my identity doesn't mean that I work it out in isolation but that I negotiate it through dialogue, partly overt, partly internalized, with others. That is why the development of an ideal of inwardly generated identity gives a new and crucial importance to recognition. My own identity crucially depends on my dialogical relations with others.

That he had already identified such problems in the 'culture of authenticity' many years before the advent of social media, and indeed predating the Web by some several years, gives cause for concern over the amplified effects of such impoverished recognitive forms within contemporary always-on contexts. But this also provides an opportunity to engage with some of the solutions laid down in a number of traditions of thought and praxis discussed at length during the course of the current study. Taylor is optimistic. He argues that it is difficult to believe that people are so locked into social and material conditions such as the atomist, instrumental, transactional relations that seem to characterise modern life that they are not able to make positive change and embrace a more authentic approach to relationships, to community and to a historical sense of self and place. He states (1991: 73) that

> [. . .] while everyone must recognize how powerfully we are conditioned by our industrial technological civilization, those views that portray us as totally locked in and unable to change our behaviour short of smashing the whole 'system' have always seemed to me wildly exaggerated.

As any reader who has read thus far would be able to discern, I have some sympathy with this view. Indeed, so does Jaron Lanier in a couple of distinct ways: expressions of his vehement anti-Marxism (2006) aside (which in some ways nonetheless align with Taylor's call to retain the current social apparatus, but transform its content), the strong individualist stance that Lanier expresses in many of his published projects (2010, 2013) has much in common with Taylor's view. Furthermore, the language that Taylor chooses here is significant for Lanier. 'Lock-in' is, of course, a technical term widely used in the field of human-machine interactions. It is used by Lanier in that sense, but he also uses it to extrapolate the trajectory of human-machine interactions, to attempt to figure out how and why human-human relationships, and the interactions individuals have within wider communities, correlate with locked-in technological and social practices. Again, in an echo of Lanier's critique of degraded social interactions on SNS platforms, discussed in some detail in previous chapters, Taylor suggests a methodology to address the 'debased' practices of misrecognition. He writes (1991: 72) that we need to

> [. . .] undertake a work of retrieval, that we identify and articulate the higher ideal behind the more or less debased practices, and then criticize these practices from the standpoint of their own motivating ideal. In other words, instead of dismissing this culture altogether, or just endorsing it as it is, we ought to attempt to raise its practice by making more palpable to its participants what the ethic they subscribe to really involves.

This necessitates a meaningful involvement in taking up an ethical position and, again, in making a leap of faith. The future may appear to offer only ever-increasing levels of inward-looking, privatised concerns. It may be the case that a variety of factors, including increased precarity, enforced mobility and jobs and situations that demand we act or behave more transactionally towards one another all characterise contemporary lifestyles, particularly in the so-called developed world. This is a depressing thought, and if taken in the rather mean spirit of much popular commentary where (particularly young) people are inwardly and narcissistically concerned with their own intensely privatised concerns, then it is true for Taylor that we are indeed running out of alternatives to reverse such trends. However, to affirm Taylor's optimism, he also contends (1991: 76–7) that:

> This perspective is different if you see these developments in the light of the ethic of authenticity. For then they don't just represent a shift in value that is unproblematic for the people concerned. Rather, you see the new, self-centred practices as the site of an ineradicable tension. The tension comes from the sense of an ideal that is not being fully met in reality. And this tension can turn into a struggle, where people try to articulate the shortfall of practice, and criticize it.

Struggle means that things can go either way, which for Taylor at least means that there is good news and bad news. But this struggle brings with it the potential to push forwards, towards the ideal, and that decline and triviality are not inevitable. And again, this suggests that same leap of faith. But this leap also requires a sense of the social imaginary – the place where Laing's 'creative relationship' is allowed to flourish and express itself to the fullest degree, and where a sense of conviviality can gain social aspects that reinforce the psychological. I am here minded of Sartre's work in *The Psychology of The Imagination* (2001). In his book, Sartre writes (2001: 169 [emphasis in original]) that

> To prefer the imaginary is not only to prefer a richness, a beauty, an imaginary luxury to the existing mediocrity, *in spite of* their unreal nature. It is also to adopt 'imaginary' feelings and actions for the sake of their imaginary nature. It is not only this or that image that is chosen, but the imaginary state with everything it implies; it is not only an escape from the content of the real (poverty, frustrated love, failure of one's enterprise, etc.), but from the form of the real itself [. . .] the very way our feelings have of developing themselves.

This is an expression of authenticity in its positive, truest sense. It is an opt-in, positive solution to what is often seen as a negative problem, demanding subtractive or censorious solutions. In the context of Web 2.0, these taken the familiar discursive form of a number of everyday issues – moral panics about children with technology, for example; the surveillance anxieties of modern state and corporate data practices; or the accompanying paternalist censorship that forms around National Webs and so-called safe spaces. Seeing the imaginary in this creative way transforms our understanding of social being from one dominated by a transactional, neoliberal economism that dominates cultural life today, to one that seems, through the imaginative world of recognition, more to do with the expression of interior lives and the potentialities of convivial, lived mutuality. That transactional culture, to which I have alluded several times throughout this book, underpins the majority of social interactions via Web 2.0 technologies through data materialisation and the fixity of image-driven social pressures. Holding up Sartre's reading of the imaginary and Laing's notion of the creative relationship with the other, one can see another path to tread.

Our intuition may tell us that we are warm, living, social, emotional, sensible, animated, thinking things – that we are, in fact, human beings, (mostly) being human. Whereas the *Black Mirror* instance at the beginning of this chapter may well be an extrapolation of existing affordances between technology, the sexual and the social, nonetheless, one can see the ways in which technological intermediaries compel us towards reified relations, amplifying an already delicate state in the intrapsychic balance between self and other. Indeed, a more materialist argument might suggest that our human relationships in general are thus in danger of becoming relations between *things* – the 'being' part of 'human being' melting into air as the objectification mechanisms of commodity-identity and reification become more prevalent. Indeed, at the height of modernity, these mechanisms were identifiable, well-known even. In *History and Class Consciousness*, for example, Georg Lukács, (1990: 83) wrote that

> The essence of commodity-structure has often been pointed out. Its basis is that a relation between people takes on the character of a thing and thus acquires a 'phantom objectivity', an autonomy that seems so strictly rational and all-embracing as to conceal every trace of its fundamental nature: the relation between people.

In this phantasmal, transactional rationality, Lukács identified commodity as a sort of *structuring principle* of everyday life, defining our sense of individuality, and well as setting the terms for social, institutional and political relations. To put it another way, our warm, lived psychology is disassembled through a reduction to 'thingness'. However, because we are not really things in the sense of inanimate, inorganic or cold things our intuition should push us towards finding a solution to accommodate the desire for recognition as whole persons with autonomous and unique interests. One way of dealing with this, tarrying with materialist terminology of commodity, is to develop the notion that commodity is a structuring principle by *reimagining commodity as a recognitive principle of mutuality*. Whether we can get to this point in our dealings with the legacy of Web 2.0 technologies, practices and principles is another question and, in my concluding remarks, I tentatively offer some explorations.

Notes

1 At time of writing, according to OpenSlate's own website, they have the ability to track over 400 million videos on YouTube, illustrating the incremental velocity of scale involved in this sector of advertising. www.openslate.com/context/ [accessed: 21/05/2018].

2 Indeed, for the range of subjects and positions taken on self-improvement and transformation, see the whole collection within which that specific work sits: Hockley and Fadina (eds) (2015).

CONCLUSION: WHAT WOULD AN ETHICS OF CONNECTIVITY LOOK LIKE?

Some final notes on the death of Web 2.0

One of the aims of this book is to contribute towards an ethics of connectivity. There are several reasons why I believe that this task is urgent in the theorising work of media and cultural studies, and, more specifically, an intervention into the theoretical constructs of psychosocial approaches to media praxis. The popular discourses of connectivity assume that it is both a good and necessary thing – for everyday life, on a personal level, and for the economy, at a political and macro level. These are familiar ideas, and so it should come as no surprise to the reader that the prevailing rhetoric of connectivity in everyday life tends to be overwhelmingly positivist. It also tends to draw heavily from an assumed and rather mechanistic technological determinist perspective, which in turn gives the ordinary consumer a specifically libertarian-futurist perspective on the uses and potential of technology in the hands of ordinary citizens. Of course, this perspective has both utopian and dystopian threads of thinking associated with it, as successive generations of thinking on the phenomenon of moral panics associated with new technology will attest. It also has political influences from both socialist-libertarianism and neoliberal-libertarian traditions. In this context, from whichever approach taken, the McLuhan-esque idea of 'global village' is a seductive one, because it lends phenomena associated negatively with globalisation a more affirmative, progressive hue. This can be understood in the sense of small-world consciousness, as well as a sense of providing the grounds necessary for justifying a multicultural 'melting pot' of ideas, freely given and exchanged, equitably shared and carrying equal status in a world that is 'connected'. At the same time, this global village idea allows for a localist, cultural specificity which can be found in the shift towards popular national discourses in most parts of the Western world, where again the notion of being 'connected' is often deemed to be crucial to personal and professional networks, of people, organisations and institutions.

This presents to us an immediate problem in establishing what connectivity is, and why an ethics of connectivity is necessary. We know that ostensibly freeing and empowering activities exist in the global communication of ideas, knowledge and resources. Gift economies, circular economies, freecycling and permaculture, conservationism and ecologies of many descriptions all exist and form part of popular praxis in many parts of the world. We know about these activities because they are given high visibility in the way that they are fundamentally related to, and driven by, an accelerated global media ecosystem. Disparate contemporary phenomena such as the Occupy movement, Anonymous and the Ice Bucket Challenge all have this in common; they were all popular phenomena facilitated by the sharing of information across social media networks by ordinary users. It is probably worth acknowledging that they *could* have existed and succeeded as trends or popular movements in a pre-social media world, or as completely offline contemporary phenomena today. However, the ease through which their proliferation took place was, at the very least, finessed through what I like to describe as 'plug-in-and-play' communications platforms, such as social networking services (SNSs) and other Web 2.0 services. This is testament to the idea that social media platforms and practices not only fulfil the needs of the marketplace but also, to an extent, the needs of individuals at the level of consumer. Marketing studies scholarship is full of examples of this premise. Dave Evans (2010), for example, frames SNSs almost exclusively in terms of next-gen business engagement. He states (2010: 4) that

> No longer satisfied with advertising and promotional information as a sole source for learning about new products and services, consumers have taken to the Social Web in an effort to share among themselves their own direct experiences with brands, products, and services to provide a more 'real' view of their research experience. At the same time, consumers are leveraging the experiences of others, before they actually make a purchase themselves.

From an empirical perspective, this is, of course entirely true. From a standpoint which considers the ethics of connectivity to be of crucial importance, particularly within the much broader context of a convergent media ecosystem, however, this purely empirical perspective is inadequate.

As I have discussed elsewhere (Singh 2017) the contemporary media ecosystem can be considered beyond older models of broadcast, networked and publication media forms. Although, perhaps, it ought to be noted, following insights from several scholars in media studies (Caldwell 2004; Jenkins 2006; Meikle and Young 2012 etc.) that older forms, institutions and power relations persist in transformed and resilient ways in this ecosystem. They exist alongside and are embedded in the architectural characteristics of an accelerated, convergent realm of connectivity.

This is a rather basic, but workable, first step towards thinking more broadly about what is frequently described as Web 2.0. That is to say, a version of the Web that is more read/writable than it is read-only, that overwhelmingly relies upon the content generated by users and one in which newer, less-visible models of revenue-generation such as data mining, data profiling and data automation and governance are to be found. We live in a world where data proliferates across a number of convergent aspects of our personal lives. This happens from financial records and credit ratings, through social media content-generation, to geolocative information and surveillance and even biometrics in identification documents such as passports; it is no exaggeration to state that we are already well into a movement towards accelerated ways of being in a digital age. Additionally, it should be noted, these are all traditionally political domains of identity, freedom and choice.

Therefore, we might say that our first problem of connectivity ethics is political in character – and this is because in contemporary media forms of communication and expression, we are dealing with power relations that assume the character of an empowering, seductive form of democratic agency for the individual, and, importantly, for the potential formation of autonomous communities of influence. Much of the information we deal with on a daily basis is available at our fingertips, in the form of multiple online accounts storing vast amounts of personal information, accessible through user-friendly interfaces and (sometimes, elegant) user-experience design. As we have seen during the course of this book, such individual agency is contingent upon the trade-off between, on one hand, the benefits of information disclosure (e.g., networking, collaboration, connectivity) and, on the other, the relative avoidance of harm through information restriction and impression management (privacy settings, multiple profiles, suitability of media for specific contexts). As Markos, Labrecque and Milne point out, 'The aggregation of disclosed information creates a digital footprint or profile of personal information, accessible online to a wide spectrum of people' (2012: 157). This aggregation leads to new privacy issues relating to digital profiles in the open, publicly visible marketplace, and also to the vague personal knowledge that disclosure of information in certain contexts is ridden with anxieties around risk. For example, in the practice of searches conducted online in recruitment processes for potential employees. This is a contract of consent familiar to many, and one which we seem to be more than willing to enter into in order to secure the free-to-access services provided by social media and Web 2.0 institutions.

There are other characteristics of the contemporary media ecosystem which help to define our sense of what connectivity is, and how it shapes the way we interact with others and with the world around us. These characteristics may also be described as political, in the sense of a political economy of connectivity. Vincent Mosco (2009) has pointed out that any political economy of communications necessarily entails the 'study of the social relations, particularly the power relations, that mutually constitute the production, distribution, and consumption of resources, including communication resources' (2009: 2). As we have seen at various moments in this book, such conditions of production were considered particularly in relation to some of the aspects of data automation. A more useful way of thinking about how political economy perspectives can advance our thinking on connectivity, and particularly its impact upon the individual at an everyday level, stems from the work of media sociologists Peter Golding and Graham Murdock (2005).

Golding and Murdock consider, in the round, 'the interplay between the symbolic and the economic dimensions of public communications [. . .] how the making of meaning is shaped at every level by the structured asymmetries in social relations' (2005: 60–2). Therefore, a fully formed political economy of connectivity would necessarily seek to engage with how social relations share a reciprocation with the creation and exchange of meaning, expressed in the realm of interpersonal communications (or, indeed, those between institutions, or individuals and institutions). And this would necessarily entail the inclusion of critiques on the economics of both relations of production and those of culture.

In terms of relations of production, we might move forward from a discussion on the role connected data plays in the automation and regulation of multileveled aspects of everyday life, and towards embedded institutional practices which govern everyday experiences of connectivity, for the vast majority of people. Perhaps traditionally associated with the preoccupations of classic thinkers of the Frankfurt School, this viewpoint considers communications and media practices as somewhat massified forms because the formal arrangements of interaction associated with such forms are: a) experienced by a majority of people in common; and b) shaped by socio-economic conditions and relations. One of the key ideas often associated with the work of Adorno and Horkheimer (2007), for example, is that 'culture industries' tend to break down the distinctions between work time and leisure time, through the emulation of work time in the scheduling, patterning and regulation of leisure time. This can be seen transparently in the way leisure time has traditionally been treated in correspondence with media entertainments; in the UK during late twentieth century, for example, television schedules became an important indicator of recognising patterns of leisure time for ordinary people. This was largely because in that context, television was such a popular mass medium, and because there were for a very long time only a small number of television network channels available to viewers, schedules could be co-ordinated around the working day. Therefore, for a number of fairly obvious reasons, audiences tended to stay massified, predictable and loyal to a number of programmes at any given time. In the UK, such mass audiences have fragmented, even as mass trends can still be predicted. This was precipitated to an extent by the introduction of deregulation of broadcasting markets following the Annan Report (1977) and the Peacock Report (1986) during the Thatcher neoliberal administration. This move in turn led to the rapid increase in available channels through corporate competition, and eventually the introduction of successive and rapid innovations in both broadcast and in personalised media leading up to and beyond the Millennium. Because of the attendant audience fragmentation, pattern recognition in media consumption is now achieved through the appropriation of personal data pulled from the use of on-demand streaming services, used by a vast global population.

However important these dimensions are, the key idea that I think relates in particular to the notion of connectivity in the context of the leisure/work distinction is the idea of *availability*. Availability, it seems to me, has a distinct dialectic that allows it to be both highly prized and freely given in contemporary Western society. Further, the dimensionality of this dialectic is unfurled to reveal a further complexity: availability involves, above all else, *time*. The coming of social media connectivity especially, but Web 2.0 interaction more generally, has led to the time-dimensionality of being-available as a default position, and a position in which we seem to be content with freely giving. Not only are we expected to be available at all times, but this semi-permanent condition of connectivity-as-availability is something that was embedded in the architecture of the technology itself. Mobile telephony means availability *where*ver one is. Smartphone and wifi technology mean consistent availability in time, because one never needs to be disconnected. This expectation is embedded in culture, evidenced through the way that concerns are raised when immediate responses to our interpersonal communications do not materialise as expected. This technological and cultural complexity has been given a specific name in social media studies: 'always-on'.

As discussed during the course of this book, always-on is the notion that several scholars use to describe various dimensions around the elision of work and leisure time across several life-boundaries. For example, it is fairly commonplace to hear the argument that the boundaries between reality and virtuality have become blurred; that the distinction between online and offline lives is somehow artificial; or that, perhaps in a more nostalgic or reactionary tone, these distinctions no longer seem to matter as much as perhaps they once did. The notion of always-on, therefore, describes the way that connectivity is assumed and ubiquitous. For example, danah boyd (2012: 71–2) writes that

> It's no longer about on or off really. It's about living in a world where being networked to people and information wherever and whenever you need it is just assumed. I may not be always-on the Internet as we think of it colloquially, but I am always connected to the network. And that's what it means to be always-on.

She argues that the real/virtual distinction is so untenable that we need to consciously declare 'off-time' in our virtual interactions. This happens in email sabbaticals, out-of-office messages, status updates on Facebook declaring a 'social media holiday', social media abstentions and so on. Interactions are ultimately incursions and tend to encroach upon our available time in the real world (Light and Cassidy 2014; Mayer-Schönberger 2011; Portwood-Stacer 2012). It is one of the many reasons why, for example, places of work tend to have policies on the use of social media during work hours. Always-on is also a powerful contribution to the culture in which these social media policies for the workplace are also often policed outside of work hours. Inevitably, there is a reputation aspect to this culture, but there is also an undeniable power dynamic at play here too.

This state of always-on also forces us to rethink what the 'network' part of 'social networking sites' actually refers to, because of the assumed connectivity, ubiquity and blurred conceptions of available time. For boyd, then, the 'network' doesn't really refer to the technology itself, but to social interactions. Technologised communication networks often replicate the functionality and practices and cultural patterns of pre-existing social networks – in her essay 'Participating in the Always-On Lifestyle' (2012) boyd uses the example of a dinner party conversation which is enhanced through intermittent reference to Wikipedia or imdb via smartphone technology and network signal provider. Immediate and assumed connection to information via a network is merely an extension of what we might assume to be a network of real-world social relations, but an extension that appears more prosthetic than hypermediate. As discussed in this book, Sherry Turkle (2011) has also written about this aspect of always-on at length. She writes about being 'tethered' to technology in such ways that it has had profound impact upon the way people ordinarily socialise in everyday life, and upon the experience of relational space. She writes (2011: 155) that, for example,

> [. . .] a train station (like an airport, a café, or a park) is no longer a communal space but a place of social collection: people come together but do not speak to each other. [. . .] When people have phone conversations in public spaces, their sense of privacy is sustained by the presumption that those around them will treat them not only as anonymous but as if absent.

The key here is to think about the habitus of individuals (i.e., probably many of us who use mobile phones frequently, including myself) who perform this absence as an exaggeration or enhancement of this absence in public spaces. If we sense that someone is listening in, we turn away. If we find that that environment in which we are sat is too noisy, or contains multiple conversations, we place a finger in the spare ear in an effort to block out all but the disembodied voice in the phone. If the phone rings or beeps when in mid-flow face-to-face conversation, we check to see who is responsible for the communication and make a split-judgement on whether to disengage from the current conversation and answer the phone's call. These are everyday occurrences, very familiar to us today, but probably unthinkable in terms of the social etiquette of even a few years ago. It therefore signifies that something has changed in the ways that social relations, on a personal level at least, are conducted. It also calls into question some of the assumptions we make about what connectivity is, in the first instance, and, in the second, our assumptions about what is happening to connectivity as praxis in accelerated contexts where real and virtual distinctions hold little weight; and also, whether those changes might be considered a good thing. In this example, the proxemics of social relations are thrown into question: a reactionary voice might say that prioritising a virtual connection over a face-to-face connection is a step in the wrong direction; a progressive voice might say that something approaching the opposite is true. However, it is just as likely that reactionary and progressive views can hold the obverse: progressives sometimes argue for the value of face-to-face time, whereas reactionary views hold that Facetime is the key to efficient interpersonal communications, particularly when it comes to workload and productivity.

Intuition tells us that connectivity in accelerated media ecosystems has something to do with our attention (in the popular or folk psychology sense of the term) and is therefore demanding of personal cognitive resources. It is related to what some commentators such as Clay Shirky have described as 'filter failure' (2008). It is not so much that the sheer amount of information available is exponentially increasing to the point where people become incapacitated, but is closer to the notion that we have yet to develop the apparatus (whether technological or cognitive) to deal with it. I would say that it is both. To what extent, say, does a switched-on phone demand of my attention, even when it lies dormant in my pocket for the entire time I conduct a face-to-face conversation with someone in the street? I *feel* that there is something that could be of interest to me in my news feed the next time I look at it and scroll down. To what extent is some part of my consciousness attending to my 'network'? I *know* that someone, somewhere in my social media friends or followers list is online *right now* – it is a certainty.

In terms of efficiency, connectivity is also related to attention in the economic sense – many of use choose to disable notifications from social media feeds on mobile apps, but the notifications settings are more than likely enabled by default. It is the business of the attention economy to keep the user engaged: eyeballs on screens consuming content in the traditional sense of 'media consumption' are augmented by the production of personal data generated through the interaction itself. Making the interaction (and therefore the production of data) as constant and consistent as possible is therefore of value to SNSs that would seek to monetise such data, and profile the user. In another sense, then, this state of connectivity returns us to the level of data automation and governance as a structuring presence of connectivity, but a kind of connectivity where the content seems to be less important that the structuring presence itself.

Whilst it also requires us to rethink the complexity involved in the relationship between connectivity as a condition, social relations and political economies of contemporary communications practices, this leads us to another problem of connectivity, then, and one fundamentally tied to the political dimension already discussed. We can say with some confidence that connectivity is a problem of psychology. As I discuss in detail over the course of this book, and indeed elsewhere (Singh 2014a, 2014b, 2017), any consideration of interpersonal communications technologies, and the practices associated with those technologies, binds the discussion of connectivity with not only general economies of cognition, but, more fundamentally, with economies of *re*-cognition, and with the psychology of personality especially. In terms of online identity mobilisation in the kinds of accelerated, convergent contexts already mentioned, this again seems to me an urgent aspect of connectivity.

Once more, we can return to Turkle, and a particular observation that forms an instructive kernel of the ideas in her book *Alone Together*. She writes (2011: 154) that

> Networked, we are together, but so lessened are our expectations of each other that we can feel utterly alone. And there is the risk that we come to see others as objects to be accessed – and only for the parts we find useful, comforting or amusing.

In this scenario, supported by Turkle's considerable record of ethnographic research in the field of social psychology, not only does it appear that loneliness increases proportionately with connectivity (in the sense of being always-on), but, additionally, social relations are diminished and we expect that a more impoverished relation will inevitably be the only one available. If this is the case, then, surely connectivity as it is assumed is not worth it? If people are reduced to objects which are accessed *only for the parts we find useful*, even if just to make ourselves feel better, then there is both a diminished sense of personhood at play here, which alone might be considered undesirable; but further, social relations are reduced to use-value. To paraphrase Jaron Lanier (2010), I have no desire to be anyone's gadget. It is, therefore, an economic question in more than one sense, because it brings into view the notion that we are moving towards a scenario where social capital in an accelerated context is built upon the necessity to treat the interpersonal encounter as an inter-*objective* encounter, rather than an inter-subjective one. The expectation is that I will be objectified, so I had better draw up my defences by objectifying the other. This is a state which is, from a philosophical perspective, perhaps not only undesirable, but is also, from a psychosocial perspective, untenable.

At length, I have examined this objectified state from the perspective of Honneth's work on the politics of recognition, through his examination of identity and the influence object-relations had on his formulation of a political take on identity formation. My particular innovation here is not only to apply Honneth's work to aspects of connectivity in the digital age, although to my knowledge there are certainly few people working in that way (the notable recent exception being, perhaps, Christian Fuchs (2016)). I additionally developed the psychological aspects of Honneth's recognition theory further. I considered how Kohut's self psychology, as well as depth approaches from Jung and existential psychology approaches to the self, such as those from Laing, can further illuminate the psychology of recognition politics in the terms set through semi-permanent conditions of connectivity.

As discussed in the final chapter to the current study, the Quantified Self movement is a popular trend where people have adopted self-tracking practices to give accurate measurements, data and visualisations of aspects of their lives, which they wish to document and analyse, possibly to share via their SNS profiles, with the goal towards 'self-improvement'. As Walker Rettberg notes, 'Quantitative self-representations can be like visualisations of big data, in that they, represent "a fantasy of knowing, or total knowledge" [. . .] We think that the numbers tell us the objective truth' (2014: 65). However, as Walker Rettberg implies, truth and accuracy can mean very different things. Self-tracking, measuring and the representational data accumulated (in the form of automated visualisations produced by a jogging app, say, and the datasets that emerge from months of daily use) can usually be said to produce a very accurate pattern of information about a very narrow aspect of oneself. Yes, I jog – but do I feel any better? Yes, my Facebook friends 'like' the filtered Instagram picture of the superfood shake I had for my breakfast, and I can assume with a degree of accuracy from this that they have given their approval presumably because it is 'good for me' – but did it taste any good? There are certain things that quantifying apps can tell us very accurately about ourselves, but other things that they are useless for telling us. The point to this exercise in critiquing quantified self is that the content of the data is less important than the ritual of performing the quantification, in a world where accuracy overrides fidelity as our primary concern.

Also under discussion in the previous chapter, Deborah Lupton (2016) takes an arguably more radical approach to Walker Rettberg. It is worth noting, in full, her observation that self-tracking has moved beyond the rationale of the consensual and personal, and into the social domains of work and the legal system. Lupton writes (2016: 121) that:

> In the persuasive computing and digital health literature, the personal data that are generated from self-tracking are represented as pedagogical and motivational – a means of encouraging self-reflection or emotional responses such as fear, guilt or shame that will lead to the desired behavioural changes. While many people may choose to engage in these types of enterprises willingly, as part of their personal goals and motivations, there is an abundant evidence in these programs that they are strongly associated with the objective of persuading people who are otherwise reluctant to participate in them. Hence the motivation for self-tracking is viewed as requiring impetus from the external agency that is attempting to change people's behaviour.

In her analysis, Lupton identifies a strand of paternalism in this conflict of motivations which we ought to both critically consider and, from an ethics perspective, guard against. However, I think that this has moved the field of inquiry beyond ethics and into the realm of political philosophy proper. Lupton goes on to identify this kind of persuasive paternalism in practice as 'nudging', which is a form of persuasion subtler than coercion, in that it is never so obvious. Nudging persuades people not only that a change in behaviour would be a good thing, but also appeals to the idea that the behaviour change is a personal motivation rather than an external one – I would go as far as to say even to the extent that one is persuaded that the idea to self-improve in a specific area is one's own idea, rather than of an external agency. This 'hidden persuasion' is of course nothing new – indeed, in *The Hidden Persuaders* (1957) Vance Packard wrote the book on the impact of subtle persuasion in consumer culture and lifestyle in the immediate postwar period. It suggests, once more, a continuity of tension between the individual and another (whether a community, an institution or a corporate entity) in terms of agency, as well as the way one views one's own agency as self-originating, that easily predates the Web. A key to understanding what Lupton means, exactly, by 'impetus from external agency', is found in her description of this paternalism as a kind of 'soft' or 'libertarian' paternalism (2016: 121–2) that

[. . .] adheres to the neoliberal model of governing populations, in which coercion is largely replaced by psychological models of behaviour that encourage people to take up self-care practices [. . .]. At its heart is the belief that, left to themselves, people would not readily take up behaviours deemed to be wise, productive and conducive to the ideal of the responsible entrepreneurial citizen.

This confirms the suspicion that we are dealing here with a political question, the orientation of which demands that we examine the motivations not just of the personal participants as a matter of consumer choices made at the empirical level, but also what the *purpose* of those kinds of choices are *for*. The neoliberal model, as we saw in Part I of this book, does of course orient itself around two central tenets. First, libertarian models of freely choosing individual actors driving markets and, second, a trust in markets to not only better inform individuals on their personal choices, but to also deliver a mechanism whereby competition in all spheres encourages wealth creation, increases prosperity and underpins conservative and traditionalist notions of national interest. One might venture to claim that, at a superficial level, this is a broadly accurate description of the political arrangement of Western societies today. Thinking about ethics as a deeper form of analysis of *ideas* than empirical forms, which describe *things* usually as they are, is a position I take to heart in this book, and is profoundly shaped by my encounters with the communitarian orientation in the work of the political philosophers Charles Taylor and Michael Sandel. It seems to me that this is necessary because of the tensions present in the praxis of the Quantified Self, particularly in its connectivity dimension where vast amounts of personal data are generated, shared, monetised, accumulated and stored by institutions and entities of influence – entities far more powerful that individuals themselves.

It has also, to my mind, profound implications for a psychology of self, where motivations of both self and other become infused with doubt. If external agencies of one description or another are 'nudging' motivations of individual actors, then the model of developed agency in Kohut's work, for example (1971, 1977, 2011), which relies upon the full recognition of autonomous motivation in oneself and in others, needs to accommodate a new kind of objectification process. It arouses an everyday suspicion of motives at an interpersonal level which reflects back up to the political realm of social relations too. As Lupton states, practices of self-tracking are 'spreading from the private realm into diverse social domains, and the implications of the self-tracking phenomenon for the politics of personal data, data practices and data materialisations' (Lupton 2016: 1). As I have stated elsewhere, the implications of Lupton's work necessitate that one considers ways in which such practices partake of a broader culture associated with self-improvement, modification and technologies of wellbeing or work productivity within relations of power (Singh 2017).

In this sense, then, the inter-objective encounters described a moment ago reconfigure social relations to account for self-regulation via data automation and governance processes. Within those processes, however, an impoverished form of agency emerges which resembles machine- rather than human-logic, and a genuinely progressive notion of human-computer interactions is replaced altogether by a newer form of agency: that of the *automaton*. This conclusion is formed through a teasing-out of the arguments concerned with describing, in rich, intersubjective terms, what the self is, and how the self relates to other selves in the social world. It therefore not only demands that the ethical implications are rethought in relation to aspects of data accumulation and use in the social realm, but also how the very functionality of connectivity in joining personal data practices to wider social forms of data automation necessitates and justifies a construction of a robust ethics of connectivity. In this book, I have outlined the steps I took towards this conclusion through a critical inquiry methodology, discussing current inadequacies in the practices and conceptualisations of digital literacy. This book has traced relevant arguments from a diversity of disciplines and approaches, chief among them communitarian ethics, depth and relational psychology, media studies and recognition theory. It is very much my hope that the synthesis of these very different approaches to such a novel arena will contribute to the transformation of thinking within the scholarship, which has long since declared the death of Web 2.0.

BIBLIOGRAPHY

Adloff, F. and S. Mau, 2006. Giving social ties: reciprocity in modern society. *Archives Européennes de Sociologie*, 47(1), pp. 93–123.

Adorno, T. W., 2003. *The Jargon of Authenticity*. London: Routledge.

Adorno, T. W. and M. Horkheimer, 2007. *Dialectic of Enlightenment: Philosophical Fragments*. Stanford, CA: Stanford University Press.

Aitkenhead, D., 2012. Interview with Michael Sandel. *Guardian*, 27 May. Available at: www.theguardian.com/books/2012/may/27/michael-sandel-reason-values-bodies [accessed: 08/03/2018].

Allen, M., 2012. What was Web 2.0? Versions as the dominant mode of internet history. *New Media & Society*, 15(2), pp. 260–75.

Allen, M., 2008. Web 2.0: an argument against convergence? *First Monday*, 13(3). Available at: http://firstmonday.org/article/view/2139/1946#p5 [accessed: 03/03/2017].

Allmer, T., 2015. *Critical Theory and Social Media: Between emancipation and commodification*. London: Routledge.

Althusser, L., 1977. *For Marx*. London: New Left Books.

Altman, R., 1985. The evolution of sound technology. In: Weis, E. and J. Belton, eds. 1985. *Film Sound: Theory and Practice*. New York: Columbia University Press.

Athique, A., 2013. *Digital Media and Society*. Cambridge: Polity.

Anderson, E., 2010. *Social Media Marketing: Game Theory and the Emergence of Collaboration*. New York: Springer.

Asikomurwa, V. and M. Mohaisen, 2015. Game theory and business intelligence in strategic business decisions – a review. *International Journal of Advanced Computational Engineering and Networking*, 3(8), pp. 101–105.

Balick, A., 2014a. How to think about psychotherapy in a digital context. In: Weitz, P., ed., 2014. *Psychotherapy 2.0: Where Psychotherapy and Technology Meet*. London: Karnac.

Balick, A., 2014b. *The Psychodynamics of Social Networking: Connected-up Instantaneous Culture and the Self*. London: Karnac.

Banaji, S. and D. Buckingham, 2013. *The Civic Web: Young People, The Internet and Civic Participation*. Cambridge, MA: MIT Press.

Baron, N. S., 2010. *Always On: Language in an Online and Mobile World*. Oxford: Oxford University Press.

Bassil-Morozow, H., 2010. *Tim Burton: The Monster and the Crowd – a post-Jungian perspective.* Hove: Routledge.

Baumer, E. P. S., Guha, S., Quan, E., Mimno, D. and G. K. Gay, 2015. Missing photos, suffering withdrawal, or finding freedom? How experiences of social media non-use influence the likelihood of reversion. *Social Media + Society,* July–December, pp. 1–14.

Baym, N., 2010. *Personal Connections in the Digital Age.* Cambridge: Polity.

Bean, R., 2009. "It's Good to Talk" – the story behind the campaign. *Campaign,* 16 September. Available at: www.campaignlive.co.uk/article/its-good-talk-story-behind-campaign/938629# [accessed: 16/08/2016].

Becker, K. and F. Stalder, eds, 2009. *Deep Search: The Politics of Search Beyond Google.* Innsbruck: Studienverlag & Transaction Publishers.

Bell, D. and B. M. Kennedy, eds, 2007. *The Cybercultures Reader* (2nd ed.). Abingdon: Routledge.

Benjamin, J., 2004. Beyond doer and done to: an intersubjective view of thirdness. *Psychoanalytic Quarterly,* 73, pp. 5–46.

Benjamin, J., 2007. Intersubjectivity, Thirdness, and Mutual Recognition. Institute for Contemporary Psychoanalysis presentation, Los Angeles, CA. Available at: http://icpla.edu/wp-content/uploads/2013/03/Benjamin-J.-2007-ICP-Presentation-Thirdness-present-send.pdf [accessed: 12/03/2018].

Benjamin, W., 1986. *Reflections.* Trans. Edmund Jephcott. New York: Schocken Books.

Berners-Lee, T., 2000. *Weaving the Web: the Past, Present and Future of the World Wide Web.* London: Texere.

Bertotti, M., Jamal, F. and A. Harden, 2014. A review of conceptualisations and meanings of "community" within and across research traditions: a meta-narrative approach. Executive Report, Connected Communities Initiative. Available at: www.ahrc.ac.uk/documents/project-reports-and-reviews/connected-communities/a-review-of-conceptualisations-and-meanings-of-community-within-and-across-research-traditions-a-metanarrative-approach [accessed: 12/03/2018].

Berry, D. M., 2008. *Copy, Rip, Burn: The Politics of Copyleft and Open Source.* London: Pluto Press.

Betts, L. R., 2016. *Cyberbullying: Approaches, Consequences and Interventions.* London: Palgrave Macmillan.

Biressi, A. and H. Nunn, 2010. "A trust betrayed": celebrity and the work of emotion. *Celebrity Studies,* 1(4), pp. 49–64.

Blau, P., 1964. *Exchange and Power in Social Life.* New York: Wiley.

Blencowe, C. et al., 2014. Immanent authority and the making of community. Executive report. Connected Communities Initiative. Available at: www.ahrc.ac.uk/documents/project-reports-and-reviews/connected-communities/immanent-authority-and-the-making-of-community [accessed: 12/03/2018].

Bogost, I., 2016. Why gamification is bullshit. In: Chun, W. H. K. and Anna Watkins Fisher, eds, 2016. *New Media, Old Media: a history and theory reader* (2nd ed.). London: Routledge. pp. 678–88.

Bollmer, G., 2012. Demanding connectivity: the performance of "true" identity and the politics of social media. *JOMEC Journal,* 1, June. Available at: https://jomec.cardiffuniversitypress.org/articles/abstract/10.18573/j.2012.10220 [accessed: 12/03/2018].

boyd, d., 2012. Participating in the always-on lifestyle. In: Mandiberg, M., ed., 2012. *The Social Media Reader.* New York: New York University Press.

boyd, d., 2014. *It's Complicated.* London: Yale University Press.

boyd, d. and J. Donath, 2004. Public displays of connection. *BT Technology Journal,* 22(4), October, pp. 71–82.

Bruns, A., 2008. *Blogs, Wikipedia, Second Life, and beyond: From production to produsage.* New York: Peter Lang.

Burgess J. and J. Green, 2009. *YouTube.* Cambridge: Polity.

Brooks, S. and P. Longstreet, 2015. Social networking's peril: cognitive absorption, social networking usage, and depression. *Cyberpsychology: Journal of Psychosocial Research on Cyberspace,* 9(4), article 5.

Branigan, E., 1986. Color and cinema: problems in the writing of history. In: P. Kerr, ed., 1986. *The Hollywood Film Industry: A Reader.* London: BFI

Burns, T., 2013. Hegel, Cosmopolitanism, and contemporary recognition theory. In: Burns, T. and S. Thompson, eds, 2013. *Global Justice and the Politics of Recognition.* Basingstoke: Palgrave Macmillan.

Burns, T. and S. Thompson, eds, 2013. *Global Justice and the Politics of Recognition.* Basingstoke: Palgrave Macmillan.

Bury, R. and J. Li, 2015. Is it live or is it timeshifted, streamed or downloaded? Watching television in the era of multiple screens. *New Media & Society,* 17(4), pp. 592–610.

Buscombe, E., 2004. Sound and colour. In: T. Schatz, ed., 2004. *Hollywood: Critical Concepts in Media and Cultural Studies Volume III – Social Dimensions: Technology, Regulation and Audience.* London: Routledge.

Caillé, A., 1994. *Don, intérêt et désintéressement: Bourdieu, Mauss, Platon et quelques autres.* Paris: La Découverte.

Caillé, A., 2011. Les indicateurs de richesse alternatifs: une fausse bonne idée? Réflexions sur les incertitudes de la gesion par le chiffre. In: A. Caillé et al., eds, 2011. *De la convivialité. Dialogues sur la societé conviviale é veni.* Paris: Éditions La Découverte, pp. 141–66.

Caldwell, J. T., 2004. Convergence television: aggregating form and repurposing content in the culture of conglomeration. In: Spigel, L. and J. Olsson, eds, 2004. *Television After TV: Essays on a Medium in Transition.* London: Duke University Press.

Cammaerts, B., 2008. Critiques on the participatory potentials of Web 2.0. *Communication, Culture & Critique,* 1, pp. 358–77.

Cannon, B., 2001. *Rethinking Normative Content of Critical Theory: Marx, Habermas and Beyond.* Basingstoke: Palgrave Macmillan.

Carah, N. and A. Dobson, 2016. Algorithmic hotness: young women's "promotion" and "reconnaissance" work via social media body images. *Social Media + Society,* October–December 2016, pp. 1–10.

Carr, N., 2008. Is Google making us stupid? What the Internet is doing to our brains. *The Atlantic* Website, July/August. Available at: www.theatlantic.com/magazine/archive/2008/07/is-google-making-us-stupid/306868/ [accessed: 15/05/2018].

Carr, N., 2010. *The Shallows: How the internet is changing the way we read, think and remember.* London: Atlantic Books.

Ceron, E., 2015. The model who quit social media reveals how much makeup was behind her perfect selfies. *Teen Vogue* Website, posted 20 November. Available at: www.teenvogue.com/story/essena-oneill-breaks-down-her-perfect-makeup-selfies [accessed: 23/01/2017].

Chen, C., 2016. Forming digital self and parasocial relationships on YouTube. *Journal of Consumer Culture* 16(1), pp. 232–54.

Chun, W. H. K. and A. W. Fisher, eds, 2016. *New Media, Old Media: a history and theory reader,* 2nd ed. London: Routledge.

Claxton, G., 2003. *Creativity: A Guide for the Advanced Learner (and Teacher).* National Association of Head Teachers Leadership Papers. Available at: https://smc-sct.wikispaces.com/file/view/Creativity+a+guide.pdf [accessed: 03/03/2018].

Click, M. A., Lee, H. and H. W. Holladay, 2013. Making monsters: Lady Gaga, fan identification, and social media. *Popular Music and Society*, 36(3), pp. 360–79.

Coleman, J. S., 1994. *Foundations of Social Theory*, volume I. Cambridge, MA: Harvard University Press.

Convivialist Manifesto. A declaration of interdependence (Global Dialogues 3). Duisburg 2014: Käte Hamburger Kolleg/Centre for Global Cooperation Research (KHK/GCR21). Available at: www.gcr21.org/fileadmin/website/daten/pdf/Publications/Convivialist_Manifesto_2198-0403-GD-3.pdf [accessed: 12/03/2018].

Coombs, D. S. and S. Collister, eds, 2015. *Debates for the Digital Age: the good, the bad, and the ugly of our online world*. Westport, CT: Prager Publishers Inc.

Cooper, M., 2008. *Essential Research Findings in Counselling and Psychotherapy: The Facts are Friendly*. London: SAGE.

Crawford, A., 2002. The myth of the unmarked net speaker. In: G. Elmer, ed., 2002. *Critical Perspectives on the Internet*. Oxford: Rowman and Littlefield.

Csikszentmihalyi, M., 1992. *Flow*. London. Random House.

Csikszentmihalyi, M., 1997. *Creativity: Flow and the Psychology of Discovery and Invention*. London: Harper Perennial.

Csikszentmihalyi, M., 2006. A systems perspective on creativity. In: J. Henry, ed., 2006. *Creative Management and Development*, 3rd ed. London: SAGE.

Curran, J., Fenton, N. and D. Freedman, 2012. *Misunderstanding the Internet*. London: Routledge.

Davis, A., 2013. *Promotional Cultures: The Rise and Spread of Advertising, Public Relations, Marketing and Branding*. Cambridge: Polity.

Deleuze, G., 1998. Having an idea in cinema. In: E. Kaufman and K. J. Heller, eds, 1998. *Deleuze and Guattari: New Mappings in Politics, Philosophy and Culture*. Minneapolis: University of Minnesota Press.

Deranty, J.-P., Petherbridge, D. and J. Rundell, eds, 2006. *Recognition, Work, Politics: New Directions in French Critical Theory*. Boston, MA: Brill.

Dewdney, A. and P. Ride, 2014. *The Digital Media Handbook*. Abingdon: Routledge.

Dewey, J. and J. A. Boydson, eds, 2008. *John Dewey – The Later Works Vol. 2: 1925–1927*. Carbondale, IL: Southern Illinois University Press.

Doyle, A., 2011. Revisiting the synopticon: reconsidering Mathiesen's "the viewer society". *Theoretical Criminology*, 15(3), pp. 283–99.

Driessens, O., 2013. Celebrity capital: redefining celebrity using field theory. *Theory and Society*, 42(5), pp. 543–60.

Duesenberry, J., 1949. *Income, Saving and the Theory of Consumer Behaviour*. Cambridge, MA: Harvard University Press.

Dutt, A. K., 2008. The dependence effect, consumption and happiness: Galbraith revisited. *Review of Political Economy*, 20(4), October, pp. 527–50.

Dyer-Witheford, N., 1999. *Cyber-Marx: Cycles and Circuits of Struggle in High Technology Capitalism*. Champaign, IL: University of Illinois Press.

Dyer-Witheford, N., 2010. Digital labour, species-becoming and the global worker. *Ephemera: Theory & Politics in Organization*. Available at: www.ephemerajournal.org/con tribution/digital-labour-species-becoming-and-global-worker [accessed: 15/07/2016].

Eagleton, T., 1991. *Ideology*. London: Verso.

Elmer, G., ed., 2002. *Critical Perspectives on the Internet*. Oxford: Rowman and Littlefield.

Ess, C., 2009. *Digital Media Ethics*. Cambridge: Polity.

Evans, D., 2010. *Social Media Marketing: The Next Generation of Business Engagement*. Oxford: Wiley Publishing.

Farr, A., 2014. Herbert Marcuse. In: E. N. Zalta, ed., 2014. *The Stanford Encyclopedia of Philosophy*. Available at: http://plato.stanford.edu/archives/fall2014/entries/marcuse/ [accessed: 15/07/2016].

Freud, S., 1911. Formulations regarding the two principles of mental functioning. *Papers on Metapsychology; Papers on Applied Psycho-Analysis*. Vol. 4 of Collected Papers. London: Hogarth and Institute of Psycho-Analysis, 1924–1950, pp. 13–21.

Fiske, J., 1989. *Reading the Popular*. London Routledge.

Flew. T., 2008. *New Media: An Introduction*, 3rd ed. Oxford: Oxford University Press.

Foster, J. B. and R. McChesney, 2011. The Internet's unholy marriage to capitalism. *Monthly Review*, 62(10). Available at: https://monthlyreview.org/2011/03/01/the-internets-unholy-marriage-to-capitalism/ [accessed: 03/03/2018].

Foucault, M., 1977. *Discipline and Punish: The Birth of the Prison*. London: Vintage.

Freeman, L. A. and A. G. Peace, 2005. *Information Ethics: Privacy and Intellectual Property*. London: Information Science Publishing

Fuchs, C., 2011. Against Henry Jenkins. Remarks on Henry Jenkins. ICA Talk, 'Spreadable Media'. *Information – Society – Technology & Media*, blog site. Available at: http://fuchs.uti.at/570/ [accessed: 12/10/2018].

Fuchs, C., 2013. *Social Media: A Critical Introduction*. London: SAGE.

Fuchs, C., 2014. *Digital Labour and Karl Marx*. London: Routledge.

Fuchs, C., 2016. *Critical Theory of Communication: New Readings of Lukács, Adorno, Marcuse, Honneth and Habermas in the Age of the Internet*. London: University of Westminster Press.

Fuchs, C. and M. Sandoval, eds, 2014. *Critique, Social Media and the Information Society*. London: Routledge.

Fuchs, C., Boersma, K., Albrechtslund, A. and M. Sandoval, eds, 2012. *Internet and Surveillance: The Challenges of Web 2.0 and Social Media*. London: Routledge.

Gackenbach, J., ed., 2007. *Psychology and the Internet: Intrapersonal, Interpersonal, and Transpersonal Implications*. London: Academic Press.

Galbraith, J. K., 1962. *The Affluent Society*. Harmondsworth: Penguin Books.

Galbraith, James K., 2008. The abiding economies of John Kenneth Galbraith. *Review of Political Economy*, 20(4), October, pp. 491–9.

Gates, K. 2011. *Our Biometric Future: Facial Recognition Technology and the Culture of Surveillance*. London: New York University Press.

Gauntlett, D., 2011. *Making is Connecting: The Social Meaning of Creativity, from DIY and Knitting to YouTube and Web 2.0*. Cambridge: Polity.

Gehl, R., 2011. The archive and the processor: the internal logic of Web 2.0. *New Media & Society*, 13(8), pp. 1228–44.

Gehring, V. V., ed., 2004. *The Internet in Public Life*. Oxford: Rowman & Littlefield.

Giota, K. G. and G. Kleftaras, 2013. The role of personality and depression in problematic use of social networking sites in Greece. *Cyberpsychology: Journal of Psychosocial Research on Cyberspace*, 7(3), article 6. Available at: https://cyberpsychology.eu/article/view/4293/3338 [accessed: 03/03/2018].

Gneezy, U. and A. Rustichini, 2000. A fine is a price. *Journal of Legal Studies*, 29(1), January, pp. 1–17.

Goffman, I., 1997. The presentation of self in everyday life. In: Lemert, C. and A. Branaman, eds, 1997. *The Goffman Reader*. Oxford: Blackwell.

Golding, P. and G. Murdock, 2005. Culture, communication and political economy. In: Curran, J. and M. Gurevitch, eds, 2005. *Mass Media and Society*, London: Hodder Education.

Gouldner, A. W., 1960. The norm of reciprocity: a preliminary statement. *American Sociological Review*, 25, pp. 161–78.

Griffin, E., 2005. *A First Look at Communication Theory*, 5th ed. Columbus, OH: MacGraw Hill Education.

Griffin, E., 2006. Anxiety/uncertainty management theory of William Gudykunst. In: E. Griffin, *A First Look at Communication Theory*, 6th ed., Columbus, OH: MacGraw Hill Education.

Gudykunst, W., 1995. Anxiety/uncertainty management (AUM) theory: current status. In: Wiseman, R. L., ed., 1995. *Intercultural Communication Theory*. Thousand Oaks, CA: SAGE.

Guildford, J. P., 1950. Creativity. *American Psychologist*, 5, pp. 444–5.

Habermas, J., 1984 [1981]. *Theory of Communicative Action, Volume One: Reason and the Rationalization of Society*. Trans. Thomas A. McCarthy. Boston, MA: Beacon Press.

Haraway, D., 2004. *The Haraway Reader*. London: Routledge.

Haraway, D., 2007. A cyborg manifesto: science, technology, and socialist-feminism in the late twentieth century. In: Bell, D. and B. M. Kennedy, eds, 2007. *The Cybercultures Reader*, 2nd ed. Abingdon: Routledge.

Harvey, D., 2005. *A Brief History of Neoliberalism*. Oxford: Oxford University Press.

Harvie, D., Layng, B. and Keir Milburn, 2014. Why are comedians, not musicians, talking 'bout a revolution? *Guardian*, 12 May. Available at: www.theguardian.com/commentisfree/2014/may/12/comedians-musicians-revolution-russell-brand-beppe-grillo-neoliberalism [access: 03/03/2018].

Hauke, C. and I. Alister, eds, 2000. *Jung and Film: Post-Jungian Takes on the Moving Image*. London Routledge.

Hauke, C. and L. Hockley, eds, 2011. *Jung and Film II –The Return: Further Post-Jungian Takes on the Moving Image*. Hove: Routledge.

Heath, S., 1980. 'The Cinematic Apparatus: Technology as Historical and Cultural Form', in de Laurentis, T. and S. Heath (eds) *The Cinematic Apparatus*. New York: St. Martin's Press. pp. 1–13.

Hegel, G. W. F., 1994 [1807]. *Phenomenology of Spirit*. Trans. and annotated Howard P. Kainz. University Park, PA: Pennsylvania State University Press

Heidegger, M., 2000. *Being and Time*. Oxford: Blackwell.

Hemanth, D. J. and S. Smys, eds, 2018. *Computational Vision and Bio Inspired Computing*. London: Springer.

Henry, J., ed., 2006, *Creative Management and Development*, 3rd ed. London: SAGE.

Herman, E. S. and N. Chomsky, 1988. *Manufacturing Consent: The Political Economy of the Mass Media*. New York: Pantheon Books.

Hill, A., 2014. Reality TV experiences: audiences, fact, and fiction. In: Ouellette, L., ed., 2014. *A Companion to Reality Television*. Oxford: Wiley-Blackwell.

Ho, S. S., Lee, E. W. J. and Y. Liao, 2016. Social network sites, friends, and celebrities: the roles of social comparison and celebrity involvement in adolescents' body image dissatisfaction. *Social Media + Society*, July–September, pp. 1–11.

Hockley, L., 2007. *Frames of Mind: A Post-Jungian Look at Cinema, Television and Technology*. Bristol: Intellect.

Hockley, L., 2014. *Somatic Cinema: The Relationship Between Body and Screen – A Jungian Perspective*. Hove: Routledge.

Hockley, L. and N. Fadina, eds, 2015. *The Happiness Illusion: How the Media Sold us a Fairytale*. Hove: Routledge.

Hockley, L. and L. Gardner, eds, 2011. *House: The Wounded Healer on Television – Jungian and Post-Jungian Reflections*. Hove: Routledge.

Hoffman, M. T., 2011. *Toward Mutual Recognition: Relational Psychoanalysis and the Christian Narrative*. Hove: Routledge.

Hogan, B., 2010. The presentation of self in the age of social media: distinguishing performances and exhibitions online. *Bulletin of Science, Technology & Society* 30(6), pp. 377–86.

Honneth, A., 1995. *The Struggle for Recognition: The Moral Grammar of Social Conflicts*. Cambridge: Polity.

Honneth, A., 2008. *Reification: A New Look at an Old Idea*. Oxford: Oxford University Press.

Honneth, A., 2012. *The I in We: Studies in the Theory of Recognition*. Cambridge: Polity.

Honneth, A. and N. Fraser, 2002. *Redistribution or Recognition? A Political-Philosophical Exchange*. London: Verso.

Hunt, E., 2015. Essena O'Neill quits Instagram claiming social media "is not real life". *Guardian*, 3 November. Available at: www.theguardian.com/media/2015/nov/03/instagram-star-essena-oneill-quits-2d-life-to-reveal-true-story-behind-images [accessed: 23/01/2017].

Hurrell, A. and L. Gomez-Mera, 2003. Entry on 'Neoliberalism'. In: McLean, I. and A. McMillan, eds, *Oxford Concise Dictionary of Politics*, 2nd ed. Oxford: Oxford University Press.

Illich, I., 1973. *Tools for Conviviality*. London: Marion Boyars.

Inwood, M., 1992. *A Hegel Dictionary*. Oxford: Blackwell.

Izod, J., 2001. *Myth, Mind and the Screen: Understanding the Heroes of Our Time*. Cambridge: Cambridge University Press.

Izod, J., 2006. *Screen, Culture, Psyche: A Post Jungian Approach to Working with the Audience*. Abingdon: Routledge.

Izod, J. and J. Dovalis, 2015. *Cinema as Therapy: Grief and Transformational Film*. Hove: Routledge.

Jacoby, M., 2006. *Individuation and Narcissism: The Psychology of Self in Jung and Kohut*. London: Routledge.

Jameson, F., 1981. *The Political Unconscious: Narrative as a Socially Symbolic Act*. Ithaca: Cornell University Press.

Jameson, F., 1988. *The Ideologies of Theory – Essays 1971–1986, Volume 2: The Syntax of History*. London: Routledge.

Jay, M., 2008. Introduction. In: Honneth, A., 2008. *Reification: A New Look at an Old Idea*. Oxford: Oxford University Press.

Jenkin, M. and L. Harris, eds, 2007. *Computational Vision in Neural and Machine Systems*. Cambridge: Cambridge University Press.

Jenkins, H., 2006. *Convergence Culture: Where Old and New Media Collide*. London: New York University Press.

Jenkins, H. et al., 2005. *Confronting the Challenges of Participatory Culture: Media Education for the 21st Century*. London: MIT Press.

Jenkins, H., Ford, S. and J. Green, 2013. *Spreadable Media: Creating Value and Meaning in a Networked Culture*. London: New York University Press.

Jenkins, H., Ito, M. and d. boyd, 2015. *Participatory Culture in a Networked Era*. Cambridge: Polity.

Jerslev, A., 2014. Talking about Angelina – celebrity gossip on the Internet. *Northern Lights*, 12(1), pp. 105–22.

Joinson, A. N., 2003. *Understanding the Psychology of Internet Behaviour: Virtual Worlds, Real Lives*. London: Palgrave Macmillan.

Joinson, A. N., 2007. Disinhibition and the Internet. In: Gackenbach, J., ed., 2007. *Psychology and the Internet: Intrapersonal, Interpersonal, and Transpersonal Implications*. London: Academic Press.

Joinson, A. N. and C. B. Paine, 2012. Self-disclosure, privacy and the Internet. In: Joinson, A. N., McKenna, K. Y. A., Postmes, T. and U.-D. Reips, eds, 2012. *Oxford Handbook of Internet Psychology*. Oxford: Oxford University Press.

Joinson, A. N., McKenna, K. Y. A., Postmes, T. and U.-D. Reips, eds, 2012. *Oxford Handbook of Internet Psychology*. Oxford: Oxford University Press.

Jung, C. G., 1953. *Two Essays on Analytical Psychology*. New York: Pantheon Books.

Jung, C. G., ed., 1964. *Man and His Symbols*. London: Aldus Books.

Katz, J. E., ed., 2008. *Handbook of Mobile Communication Studies*. London: MIT Press.

Kaun, A. and F. Stiernstedt, 2014. Facebook time: technological and institutional affordances for media memories. *New Media & Society*, 16(7), pp. 1154–68.

Keen, A., 2007. *The Cult of the Amateur: How blogs, MySpace, YouTube and the rest of today's user-generated media are killing our culture and economy*. London: Nicholas Brealey Publishing.

Kerr, P., ed., 1986. *The Hollywood Film Industry: A Reader*. London: BFI

Kieffer, C., 2013. *Mutuality, Recognition and the Self. Psychoanalytic Reflections*. London: Karnac.

Kieran, M., 1999. *Media Ethics: A Philosophical Approach*. London: Praeger.

Kimbles, S. L., 2000. The cultural complex and the myth of invisibility. In: T. Singer, ed., 2000. *The Vision Thing*. London: Routledge.

Kohut, H., 1971. *The Analysis of the Self*. PLACE: International Universities Press.

Kohut, H., 1977. *The Restoration of The Self*. London: University of Chicago Press.

Kohut, H., 2011 [1979]. Four basic concepts in self psychology. In: P. H. Ornstein, ed., *The Search for the Self: Selected Writings of Heinz Kohut 1978–1981*. London: Karnac.

Kojève, A., 1969. *Introduction to the Reading of Hegel*, trans. J. Nichols. Ithaca, NY: Cornell University Press.

Kowalski, Robin M., Limber, Susan P., Agatston and W. Patricia, 2012. *Cyberbullying: Bullying in the Digital Age*, 2nd ed. Oxford: Wiley-Blackwell.

Kracauer, S., 1968. *Theory of Film: The Redemption of Physical Reality*. Oxford: Oxford University Press.

Krüger, S. and J. Johanssen, 2014. Alienation and digital labour – a depth-hermeneutic inquiry into online commodification and the unconscious. *Triple C: Communication, Capitalism and Critique*, 12(2), pp. 632–47.

Kuksa, I. and T. Fisher, eds, 2017. *Design for Personalisation*. Abingdon: Routledge.

Lagore, J., 2015. Self promotion for all! Content creation and personal branding in the digital age. In: Coombs, D. S. and S. Collister, eds, 2015. *Debates for the Digital Age: the good, the bad, and the ugly of our online world*. Westport, CT: Praeger Publishers Inc.

Lamdin, D. J., 2008. Galbraith on advertising, credit, and consumption: a retrospective and empirical investigation with policy implications. *Review of Political Economy*, 20(4), October, pp. 595–611,

Lange, P. G., 2014. *Kids on YouTube: Technical Identities and Digital Literacies*. Walnut Creek, CA: Left Coast Press.

Lanier, J., 2006. Digital Maoism: the hazards of the new online collectivism. *Edge*. Available at: www.edge.org/3rd_culture/lanier06/lanier06_index.html [accessed: 02/03/2018].

Lanier, J., 2010. *You Are Not a Gadget: A Manifesto*. New York: Vintage.

Lanier, J., 2013. *Who Owns the Future?* London: Allen Lane.

Lapidot-Lefler, N. and Barak, A., 2015. The benign online disinhibition effect: Could situational factors induce self-disclosure and prosocial behaviors? *Cyberpsychology: Journal of Psychosocial Research on Cyberspace*, 9(2), article 3.

Lashley, M. C., 2013. *Making Culture on YouTube: Case Studies of Cultural Production on the Popular Web Platform*. Doctoral Thesis. University of Georgia.

Learmonth, M., 2013. Digitas unveils tool to find YouTube stars before they're stars: a long tail of YouTube stars is out there but how to find them? *Advertising Age*, 2 May. Available at: http://adage.com/article/special-report-tv-upfront/digitas-unveils-tool-find-nascent-youtube-stars/241262/ [accessed: 18/07/2016].

Leitch, T., 2014. *Wikipedia U: Knowledge, Authority, and Liberal Education in the Digital Age*. Baltimore, MD: Johns Hopkins University Press.

Lessig, L., 2004. *Free Culture: How big media uses technology and the law to lock down culture and control creativity*. London: The Penguin Press.

Lessig, L., 2008. *Remix: Making art and commerce thrive in the hybrid economy*. London: Bloomsbury.

Levine, R., 2011. *Free Ride: How the internet is destroying the culture business, and how the culture business can fight back*. London: The Bodley Head.

Lévy, P., 1999. *Collective Intelligence: Mankind's Emerging World in Cyberspace*. Trans. R. Bononno. Cambridge, MA: Perseus Books.

Lewallen, J. and E. Behm-Morawitz, 2016. Pinterest or thinterest?: Social comparison and body image on social media. *Social Media + Society*, January–March, pp. 1–9.

Light, B. and E. Cassidy, 2014. Strategies for the suspension and prevention of connection: Rendering disconnection as socioeconomic lubricant with Facebook. *New Media & Society*, 16(7), pp. 1169–84.

Lister, M. et al. 2003. *New Media: A Critical Introduction*. London: Routledge.

Lovink, G., 2008. *Zero Comments: blogging and critical Internet culture*. London: Routledge.

Lovink, G., 2011. *Networks without a Cause: A Critique of Social Media*. Cambridge: Polity.

Lovink, G., 2016. *Social Media Abyss: Critical Internet Cultures and the Force of Negation*. Cambridge: Polity.

Lupton, D., 2016. *The Quantified Self*. Cambridge: Polity.

Lukacs, G., 1990. *History and Class Consciousness*. London: Merlin Press.

Lysaker, O. and J. Jakobsen, eds, 2015. *Recognition and Freedom: Axel Honneth's Political Thought*. Boston, MA: Brill.

Mandiberg, M., ed., 2012. *The Social Media Reader*. New York: New York University Press.

Margalit, A., 2001. Recognizing the brother and the other. In: Honneth, A. and A. Margalit, 2001. *Recognition. Proceedings of the Aristotlean Society*. Supplementary Volumes, 75, pp. 127–39.

Marcuse, H., 1955. *Eros and Civilization: A Philosophical Inquiry into Freud*. Boston: Beacon Press.

Marcuse, H., 1968. *One Dimensional Man*. London: Sphere Books.

Markos, E., Labrecque, L. I. and G. R. Milne, 2012. Web 2.0 and consumers' digital footprint. *Online Consumer Behavior: Theory and Research in Social Media, Advertising and E-Tail*, 157, pp. 157–82.

Marshall, P. D., 2014. *Celebrity and Power: Fame in Contemporary Culture*. Minneapolis: University of Minnesota Press.

Mason, R., 1986. Four ethical issues of the information age. *Management Information Systems Quarterly*, 10(1), March, pp. 5–12.

Mathiesen, T., 1997. The viewer society: Michel Foucault's "Panopticon" revisited. *Theoretical Criminology*, 1(2), pp. 215–34.

Mayer-Schönberger, V., 2011. *Delete: The Virtue of Forgetting in the Digital Age*. Princeton, NJ: Princeton University Press.

McChesney, R., 2013. *Digital Disconnect: How Capitalism Is Turning the Internet against Democracy*. New York: The New Press.

McCormick, K., 1983. Duesenberry and Veblen: the Demonstration Effect revisited. *Journal of Economic Issues*, 17(4), pp.1125–9.

McQueen, P., n.d. Entry on 'Social and Political Recognition'. *Internet Encyclopedia of Philosophy*. Available at www.iep.utm.edu/recog_sp/ [accessed: 16/08/2016].

McQuillan, M., G Macdonald, S. Thomson, and R. Purves (eds) *Post-Theory: New Directions in Criticism*. Edinburgh: Edinburgh University Press.

Mead, G. H., 1970. *Mind, Self and Society*. Chicago: Chicago University Press

Meikle, G., 2016. *Social Media: Communication, Sharing, and Visibility*. Abingdon: Routledge.

Meikle, G. and S. Young, 2012. *Media Convergence: Networked Digital Media in Everyday Life*. London: Palgrave Macmillan.

Mill, J. S., 1974. *On Liberty*. Harmondsworth: Penguin Books.

Mill, J. S., 2000. *Principles of Political Economy*. Ontario: Batoche Books.

Mendelson, M. and Z. Papacharissi, 2011. Look at us: collective narcissism in college student Facebook photo galleries. In: Papacharissi, Z., ed., 2011. *A Networked Self: Identity, Community and Culture on Social Network Sites*. Abingdon: Routledge.

Merleau-Ponty, M., 1964. *Sense and Non-Sense*. Evanston, IL: Northwestern University Press.

Moore, P. and A. Robinson, 2015. The quantified self: What counts in the neoliberal workplace. *New Media & Society*, 18(11), pp. 2774–92.

Mosco, V., 2009. *The Political Economy of Communication*. London: SAGE.

Mosco, V., 2014. *To the Cloud: Big Data in a Turbulent World*. Paradigm Press.

Mourlas, C. and P. Germanakos, eds, 2009. *Intelligent User Interfaces: Adaptation and Personalization Systems and Technologies*. London: Information Science Reference.

Navarro, R., Yubero, S. and E. Larranaga, eds, 2016. *Cyberbullying Across the Globe: Gender, Family, and Mental Health*. New York: Springer.

O'Neill, S. and N. H. Smith, eds, 2012. *Recognition Theory as Social Research: Investigating the Dynamics of Social Conflict*. Basingstoke: Palgrave Macmillan.

O'Reilly, T., 2005. What is Web 2.0? Design patterns and business models for the next generation of software. Available at: www.oreilly.com/pub/a/web2/archive/what-is-web-20.html [accessed: 12/03/2018].

O'Reilly, T., 2006. Levels of the game: the hierarchy of Web 2.0 applications. Available at: http://radar.oreilly.com/2006/07/levels-of-the-game-the-hierarc.html [accessed: 12/03/2018].

Oberlander, J., 2017. Who is really in control? Pitfalls on the path to personalisation and personality. In Kuska, I. and T. Fisher, eds, 2017. *Design for Personalisation*. Abingdon: Routledge.

Ogden, T. H., 1992. *The Matrix of the Mind: Object Relations and the Psychoanalytic Dialogue*. London: Karnac.

Ogden, T. H., 1994. *Subjects of Analysis*. London: Karnac.

Ornstein, P. H., 2011. The evolution of Heinz Kohut's psychoanalytic psychology of the self. In Kohut, H., 2011. *The Search for the Self: Selected Writings of Heinz Kohut 1978–1981*. London: Karnac.

Packard, V., 1957. *The Hidden Persuaders*. Harmondsworth: Pelican.

Papacharissi Z., 2010. *A Private Sphere*. Cambridge: Polity.

Papacharissi Z., ed., 2011. *A Networked Self: Identity, Community and Culture on Social Network Sites*. London: Routledge.

Pariser, E., 2011a. *The Filter Bubble: What the Internet is Hiding from You*. New York: Penguin Press.

Pariser, E., 2011b. The troubling future of Internet search. *The Futurist*, 45(5), Sep–Oct.

Paterson, M., 2006. *Consumption and Everyday Life*. Abingdon: Routledge.

Penny, L., 2013. *Cybersexism: Sex, Gender and Power on the Internet*. London: Bloomsbury.

Petherbridge, D., ed., 2011. *Axel Honneth: Critical Essays with a reply by Axel Honneth*. Leiden: Brill.

Petherbridge, D., 2013. *The Critical Theory of Axel Honneth*. Lanham, MD: Lexington Books.

Portwood-Stacer, L., 2012. Media refusal and conspicuous non-consumption: The performative and political dimensions of Facebook abstention. *New Media & Society*, 15(7), pp. 1041–57.

Reilly, S., 2000. Entry on neo-liberalism. In: Bullock, A. and S. Trombley, eds, 2000. *The New Fontana Dictionary of Modern Thought*, 3rd ed. London: HarperCollins Publishers.

Rheingold, H., 2002a. *Smart Mobs – The Next Social Revolution: Transforming Culture and Communities in the Age of Instant Access*. New York: Basic Books.

Rheingold, H., 2002b. Smart Mobs summary. *Edge*. Available at: www.edge.org/3rd_cul
ture/rheingold/rheingold_print.html [accessed: 12/03/2018].

Rheingold, H., 2012. *Net Smart: How to Thrive in an Online World*. London: MIT Press.

Reisman, D., 1965. *The Lonely Crowd*. London: Yale University Press.

Rojek, C., 2015. *Presumed Intimacy: Para-Social Relationships in Media, Society and Celebrity
Culture*. Cambridge: Polity.

Royce, J., 1898. The psychology of invention. *Psychological Review*, 5(2), pp. 113–44.

Runco, M. A. and G. J. Jaeger, 2012. The standard definition of creativity. *Creativity
Research Journal*, 24(1), pp. 92–6.

Samuels, A., 1993. *The Political Psyche*. London: Routledge.

Sandel, M., 2012. *What Money Can't Buy: The Moral Limits of Markets*. London: Allen Lane.

Sandel, M., 2013. In conversation with A. C. Grayling. Royal Geological Society, London.
8 May, 2013. Available at: www.youtube.com/watch?v=ea787aGCuK0 [accessed:
12/09/2016].

Sandoval, M., 2013. Foxconned labour as the dark side of the information age: working conditions at Apple's contract manufacturers in China. *tripleC: Communication,
Capitalism & Critique. Open Access Journal for a Global Sustainable Information Society*, 11(2),
pp. 318–47.

Sartre, J.-P., 2001. *The Psychology of The Imagination*. London: Routledge.

Schatz, T., ed., 2004. *Hollywood: Critical Concepts in Media and Cultural Studies Volume III –
Social Dimensions: Technology, Regulation and Audience*. London: Routledge.

Scholz, T., ed., 2013. *Digital Labor: The Internet as Playground and Factory*. London: Routledge.

Seveg, E., 2010. *Google and the Digital Divide: The bias of online knowledge*. Oxford: Chandos.

Senft, T. M., 2008. *Camgirls: Celebrity and Community in the Age of Social Networks*. New
York: Peter Lang.

Shirky, C., 2008. It's not information overload, it's filter failure. Public talk, Web 2.0 *Expo*.
Available at: www.youtube.com/watch?v=LabqeJEOQyI [accessed: 12/03/2018].

Shirky, C., 2010. *Cognitive Surplus: Creativity and Generosity in a Connected Age*.
Harmondsworth: Penguin.

Siebers, J. and E. Fell, 2014. An exploration of the relation between the concepts of "community" and "future" in philosophy. Executive Report. Connected Communities
Initiative. Available at: www.ahrc.ac.uk/documents/project-reports-and-reviews/
connected-communities/an-exploration-of-the-relation-between-the-concepts-
of-community-and-future-in-philosophy [accessed: 12/03/2018].

Singh, G., 2014a. Recognition and the image of mastery as themes in *Black Mirror* (Channel
4, 2011–present: an eco-Jungian approach to "always-on" culture). *International Journal
of Jungian Studies*, 6(2), pp. 120–32.

Singh, G., 2014b. *Feeling Film: Affect and Authenticity in Popular Cinema*. Hove: Routledge.

Singh, G., 2015. The myth of authentic self-actualisation: happiness, transformation and
reality TV. In: L. Hockley and N. Fadina, eds, 2015. *The Happiness Illusion: How the
media sold us a fairytale*. Hove: Routledge.

Singh, G., 2017. YouTubers, online selves and the performance principle: notes from a
post-Jungian perspective. *CM: Communication and Media Journal*, 11(38), pp. 205–32.

Singh, G., 2018. Wupocalypse now: supertrolls and other risk anxieties in social media
interactions. In: Sampson, T., Ellis, D. and S. Maddison, eds, 2018. *Affect and Social
Media*. Rowman and Littlefield. Radical Cultural Studies series (in press).

Singer, T., ed., 2000. *The Vision Thing*. London: Routledge.

Singer, T., 2004. The cultural complex and the archetypal defences of the group spirit. In:
Singer, T. and S. L. Kimbles, eds, 2004. *The Cultural Complex: Contemporary Jungian
Perspectives on Psyche and Society*. Hove: Routledge

Singer, T. and S. L. Kimbles, eds, 2004. *The Cultural Complex: Contemporary Jungian Perspectives on Psyche and Society*. Hove: Routledge

Smith, N. H., 2012. Introduction: a recognition-theoretical research programme for the social sciences. In: O'Neill, S. and Nicholas H. Smith, eds, 2012. *Recognition Theory as Social Research: Investigating the Dynamics of Social Conflict*. Basingstoke: Palgrave Macmillan

Snickars, P. and P. Venderau, eds, 2009. *The YouTube Reader*. London: Wallflower.

Sorbring, E., Skoog, T. and M. Bohlin, 2014. Adolescent girls' and boys' well-being in relation to online and offline sexual and romantic activity. *Cyberpsychology: Journal of Psychosocial Research on Cyberspace*, 8(1), article 7. Available at: https://cyberpsychology. eu/article/view/4298/3346 [accessed: 12/03/2018].

Spangler, T., 2014. YouTube multichannel network was target of Relativity's surprise $1.1 billion bid of mostly stock. *Variety*, 14 April. http://variety.com/2014/biz/ news/relativity-offers-up-to-900-million-for-maker-studios-in-bid-to-outflank-dis ney-1201156736/ [accessed: 15/07/2016].

Spigel L. and Olsson L., eds, 2004. *Television After TV: Essays on a Medium in Transition*. London: Duke University Press.

Spink, A. and M. Zimmer, eds, 2008. *Web Search: Multidisciplinary Perspectives*. Berlin: Springer.

Sproull, L. and S. Kiesler, 1986. Reducing social context cues: electronic mail in organizational communications. *Management Science*, 32(11), pp. 1492–1512.

Stallman, R. M., 2001. *Free Software, Free Society: Selected Essays of Richard M. Stallman*. J. Gay, ed., 2001. Boston, MA: GNU Press.

Stallman, R. M., 2004. *Free Software, Free Society: Selected Essays of Richard M. Stallman*, 2nd ed. Boston, MA: GNU Press.

Stein, M. I., 1953. Creativity and culture. *Journal of Psychology*, 36, pp. 311–322.

Sternberg, R. J., 2006. The nature of creativity. *Creativity Research Journal*, 18(1), pp. 87–98.

Stever, G. S., 2011. Fan behavior and lifespan development theory: explaining para-social and social attachment to celebrities. *Journal of Adult Development*, 18, pp. 1–7.

Stewart, C. T., 2008. *Dire Emotions and Lethal Behaviours: Eclipse of the Life Instinct*. Hove: Routledge.

Storr, A., 1998. *The Essential Jung*. London: Fontana.

Sturken. M. and L. Cartwright, 2000. *Practices of Looking: An Introduction to Visual Culture*. Oxford: Oxford University Press.

Suler, J., 2004. The online disinhibition effect. *International Journal of Applied Psychoanalytic Studies*, 2(2), pp. 184–8.

Surowiecki, J., 2004. *The Wisdom of Crowds: Why the Many Are Smarter Than the Few and How Collective Wisdom Shapes Business, Economies, Societies and Nations*. London: Abacus.

Taylor, C., 1991. *The Ethics of Authenticity*. London: Harvard University Press.

Terranova, T., 2004. *Network Culture: Politics for the Information Age*. London: Pluto Press.

Thompson, K., 1998. *Moral Panics*. London: Routledge.

Turkle, S., 2008. Always-on/always-on-you: the tethered self. In: Katz, J. E. ed., 2008. *Handbook of Mobile Communication Studies*. London: MIT Press.

Turkle, S., 2011. *Alone Together: Why We Expect More from Technology and Less From Each Other*. New York: Basic Books

Turkle, S., 2015. *Reclaiming Conversation: The Power of Talk in a Digital Age*. New York: Penguin Books.

Vallor, S., 2016. *Technology and the Virtues: A Philosophical Guide to a Future Worth Wanting*. Oxford: Oxford University Press.

Van Dijc, J. and D. Nieborg, 2009. Wikinomics and it discontents: a critical analysis of Web 2.0 business manifestos. *New Media & Society*. 11(5), pp. 855–74.

Van Dijck, J., 2013. *The Culture of Connectivity: A Critical History of Social Media.* Oxford: Oxford University Press.

Van Dijk, J. A. G. M., 2005. *The Deepening Divide: Inequality in the Information Society.* London: SAGE.

Vandebosch, H., Simulioniene, R. Marczak, M., Vermeulen, A. and L. Bonetti, 2013. The role of the media. In: P. Smith and G. Steffgen, eds, 2013. *Cyberbullying through the new media.* London: Psychology Press.

Vannoy Adams, M., 2004. *The Fantasy Principle: Psychoanalysis of the Imagination.* Hove: Brunner-Routledge.

Veblen, T., 1899. *The Theory of the Leisure Class: An Economic Study of Institutions,* 2007 edition. Teddington: The Echo Library.

Waddell, T., 2006. *Mis/takes: Archetype, myth and identity in screen fiction.* Hove: Routledge.

Walker Rettberg, J., 2008. *Blogging.* Cambridge: Polity.

Walker Rettberg, J., 2014. *Seeing Ourselves Through technology: How we use selfies, blogs and wearable devices to see and shape ourselves.* Basingstoke: Palgrave Macmillan.

Wallace, P., 1999. *The Psychology of the Internet.* Cambridge: Cambridge University Press.

Weber, M., 2001. *The Protestant Ethic and the Spirit of Capitalism.* Abingdon: Routledge Classics.

Webster, F., 2002. The information society revisited. In: L. Lievrouw and S. Livingstone, eds, 2002. *Handbook of new media: social shaping and social consequences of ICTs.* London: SAGE.

Webster, J. G., 2014. *The Marketplace of Attention: How Audiences Take Shape in a Digital Age.* London: MIT Press.

Weis, E. and J. Belton, eds, 1985. *Film Sound: Theory and Practice.* New York: Columbia University Press.

Weitz, P., ed., 2014. *Psychotherapy 2.0: Where Psychotherapy and Technology Meet.* London: Karnac.

Wechsler, H., 1990. *Computational Vision.* London: Academic Press.

Widyanto, L. and M. Griffiths, 2007. Internet addiction: does it really exist? (Revisited). In: Gackenbach, J., ed., 2007. *Psychology and the Internet: Intrapersonal, Interpersonal, and Transpersonal Implications.* London: Academic Press.

Winnicott, D. W., 1956. On transference. *International Journal of Psychoanalysis,* 37, pp. 386–8.

Winnicott, D. W., 1965. *The Maturational Process and the Facilitating Environment: Studies in the Theory of Emotional Development.* New York: International University Press.

Winston, B., 1986. *Misunderstanding Media.* London: Routledge and Kegan Paul.

Winston, B., 1996. *Technologies of Seeing: Photography, Cinematography and Television.* London: BFI.

Winston, B., 1998. *Media Technology and Society, a History: From the Telegraph to the Internet.* London: Routledge.

Zelenkauskaite, A., 2016. Remediation, convergence, and big data: conceptual limits of cross-platform social media. *Convergence,* 22(1), pp. 1–16.

Zurn, C., 2015. *Axel Honneth.* Cambridge: Polity.

Zylinska, J., 2009. *Bioethics in the Age of New Media.* London: MIT Press.

INDEX

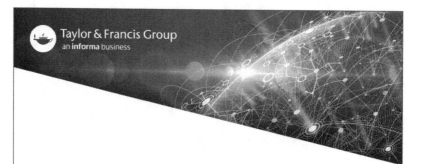